Acknowledgments

A big thank you to our fellow Scholastic authors with whom we collaborated on a few strategies inspired by their own books: Lindsay Kemeny, Lily Howard Scott, Melissa Loftus, Lori Sappington, Molly Ness, and Katie Pace Miles. You were all a wealth of knowledge, and it was our honor to rub elbows with you. Thank you, Karrissa and Sarah, for helping to inspire two of our strategies!

Thank you to Anna Harwood for allowing us to take photographs in your incredible school. I've never known anyone to fight harder for kids than you. Elizabeth, Tammi, and Taylor, the photoshoot couldn't have happened without you. Thank you to the students in Gloucester County for allowing us to shine a light onto your brilliance: Ember, Laeryn, Renly, Jolyn, Harvey, Henry, Lincoln, Theo, Jarren, Anniston, Aubrey, Maddie, Luna, Parker, Grayson, and Skyler. Children like you are the reason we love to teach. To our amazing photographer, Kelly Marderosian, thank you for bringing these strategies to life. Thank you to Remi, Gaige, Rickee, Ivy, Jackson, Jaymes, and Mrs. Taryn Wilson for also being in some of the photos in the book!

Special thanks to Chase Young, Joseph Pizzo, Melissa Loftus, Lori Sappington, Molly Ness, William Nichols, Kathy Roe, Patricia Braden, Melanie Kuhn, Lily Howard Scott, and Katie Pace Miles for your enthusiasm and belief in this project to bring the magic of words to students' ears and mouths, which you so kindly expressed in your endorsements.

CONTENTS

Timothy V. Rasinski,
Melissa Cheesman Smith
& Savannah Campbell

THE MEGABOOK

Strategies to Boost Word Learning for Reading, Writing, Speaking & Listening

VOCABULARY

SCHOLASTIC

To the amazing teachers I have had the privilege of knowing, working with, and learning from over the past half century. Every day you make the world a better place for children, their families, and the world. Thank you for all you do.

—TVR

To my three kids, who each have their own relationship with words. My daughter Londyn, who uses words to connect, socialize, and create relationships. My son Jaymes, who is always curious about the nuance and precision of his words and has a developed vocabulary as his nose was always in a book growing up. And finally, my son Jackson, whose words come from his heart, always careful and kind with his words, attentive to how they will be received. I love the way you use language to express yourselves, matching exactly who you are.

—MCS

For my mom, Teresa. Without your unyielding love and faith in me, nothing I've become would have ever been possible.

—SC

Senior Vice President and Publisher: Tara Welty
Executive Editorial Director: Sarah Longhi
Editor-in-Chief: Raymond Coutu
Production Editor: Danny Miller
Assistant Editor: Samantha Unger
Creative Director: Tannaz Fassihi
Interior design: Maria Lilja

Photos ©: 31, 42, 47, 95–96, 103–106, 137, 141–144, 146–149, 151–154, 159, 217, 229, 235, 238: © Getty Images and Shutterstock.com. All other photos courtesy of the author. Icons created by The Noun Project.

Credits: 284–285: "Idiom Word Ladders" from *Daily Word Ladders: Idioms (Grades 4+)* © 2020 by Timothy V. Rasinski & Melissa Cheesman Smith. Used by permission. All rights reserved.

ISBN 979-8-225-02373-7

1 2 3 4 5 6 7 8 9 10 150 35 34 33 32 31 30 29 28 27 26

Scholastic Inc., 557 Broadway, New York, NY 10012

Strategies for Learning Words We Provide

CHAPTER 3: WISE = STUDENT TOOLS FOR DETERMINING MEANING

Strategies for Using Context Clues

Strategies for Using Morphology

INTRODUCTION

"I am not what I seem. I am the words I speak."

—Sandra Cisneros

Envision two third-grade students sitting together, each holding the book *What If You Could Sniff Like a Shark?*, engaged in a conversation about the text as part of their oceanography science unit. This content-rich book will take several days for students to read, and Mrs. Baldwin started the day's reading lesson by introducing challenging, content-specific vocabulary that the students will encounter as they read: *shape-shift, cells, Fahrenheit* (°F), *lifespan, siphon, predators,* and *prey*. She also introduced some more general words from the book that students might encounter in other texts or everyday conversations: *develop, inflate, adaptation,* and *reaction*. She provides student-friendly definitions of the words and has students practice pronouncing them, ensuring success when reading aloud with their partner.

Mrs. Baldwin asks students to note any shark body part they encounter, write it on a sticky note with an arrow, and place it in the book. She models how to record the first body part, "dorsal fin," before students try it themselves and put their first sticky note in their book. With this activity, Mrs. Baldwin builds background knowledge about sharks. *What If You Could Sniff Like a Shark?* is one of several ocean-related texts Mrs. Baldwin has chosen because she knows the importance of having children read widely, to build not only background knowledge but also vocabulary. To that end, she provides a diverse set of texts and language experiences on the topic. Her students have watched video clips about the ocean, engaged in conversations and texts about ocean life, and written reports about their favorite sea creatures.

This engaging work is at the heart of high-quality vocabulary instruction: creating a classroom where children are exposed to a variety of language experiences throughout the day—diverse, meaningful exposures that help students develop a deep understanding of key vocabulary (Graves, 2016).

Education writer Natalie Wexler (2019) emphasizes, "The most important factor in determining whether readers can understand a text is how much relevant vocabulary or background knowledge they have" (p. 46). Vocabulary is essential to language as well as to reading comprehension because, as Michael Graves (2016) emphasizes, unfamiliar words can create significant barriers to understanding complex text. Vocabulary and comprehension share a symbiotic relationship—a strong vocabulary directly supports a reader's ability to comprehend text, while repeated exposure to rich text expands vocabulary knowledge.

Why Is Vocabulary Important?

Vocabulary is the foundation of literacy and effective communication. A strong vocabulary enables students to access, process, and express concepts clearly when speaking and writing. While vocabulary and reading comprehension are often approached separately in an instructional setting, the two are inextricably linked. The National Reading Panel (2000) states that "vocabulary is generally tied closely to individual words while comprehension is more often thought of in much larger units. To get to the comprehension of larger units requires the requisite processing of the words. Precisely separating the two processes is difficult, if not impossible" (pp. 4–15). Without comprehension at the word level, comprehension at the sentence, paragraph, and whole-text level becomes nearly impossible. After all, how can you understand a text if you don't know the meanings of the words within it?

Reading comprehension can and does break down at the word level. That means our students must be able to read words (i.e., decode them) AND understand their meaning in print for comprehension to occur. Decoding allows students to access the print, while vocabulary knowledge and word-learning strategies equip them to make meaning from what they read. In other words, vocabulary does not just support comprehension, it is the very foundation upon which it is built.

Imagine you're reading an online news article about global responses to a public health crisis. The text explains how infection outbreaks *emerge*, how quickly the number of infections can *escalate* under certain conditions, and how governments and organizations might *mobilize* resources to stop the spread. The article also discusses the *ramifications* of outbreaks for communities and health care systems. If you already know what those italicized words mean and understand their nuances, the article's core ideas are accessible and you're able to learn about the global responses to public health crises. But if those words are unfamiliar, you may struggle to construct meaning from the article, leading to confusion, misinterpretation of ideas, or disengagement, and you're likely to stop reading the article.

Without a robust vocabulary, even the best decoders cannot fully achieve the end goal: comprehending what they read or hear.

What Are the Elements of "WISE" Vocabulary Instruction?

A comprehensive approach to vocabulary instruction should contain and integrate the following four core elements.

Word Consciousness

First, varied language experiences, where students are curious about words they encounter and precise about words they choose, are the marker of a classroom centered around **word consciousness**, an essential component of a vocabulary-rich classroom (Graves, 2016; Scott et al., 2008; Beck et al., 2013). Word conscious students notice and use interesting and precise language in writing and speaking. See Chapter 1 for more on word consciousness.

Individual-Word Learning

Second, facilitating **individual-word learning** is a must to increase student vocabulary. According to Beck, McKeown, and Kucan (2013), effective vocabulary instruction focuses on frequently encountered academic words and provides multiple exposures to them in meaningful contexts. Direct, repeated exposure to new vocabulary allows for deeper understanding of words and helps store that vocabulary in long-term memory (Stahl & Nagy, 2006; Altalhab, 2018). Directly teaching words in content areas or units of study is also essential because it enables students to engage more confidently with grade-level academic texts and discussions. See Chapter 2 for more on individual-word learning.

Student Tools for Determining Meaning

Third, students need instruction and practice in using **tools for determining meaning** when they encounter unknown words while reading and conversing with others. Using context clues, morphology, and reference materials are three proven strategies that aid students' independence in deciphering the meaning of unfamiliar words (Nagy & Scott, 2000; Graves, 2016). See Chapter 3 for more on student tools for determining meaning.

Exploration of Word Relationships

Lastly, students need time to deepen their understanding of words they are familiar with by **exploring word relationships**, such as multiple-meaning words, homophones, and figurative language. This type of exploration is essential in building a deeper understanding of language (Baumann & Kame'enui, 1991; Blachowicz & Fisher, 2010; Stahl & Nagy, 2006). See Chapter 4 for more on the exploration of word relationships.

This book is structured around those four core elements, which are explored in greater detail in the chapter introductions.

What Does the Science of Reading Say About Vocabulary Instruction?

The term "science of reading" has gained widespread recognition among educators. But what is the science of reading, and what does it have to say specifically about vocabulary?

First, it is important to note what the science of reading is NOT. It is not a program, it is not an initiative, and it is not based on a single research article. Instead, the science of reading is a body of interdisciplinary research from fields such as literacy education, cognitive psychology, neuroscience, linguistics, and developmental psychology. This research has spanned decades, giving insight into how children learn to read and comprehend.

Best practices emerge when a convergence of evidence supports a particular topic, such as vocabulary. Scientific conclusions must be determined with the understanding that research is constantly evolving. As new findings arise, it is essential to remain grounded in research, to adapt instructional approaches accordingly, and to continuously deepen knowledge about how children learn to read.

But what does the science of reading say about teaching vocabulary specifically? The National Reading Panel's findings on vocabulary, along with additional research (Graves, 2016; Beck et al., 2013), present useful information and direction for vocabulary instruction. First, vocabulary plays a critical role in comprehension. A great vocabulary bank aids in comprehension, and strong comprehension helps students increase vocabulary through context (Moats, 2004). Simply put, when we teach vocabulary, we are also teaching comprehension.

Another key understanding around vocabulary instruction is that vocabulary should be taught both directly and indirectly. Vocabulary knowledge is one of the strongest predictors of reading comprehension and overall academic success (Graves, 2016). Once students enter school, their reading vocabulary increases by 3,000–4,000 words per year (Graves, 2016). It is impossible to teach that many words explicitly in a school year. So while explicit instruction is essential, it is not the only type of instruction students should receive.

Furthermore, a single exposure to a word will not enable students to understand the word in a rich and meaningful way. Instead, students should have multiple exposures to words in a variety of contexts (National Reading Panel, 2000; Peters, 2014). It is only when students have repeated exposure to words, as well as rich, varied, contextual experiences with words, that they will grow their vocabulary banks to the size needed for proficient reading, writing, listening, and speaking.

Finally, the role of wide reading—reading diverse texts on a topic to build knowledge—cannot be overstated. Over time, wide reading provides the most significant contribution to a child's vocabulary development (Graves, 2016). Explicit instruction alone is not enough for students to increase their vocabulary by up to 4,000 words a year. Once children can read, they need to be given substantial time to read. By the end of high school, the average student will have acquired about 50,000 words in their reading vocabulary (Graves, 2016, p.4). By combining explicit and varied instruction with opportunities for wide reading, you create the conditions students need to become proficient readers and writers with expansive vocabularies.

What Are the Three Tiers of Vocabulary—and Why Do They Matter?

"The limits of my language mean the limits of my world."

— Ludwig Wittgenstein

Researcher Isabel Beck categorized the words we acquire and use into three tiers based on their frequency of use and complexity. This provides foundational knowledge for word instruction, informing you about which types of words to prioritize for instruction (Beck et al., 2013).

Tier 1 words are common, everyday words with simple meanings, such as *sing*, or function words like *this*. They make up a large portion of typical language interactions that students engage in at a young age or when acquiring foundational language skills. A child will quickly learn the word *dog* through conversations when interacting with a pet at home. Language-rich homes provide a strong foundation of Tier 1 words, setting the stage for success in kindergarten (Hart & Risley, 1995; Zukowski, 2020; Blachowicz & Cobb, 2021; Golinkoff et al., 2019; Hoff, 2003). Once in the classroom, typical language interactions further develop a student's growing Tier 1 vocabulary.

Tier 2 words are more precise and nuanced, enabling students to read texts with greater comprehension and engage in deeper conversations. They appear frequently in grade-level texts and academic language interactions. They are wide-ranging and not tied to one specific subject. As such, they are used most frequently in vocabulary instruction because they are critical for reading comprehension and language development. Students might say they feel *sad* their cat died, but with knowledge of Tier 2 words, they might say they feel *heartbroken*, which carries a deeper, more nuanced meaning. Knowledge of Tier 2 words enhances students' ability to understand and express complex ideas (Beck et al., 2013).

Tier 3 words are specialized words that students typically encounter in content areas, so they are less common than Tier 1 or 2 words. That said, they are vital for students to learn explicitly within the context of a particular subject, such as *civil rights* in social studies, *mitosis* in science, and *hypotenuse* in mathematics. Developing an understanding of Tier 3 words is essential for students to grasp and engage more deeply with subject-specific content (Beck et al., 2013).

Tiers of Vocabulary

Category	Tier 1 Words	Tier 2 Words	Tier 3 Words
Type of Word	**Common**	**Precise**	**Specialized**
Definition	Everyday words naturally encountered in oral and written language	Academic words that students need to communicate precisely and clearly	Specialized words unique to the content areas
Examples	*happy, jump, table, sunlight, purple*	*absurd, mention, compassionate, dainty, scurried*	*photosynthesis, peninsula, metaphor, democracy, integer*
Criteria for Selecting Words	If needed, words that build missing foundational oral language skills or words that correct expressive and receptive student misconceptions	Academic words that students will encounter frequently or are difficult to define with morphology or context clues	Content-specific words that are essential to develop background knowledge within a unit of study
How Words Are Acquired	Primarily through incidental oral language interactions	Through explicit individual-word instruction that provides multiple, frequent exposures in context	Through explicit instruction by the teacher or through the use of student tools

(Beck et al., 2013; Graves, 2016)

You'll notice a sampling of word types in the paragraph below. Most of the words are Tier 1 words that students encounter in everyday interactions. Mixed in are Tier 2 words, such as *accurately* and *consistency*, which show up across subjects and deserve focus during instruction. You'll also see a few Tier 3 words, such as *knead* and *fermentation*, which are content-specific terms and are imperative to comprehend the paragraph fully.

Tier 1 **Tier 2** **<u>Tier 3</u>**

Baking bread requires a special ingredient called **<u>yeast</u>**, which helps the dough to **rise** and grow bigger. We must **measure** the flour and water **accurately** to make sure the **<u>dough</u>** has the right **consistency** before we **<u>knead</u>** it. The **<u>fermentation</u> process** is what causes the dough to expand and turn into a big, edible loaf of goodness!

How Do Expressive Language and Receptive Language Relate to Vocabulary?

Expressive language is the ability to communicate thoughts and ideas through speaking, writing, or other forms of expression. We produce language to convey meaning effectively. In contrast, *receptive language* is the ability to understand spoken or written communication (Owens, 2020; Paul & Norbury, 2012).

Language Domains

	RECEPTIVE Input: Ability to understand	**EXPRESSIVE** Output: Ability to communicate
ORAL Interact With People	**LISTENING** • read-alouds • presentations • videos • discussions	**SPEAKING** • sharing • presenting • conversing • asking and answering questions
PRINT Interact With Text	**READING** • shared reading • choral reading • echo reading • independent reading • literature club/study	**WRITING** • descriptive writing • informational writing • opinion/argument writing • narrative writing

Vocabulary plays a crucial role across all language domains (reading, writing, speaking, and listening), as it is the foundation for successful communication and comprehension.

In Reading

Students rely on their understanding of word meanings to make sense of what they read (Snow, 2010). Beck, McKeown, and Kucan (2013) emphasize that vocabulary knowledge, along with background knowledge, is a strong predictor of reading comprehension, as readers with larger vocabularies are better able to construct meaning from texts. Without a large vocabulary, students will struggle to comprehend texts, ultimately limiting their overall academic achievement (National Reading Panel, 2000; Schuth et al., 2017; Quinn et al., 2015). Developing students' vocabulary is, therefore, essential for enhancing reading proficiency and promoting overall literacy development. A strong vocabulary not only helps in understanding individual words, but also interpreting ideas, making inferences, and following complex arguments—all of which are crucial for successful reading.

In Writing

Vocabulary knowledge is equally important to writing, as it directly influences students' ability to articulate and elaborate on their thinking, choose precise and effective language, and structure their pieces. Students with large vocabularies are better able to express their ideas with clarity and sophistication, resulting in higher-quality written work (Scott, Nagy, &

Flinspach, 2008). A rich vocabulary provides students with a broader range of words to convey their thoughts accurately, enhancing their overall writing proficiency. Where reading requires receptive vocabulary knowledge, writing requires expressive vocabulary knowledge.

In Speaking

Although vocabulary instruction has traditionally been most closely tied to reading and writing, it is equally vital to speaking and listening. Speaking skills, in particular, are greatly enhanced by a broad vocabulary because students are better able to engage in meaningful, nuanced conversations and demonstrate a richer understanding of language and content (Kieffer & Lesaux, 2012). Nagy and Townsend (2012) highlight that vocabulary knowledge is a key driver of oral language development, as it enables students to engage in discussions, ask and answer questions, and articulate their ideas effectively.

In Listening

Similarly, listening comprehension is deeply connected to vocabulary knowledge, as listeners must understand words they hear in order to process spoken language. Without a strong vocabulary, students may struggle to keep up with discussions, understand instruction, and make sense of other forms of oral communication. Providing vocabulary instruction that nurtures speaking and listening skills not only strengthens students' communication abilities, but also enhances their overall academic achievement by promoting active participation and engagement in classroom discourse (Beck et al., 2013).

In sum, vocabulary plays an integral role in all four language domains: reading, writing, speaking, and listening. The instructional approaches featured in this book will work to increase and improve students' vocabularies in all these domains. The domains are notated on the side of each Strategy Page.

How Do Students Acquire Vocabulary?

When students are exposed to a new word incidentally or instructionally, their understanding of that word goes from unknown to **shallow**, where students can recognize and understand a word within a limited context (Beck et al., 2013; Nagy & Scott, 2000).

With repeated exposure to the word and additional instruction, students develop a more **familiar** understanding of a word's definition and connotation (Stahl & Nagy, 2006; Graves, 2016).

Over time, repeated encounters with a word in various contexts lead to a **nuanced** understanding of it, where students come to know the word well enough to use it to express ideas and reasoning (Beck et al., 2013; Blachowicz & Fisher, 2010).

As students develop a **deep**, rich understanding, the word becomes integrated into their vocabulary to be used in multiple contexts (Graves, 2016; Stahl & Nagy, 2006).

Repeated exposure to words through receptive and expressive language experiences transforms shallow knowledge into deep knowledge. Along with explicit instruction, it moves students from mere recognition of words to receptive and expressive use of words (Beck et al., 2013). Vocabulary acquisition is not a single event but rather, without question, a layered, evolving experience that builds word acquisition over time (Baumann & Kame'enui, 1991).

Stages of Vocabulary Acquisition

WORD ACQUISITION

NUMBER OF EXPOSURES ⟶

1	2	3	4	5	6	7	8	9	10	11	12	13	14	15	16	17	18	19	20

RECEPTIVE		EXPRESSIVE	
SHALLOW	**FAMILIAR**	**NUANCED**	**DEEP**
Understands in a limited context	Understands in a general context with definition and connotation	Understands and uses with conscious effort in limited contexts	Understands rich, decontextualized meanings and uses effortlessly in multiple contexts

Numbers are approximate and based on an average from numerous studies. Factors such as student acquisition rate, complexity of a word, and level of context in an encounter can vary the number of exposures needed for each stage. (Graves, 2016 and Beck et al., 2013)

Vocabulary acquisition occurs daily in students' lives. Let's dive into learning opportunities that help students to move from *shallow* to *deep* understanding of words.

- **Incidental word learning** refers to the process of acquiring vocabulary naturally through exposure to language in conversations and everyday experiences (Beck et al., 2013). According to Beck et al. (2013), this type of learning happens in informal or social settings, and when students are reading widely and independently, often without purposely focusing on the words themselves.
- **Explicit vocabulary instruction** involves teaching carefully selected words that are critical for comprehension and academic success. Those words often come from a book study or content-area unit of study. Teachers typically provide a student-friendly definition of a word before engaging students in a variety of meaningful, contextualizing activities to reinforce their understanding of that word. Explicit instruction also involves teaching strategies for determining word meanings, such as using context clues, analyzing morphemes, and consulting reference materials, which helps students unlock unfamiliar words independently. In addition, explicit instruction involves exploring word relationships by focusing on figurative language, multiple-meaning words, and homophones to deepen students' understanding of and flexibility with language (Fisher & Frey, 2014; Graves, 2016). You'll find activities and strategies for explicit instruction throughout this book.
- **Implicit vocabulary instruction** involves acquiring vocabulary during discussions, read-alouds, field trips, collaborative classroom experiences, and spontaneous teachable moments throughout the school day. Rather than directly teaching specific words, teachers purposely introduce and clarify word meanings as opportunities arise, allowing students to absorb vocabulary through meaningful interactions (Graves, 2016). Although implicit vocabulary instruction is not something that's typically planned, it can be a key part of the curriculum in the directions and feedback you give, the curiosity about words you encourage, and other everyday interactions you have with students when vocabulary learning opportunities arise.

What's the Best Way to Assess Vocabulary Knowledge?

Vocabulary assessment can be complex. While there are some commercially available tools, few are user-friendly or provide the kind of precise, actionable data you need to plan effective instruction. Students need to know thousands of words, an impossible task to comprehensively assess. Assessing even a small sampling of these words may provide a general idea of students' vocabulary development, but how would this guide instruction? To get a real sense of what's working, the best way to measure vocabulary knowledge is to look at our WISE components:

Word Consciousness

Because of the metacognitive nature of word consciousness, it may be measured qualitatively by using a survey, self-awareness scale, or observations of behaviors. In Chapter 1, on page 21, we offer a chart that gives you a glimpse into how word consciousness can be measured.

Individual-Word Learning

The teacher is responsible for choosing which words to teach and to what degree to teach them explicitly (Beck et al., 2013). The old-fashioned method of simply having students match a word with its definition only tests their ability to memorize rather than truly understand and apply that word (Marzano, 2004). A more effective approach is to present students with real-life scenarios where they would need to understand the word receptively or use it expressively, such as "What might you wear if you had to go outside on a *frigid* day?" This approach requires a more meaningful demonstration of vocabulary knowledge that reflects comprehension and predicted receptive understanding or expressive use (Graves, 2016).

Student Tools for Determining Meaning

Context clues, morphology, and reference sources are tools students can use for determining meaning. The use of context clues to determine meaning is best assessed during small-group instruction. As students find meaning using context clues, an informal observation by you is the best way to determine if students are applying that strategy well. To assess morphology, design tasks that require students to break down words into their meaningful parts and explain how those parts contribute to word meaning (Beck et al., 2013). Tasks such as breaking words into meaningful parts or changing them into related forms are exercises that help you assess students' ability to work with morphemes in context (Graves, 2016; Carlisle, 2010a). For example, asking a student to split a word (*reconstruction* into *re-con-struct-ion*) or providing a base word and asking them to generate related forms (turning *teach* into *teacher, teaches, teaching, reteach*) provides valuable information about a child's morphological understanding (Rasinski et al., 2020).

Exploration of Word Relationships

Word relationships, such as synonyms, multiple-meaning words, homophones, connotations, and figurative language, can be initially taught and assessed as isolated skills. Let's take synonyms for example. When teaching synonyms in the primary grades, you may define synonyms and give examples before you have students practice coming up with them. You could then assess students by having them find synonyms for boring words in sentences, or matching up two words that are synonyms. In the upper grades, understanding word relationships becomes more complex because instruction tends to focus on the nuances between and among words, and not just their similarities and differences. So you might assess students by having them apply a "just right" word to a context-rich sentence (Graves, 2016). Ultimately, explicit instruction followed by an assessment aligned to that instruction is the most effective way to determine understanding of word relationships. However, the ultimate goal is for students to take these individual skills and use them to build a richer, more comprehensive vocabulary that helps them express their ideas clearly and accurately as well as understand oral communication.

Five Tips for Creating Vocabulary Assessments

1. **Incorporate Contextual and Real-Life Scenarios** Write questions that require students to choose the correct word within the context of a sentence or a real-life scenario. Assessing vocabulary in context shows us whether students truly understand how a word functions in a sentence (Beck et al., 2013). Tying assessments to authentic situations makes it more meaningful and gives students the opportunity to apply words in real situations (Graves, 2016).

2. **Assess Receptive and Expressive Vocabulary** Vocabulary assessments should be designed to evaluate not only students' ability to understand words in reading, but also their ability to use words meaningfully in writing, speaking, and listening contexts, ensuring a comprehensive assessment of their language proficiency (Li et al., 2024). Include questions that assess how well students understand words while reading (receptive) and use words in writing (expressive) (Graves, 2016).

3. **Focus on Tier 2 Words** Target words that students are likely to encounter frequently in a variety of academic and real-world contexts. This ensures that the vocabulary they learn is relevant and will support their overall language development (Nation, 2013).

4. **Require Strategy Use** Incorporate questions about word relationships such as synonyms, antonyms, homonyms, and nuances, which enables you to assess whether students see how words connect and strengthens their ability to understand and apply vocabulary in diverse contexts (Snow, 2010). Also, incorporate questions that require students to infer the meaning of words from surrounding text, testing their ability to use context clues (Beck et al., 2013).

5. **Align Assessments With Instruction and Standards** Any vocabulary assessment should align with how you taught the words and what standards you addressed. Assess what you teach, in other words. If you introduced vocabulary through context, your assessment should emphasize contextual understanding of those words rather than rote memorization (Snow, 2010).

How Does *The Megabook of Vocabulary* Fit Within Your Reading Program?

We wrote *The Megabook of Vocabulary* with flexibility in mind so it could be used with any core reading program, or as a guide in classrooms without a required curriculum. The research-based strategies it contains are not about adding more to your already full plate. Instead, they are designed to make planning and implementing instruction easy and effective. Whether you are using a basal, a reading anthology, a district-created scope and sequence, or crafting your own curriculum from various resources, *The Megabook of Vocabulary* will help you embed meaningful vocabulary instruction within your existing framework.

Every core reading program includes lists of vocabulary words to teach. This book offers practical strategies you can use with words from your curriculum, your own words, or the words we provide. These strategies are designed to offer the multiple, contextual, meaningful exposures your students need to understand and retain new vocabulary. Additionally, we've included a variety of instructional routines and word lists, ensuring that no matter how much time you have, you can still deliver effective and purposeful vocabulary instruction.

The Megabook of Vocabulary helps you work smarter within your existing curriculum, while meeting building, district, and state mandates in authentic, meaningful ways.

A Close-Up Look at a Strategy Page

The strategy sections in each chapter begin with a page that spells out clearly everything you need to do to plan for, carry out, and extend instruction. Most of the strategy pages are immediately followed by word lists or student practice pages that can be photocopied and/or downloaded by scanning this QR code or visiting scholastic.com/megabookvocabresources.com. All essential materials are provided!

Pinpoints the language domains that stand to benefit the most from the strategy: reading, writing, speaking, and/or listening.

CHAPTER 3
Student Tools for Determining Meaning

Strategies for Using Morphology

LANGUAGE DOMAINS

Reading ✓

Writing ✓

Speaking ✓

Listening ✓

3.F Suffix Spin

Create word cards for the most frequently used suffixes (*-s*, *-es*, *-ing*, and *-ed*) and display them in a pocket chart with the base word cards from the materials list, or choose your own base words that don't require a spelling change when a suffix is added. On cardstock, copy the Suffix Spinner on page 189 and cut it out; then provide students with a paper clip and pencil to use the spinner. One student at a time spins the spinner and selects a base word from the pocket chart. Then other students write the base word with the suffix on dry-erase boards and hold up answers for you to see. Students can turn and share with a partner a sentence containing that word.

Explains what the strategy is and how to implement it.

Materials	• Suffix Spinner, page 189 • base word cards; create cards with these words on them: *cat, jump, help, sing, swim, box, wish, push, talk, match* • dry-erase boards and markers • paper clips and pencils
Grade Band	K–3
Length of Activity	10 minutes
Differentiation Ideas	• **Striving Learners and English Learners:** Use the same spinners and base word cards in small groups before the whole-group activity. • **English Learners:** Provide images for each of the base word cards, or ask a student to draw a picture on each card to represent the meaning.
Extension Ideas	Instead of using the recommended base words, provide students with examples where the spelling changes (e.g., double consonant, e-drop, *y* change).
Answers	cats, jumps, helps, sings, swims, boxes, wishes, pushes, talks, matches, jumping, helping, singing, swimming, boxing, wishing, pushing, talking, matching, jumped, helped, boxed, wished, pushed, talked, matched

Lists the materials to gather prior to instruction.

Specifies the amount of time it will likely take to carry out instruction. Strategies range from quick bursts of learning to rich, weeklong projects.

Offers ways to enrich instruction—and build on it.

Identifies the grades for which the strategy is intended. If necessary, adapt strategies and texts for your grade.

Suggests ways to adapt the strategy for striving learners, English learners, and/or thriving learners.

Strategies for Developing a Curiosity About Words, pages 22–47

Strategies for Choosing the Right Expressive Words, pages 48–71

Chapter 1 downloadables are available here.

CHAPTER 1

Word Consciousness

"Words mean more than what is set down on paper. It takes the human voice to infuse them with deeper meaning."

—Maya Angelou

Word consciousness enhances students' ability to comprehend and express language with precision and intention. It refers to students' *awareness of, curiosity about, appreciation of,* and *enthusiasm for* words, as well as their understanding of how words shape communication. Engagement with language, especially through rich vocabulary interactions and instruction, significantly contributes to later academic success (Cunningham & Stanovich, 1997). Children who actively engage with words—whether by pondering their meanings or using them proactively—are more likely to develop strong reading and writing skills, which in turn influences their overall literacy development (Beck & McKeown, 2007a). Neugebauer and colleagues (2017) found that teacher talk that reinforced kindergartners' use of words, affirmed their understanding of word meanings, and helped them make personal connections to vocabulary was positively associated with gains in general vocabulary knowledge by the end of the school year. Lane and Allen (2010) found that a word-rich classroom environment maximizes students' opportunities to learn new words, and that the teacher's use of sophisticated language provides an important model for children's vocabulary development.

The goal of fostering word consciousness is not to just increase students' vocabularies, but also to get them thinking critically about words on a regular basis. When students are aware of the power and complexity of words, they are more likely to use precise language and communicate effectively (Graves, 2016). This metacognitive approach supports students' ability to express ideas clearly, persuasively, and with intention. It leads them to a deeper understanding of words while reading, writing, speaking, and listening.

A word-conscious classroom encourages children to experiment with words, think critically about their meanings, and use them precisely in written and spoken communication. When you engage students in discussions about the meanings of words in texts, they significantly increase their vocabulary knowledge and use more precise words when writing and speaking (Beck & McKeown, 2007a). By integrating word consciousness into daily learning, you help students build a lasting curiosity about language that fuels vocabulary development and academic success.

The chart below explains what the expressive and receptive levels of word consciousness might look like in students.

WORD CONSCIOUSNESS LEVELS

RECEPTIVE LANGUAGE: READING and LISTENING When students encounter a word they do not know, they…		
continue without pause or hesitate briefly then simply move on	pause and recognize that they don't know what the word means, trying to figure it out if there is an effortless way to grasp the meaning, or otherwise move on	stop and use word-learning strategies, recognizing that the word may be important for comprehension, but also satisfying their own curiosity about language
inattentive	**aware**	**mindful**

EXPRESSIVE LANGUAGE: WRITING and SPEAKING When students communicate ideas, they…		
use basic vocabulary, lacking specificity	use synonyms for everyday words to fit the situation, but their word choice is usually limited to the first word they think of that might fit	choose words from a well-maintained vocabulary bank with attention to the nuance and connotation of a word to communicate precise ideas for a specific audience
inattentive	**aware**	**mindful**

LANGUAGE DOMAINS

Reading

Writing

Speaking

Listening

1.A **Label the Room**

Turn everyday objects into powerful vocabulary boosters by labeling them. With labels, you create a connection between spoken and written language, reinforcing vocabulary recognition and usage. For students just learning to read and spell, labels provide additional exposures to words, which assist students with retention of high-utility words. Choose objects around the room that are commonly used and referred to in conversation. Make your instruction interactive by pointing out labels during conversations, playing games that involve finding or using the labeled words, and encouraging students to use the labels to spell the names of everyday objects correctly.

Common and useful labels: *door, window, desk, chair, table, carpet/rug, whiteboard, chalkboard, bulletin board, wall, floor, ceiling, lights, clock, trash can, recycling bin, bookshelf, book, notebook, folder, binder, paper, pencil, eraser, crayons, markers, colored pencils, ruler, scissors, glue, tape, stapler, hole puncher, calculator, computer, laptop, tablet, mouse, keyboard, monitor, printer, projector, headphones, cubby, locker, classroom library, cabinet, reading corner, writing station, art station, math center, calendar, water fountain*

Materials	teacher-created labels for important objects around and near the classroom
Grade Band	K–1
Length of Activity	This is an organizational activity.
Differentiation Ideas	• **Striving Learners:** Encourage students to walk around the room to practice reading the words aloud. • **English Learners:** Write labels in English and your students' native language(s). Practice labels daily with students, and encourage them to refer to labels during speaking and writing exercises.
Extension Ideas	• Consider labeling more complex objects with a different-color card. • Show syllable division of each word in an unobtrusive manner, for example: *class-room li-brar-y* underneath the phrase.

1.B Environmental Print Hunt

Even before students can decode words, they often recognize signs and logos by sight, which helps bridge the gap between environmental print and reading. Collect and display signs and logos from everyday, well-known businesses to turn them into a powerful tool for building early literacy. Use those graphics to spark conversations by asking questions such as: "Who's seen this one before?" or "What do you think it says?". Invite students to "read" the logos aloud and search for familiar letters, sounds, or patterns. Encourage them to be on the lookout for signs and logos outside of school, too, in their neighborhoods, while shopping, and at mealtimes.

Materials	pictures of well-known business signs and logos in the area
Grade Band	K–1
Length of Activity	15 minutes

Differentiation Ideas	• **Striving Learners:** Limit the number of signs and logos you preview at once. Start with the MOST well-known ones (e.g., Walmart, McDonald's, Target, etc.) and gradually add in more.
	• **English Learners:** Offer sentence frames to discuss the signs and logos, such as:
	  • *I recognize the letter ________.*
	  • *This logo came from ________.*
	  • *I saw this sign at ________.*

Extension Ideas	• Create a pretend-play center with store signs, menus, and flyers where students "shop" and practice recognizing words. • Have students find other business signs and logos that they know how to "read" with their families, as a take-home activity. • Ask students to bring in labels, food boxes, or print advertisements they can collect at home or in their communities. • Ask students to categorize the businesses in various ways, such as type of the business (e.g., restaurant, grocery store, fitness center) or the first sound in the business's name.

LANGUAGE DOMAINS

Reading

Writing

Speaking

Listening

Strategies for Developing a Curiosity About Words

LANGUAGE DOMAINS

Reading

Writing

Speaking

Listening

1.C Word Associations Game

In Word Associations, students must guess a "Star Word" based on clues. The quicker they guess a Star Word, the more points their team gets! Put students into small groups and give each group a dry-erase board, marker, and eraser. Read aloud the first Clue Word from the Word Association Sets on pages 25–27 and then have students work together to guess the Star Word in Column 1 by writing it down on the dry-erase board, or for younger students not yet reading or writing, have them whisper their answers to you. Once all groups have written down a response, ask them to reveal their answers. If no group guesses correctly, students erase their boards and continue on through the remaining Clue Words. Once a group identifies the correct Star Word, move on to the next. Keep track of points, and note that multiple groups may score in a single round.

Points

Guessed correctly on:

- 1st Clue Word: 5 points
- 2nd Clue Word: 4 points
- 3rd Clue Word: 3 points
- 4th Clue Word: 2 points
- 5th Clue Word: 1 point

Word Associations Game, Grades K–1

Word Associations Set A

☆ STAR WORD	CLUE WORDS *read aloud one at a time*				
	5 points	**4 points**	**3 points**	**2 points**	**1 point**
castle	king	queen	moat	knight	tower
jungle	trees	monkey	wild	vines	animals
rocket	space	blast	astronaut	moon	launch
turtle	shell	slow	green	pond	swim
rainbow	colors	sky	rain	bright	arc
clock	hands	numbers	time	tick	alarm
balloon	float	air	pop	party	string
snowman	winter	cold	carrot	build	white
firetruck	red	siren	hose	rescue	ladder
drum	music	beat	sticks	loud	play
swing	park	seat	push	high	fun
umbrella	rain	cover	open	dry	handle
island	water	beach	sand	palm	boat
moon	night	round	stars	shine	sky
glove	hand	fingers	winter	warm	wear

25

Materials	• Word Associations Set A, Grades K–1, page 25 • Word Associations Set B, Grades 2–3, page 26 • Word Associations Set C, Grades 4–5, page 27 • dry-erase boards, markers, and erasers for small groups
Grade Band	K–5
Length of Activity	10 minutes
Differentiation Ideas	**Striving Learners and English Learners:** Write the Clue Words on the board so they can see the spelling of the word as you announce it. You can also provide picture clues for each Clue Word to reinforce word meanings.
Extension Ideas	• Have each small group write its own Word Association Set to share with the class. Before writing, discuss what makes a good set of clues (e.g., the most obvious word should be last; the first one should be general so it doesn't give away the Star Word too easily). • Use words from a current content area text or unit of study to create your own Word Association Sets.

Word Associations Set A

☆ STAR WORD	CLUE WORDS *read aloud one at a time*				
	5 points	**4 points**	**3 points**	**2 points**	**1 point**
castle	king	queen	moat	knight	tower
jungle	trees	monkey	wild	vines	animals
rocket	space	blast	astronaut	moon	launch
turtle	shell	slow	green	pond	swim
rainbow	colors	sky	rain	bright	arc
clock	hands	numbers	time	tick	alarm
balloon	float	air	pop	party	string
snowman	winter	cold	carrot	build	white
firetruck	red	siren	hose	rescue	ladder
drum	music	beat	sticks	loud	play
swing	park	seat	push	high	fun
umbrella	rain	cover	open	dry	handle
island	water	beach	sand	palm	boat
moon	night	round	stars	shine	sky
glove	hand	fingers	winter	warm	wear

Word Associations Set B

☆ STAR WORD	CLUE WORDS *read aloud one at a time*				
	5 points	**4 points**	**3 points**	**2 points**	**1 point**
compass	direction	north	needle	map	travel
volcano	lava	mountain	ash	eruption	magma
octopus	ocean	tentacles	ink	suction	eight
echo	sound	repeat	canyon	loud	voice
treasure	gold	chest	pirate	map	jewels
cactus	desert	prickly	green	plant	thorns
penguin	cold	waddle	ice	black-and-white	Antarctica
telescope	stars	magnify	space	lens	observe
igloo	snow	cold	ice	shelter	blocks
chameleon	color	change	lizard	camouflage	reptile
parachute	jump	float	sky	air	land
horizon	sunset	sky	far	ocean	line
maze	puzzle	path	walls	lost	exit
tornado	wind	storm	destruction	spin	funnel
lightning	storm	thunder	flash	electricity	strike

Word Associations Set C

☆ STAR WORD	CLUE WORDS *read aloud one at a time*				
	5 points	**4 points**	**3 points**	**2 points**	**1 point**
meteor	space	rock	burn	sky	streak
coral	ocean	colorful	fish	underwater	reef
fossil	dinosaur	bones	ancient	rock	preserved
hurricane	storm	wind	rain	powerful	destruction
lantern	light	glow	carry	candle	dark
harbor	boats	water	dock	ships	bay
glacier	ice	frozen	mountain	slow	cold
mansion	large	house	rich	rooms	fancy
eruption	volcano	explosion	lava	ash	sudden
canyon	deep	rock	river	walls	nature
telescope	stars	see	magnify	space	lens
orbit	planet	path	sun	move	around
blueprint	plan	building	design	paper	drawing
parade	march	floats	music	celebration	people
icicle	winter	frozen	cold	hanging	drip

Strategies for Developing a Curiosity About Words

LANGUAGE DOMAINS

Reading

Writing

Speaking

Listening

1.D Weekly Word Quests

Weekly Word Quests encourage students and staff to engage actively with words. Every week, a selected teacher presents an age-appropriate, word-related challenge to all students, such as, "Find words with a prefix meaning *again*." Use the Weekly Word Quests examples on pages 29–30. Each teacher then receives a name tag with a word, with some that meet the requirement (*redecorate*) and others that don't (*reaching*). The words are also posted outside each classroom, allowing students another way to discover them. Throughout the week, students casually explore name tags and classroom displays to find words that match the required task before sharing their findings at the end of the week.

Materials	• name-tag stickers or 2-x-4 mailing labels (one for each participating teacher) • sheet protectors (for outside each teacher's door) • Weekly Word Quests examples, pages 29–30
Grade Band	K–8
Length of Activity	Varies
Differentiation Ideas	• **Striving Learners:** Adapt the challenge based on students' skill levels. If a requirement is too advanced, it can be modified using the same words, but focusing on a simpler feature such as a digraph, vowel team, ending, or syllable count. • **English Learners:** Write the words in English and in your students' native language(s) to allow all students access to the challenge, when appropriate. Utilizing images on the displays outside the classroom can provide additional support. • **Thriving Learners:** After completing the first quest, students tackle an extra question, such as identifying a different word part, meaning, or usage.
Extension Ideas	**Word Scavenger Hunt:** Ask students to search for correct words that are NOT displayed as part of the challenge. Have students search for words that fit the challenge in books, signs, or their surroundings. They can write down words they find and share during a class discussion.
Answers	Answers integrated in Weekly Word Quests examples, pages 29–30

Example 1: Find words that mean the opposite of the underlined word in the sentence. *The massive skyscraper towered over the city.*

Correct Answers		Distractors/Incorrect Answers	
• tiny • little • small • miniature • teeny	• slight • undersized • minuscule • puny • petite	• colossal • tremendous • gigantic • huge • large	• big • vast • enormous

Example 2: Find words that have a suffix AND a prefix.

Correct Answers		Distractors/Incorrect Answers	
• unlucky • unhelpful • replayed • unbelievable • pretreatment • unreadable • rereading	• indescribable • rereads • previews • misspelled • dishonestly • triangles • bicycles	• replay • disagree • preheat • subway • misstep • outrun • freedom	• childhood • beautiful • simply • heavy • teacher • garland • mindful

Example 3: Find words with a prefix that means "back or again."

Correct Answers		Distractors/Incorrect Answers	
• remind • resend • renew • rematch • report	• restart • restocked • retrace • reword • reuse	• reach • ready • rent • reef • reader	• really • rental • reaped • reptile • reckon

Example 4: Find words that are synonyms for *happy.*

Correct Answers		Distractors/Incorrect Answers	
• joyful • cheerful • glad • content • satisfied	• ecstatic • overjoyed • elated • blissful • thrilled	• sad • unhappy • miserable • upset • heartbroken	• devastated • gloomy • displeased • troubled • uneasy

Example 5: Find words with the same vowel sound as *play*.

Correct Answers		Distractors/Incorrect Answers	
• waiting • snake • game • flake • stray	• trail • weight • paint • sway • day	• apple • Alaska • patchy • camera • crashing	• pasta • swamped • hand • stamp • salad

Example 6: Find rhyming words.

Correct Answers	
• cat, bat, hat • dog, fog, log • run, fun, sun • happy, snappy, sappy • water, daughter • silly, chilly	• throat, coat • kitten, mitten • money, sunny, bunny • mug, hug, rug • reflection, direction, connection • brother, mother

Example 7: Find words where *-ly* has the same meaning as in *happily*.

Correct Answers		Distractors/Incorrect Answers	
• quickly • gently • kindly • softly • loudly	• quietly • carefully • happily • brightly • mindfully	• lily • fly • family • sly • only	• jolly • jelly • ally • belly • gully

Example 8: Find words with a schwa.

Correct Answers		Distractors/Incorrect Answers	
• about • banana • chocolate • Alaska	• sofa • pilot • again • elephant • animal	• playground • snowman • moonlight • midnight	• windmill • popcorn • rainbow • candy • birdhouses

Strategies for Developing a Curiosity About Words

1.E **Charades**

Charades provides students with an opportunity to solidify their word learning in a fun, game-like way. Copy, cut out, and fold selected Charades Word Cards on pages 32–33 (or use vocabulary words you've taught). Divide the class into two teams and place the cards in a bowl or hat. Have a player on one team draw a card and silently act out the word or phrase while the team tries to guess the word within a specified time, perhaps 30 or 60 seconds. If guessed correctly, that team earns a point. Then the other team takes a turn. Continue until all cards have been used or time is up. The team with the most points wins!

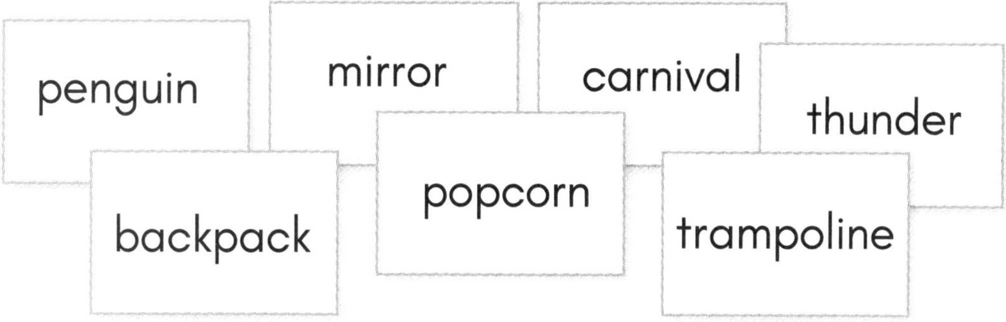

Materials	• Charades Word Cards Set A, Grades K–3, page 32 • Charades Word Cards Set B, Grades 4–8, page 33
Grade Band	K–8
Length of Activity	10–15 minutes per game
Differentiation Ideas	**Striving Learners and English Learners:** Either whisper the word to students before playing or include picture clues with the word.
Extension Ideas	• Permit students to come up with their own words for their peers. • Send home as an "at-home activity" for parents to use with their children as a way to support oral language development and family involvement.

LANGUAGE DOMAINS

Reading

Writing

Speaking

Listening

Charades Word Cards Set A

camping	waterfall	superhero	shovel
suitcase	clown	scooter	embarrassed
penguin	fog	carnival	tug-of-war
weightlifting	mirror	hot air balloon	escape
frighten	detective	backpack	mummy
hot dog	helicopter	rainbow	trampoline
scarf	popcorn	worried	skip
thunder	jealous	flashlight	calculator

Charades Word Cards Set B

marathon	flash mob	meteor shower	treasure map
DJ	haunted house	hopscotch	lion tamer
tarantula	washing the car	origami	working out
detective	horseback riding	shopping spree	cliff diving
ice sculpture	news	rock climbing	secret handshake
snowman	dance battle	laser tag	landing on the moon
couch potato	spaghetti	ziplining	jealous
shark tank	paparazzi	speed walking	cooking show

CHAPTER 1
Word Consciousness

Strategies for Developing a Curiosity About Words

LANGUAGE DOMAINS

Reading

Writing

☐

Speaking

Listening

1.F Elevating Everyday Conversations

This strategy allows you to help elevate vocabulary in oral discussions by replacing simple, familiar words with more academic ones. Begin by selecting a category from the Academic Word Lists on page 35, such as "Thinking and Problem-Solving Words." Use words from the selected list several times throughout the day. With your first use of a word, ask students to repeat it and provide them with a simple definition. For example, tell students to repeat the word *identify*, then explain, "*Identify* means to figure out what something is." Find times throughout the week to use words from the selected list, such as saying "Let's *identify* which resource we have today" or "Who can *identify* the page we are currently on in our story?" Throughout the week, use tone, gestures, visual cues, or synonyms to continue reinforcing the Academic Word Lists vocabulary. Over time, utilizing these words most often seen in written texts will become a part of students' everyday vocabulary. (Strategy inspired by Lindsay Kemeny's *7 Mighty Moves*.)

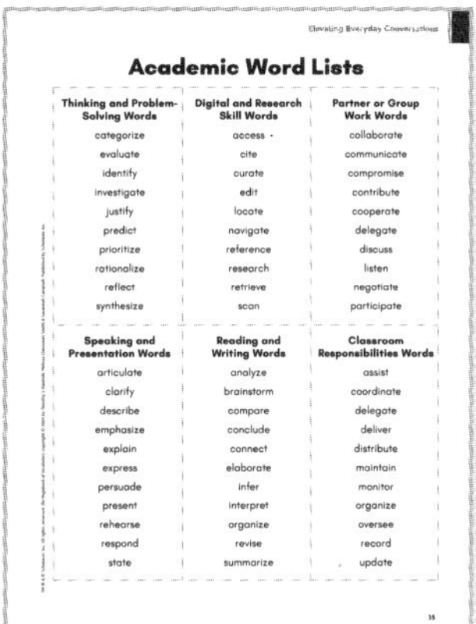

Elevating Everyday Conversations

Academic Word Lists

Thinking and Problem-Solving Words	Digital and Research Skill Words	Partner or Group Work Words
categorize	access	collaborate
evaluate	cite	communicate
identify	curate	compromise
investigate	edit	contribute
justify	locate	cooperate
predict	navigate	delegate
prioritize	reference	discuss
rationalize	research	listen
reflect	retrieve	negotiate
synthesize	scan	participate

Speaking and Presentation Words	Reading and Writing Words	Classroom Responsibilities Words
articulate	analyze	assist
clarify	brainstorm	coordinate
describe	compare	delegate
emphasize	conclude	deliver
explain	connect	distribute
express	elaborate	maintain
persuade	infer	monitor
present	interpret	organize
rehearse	organize	oversee
respond	revise	record
state	summarize	update

35

Materials	Academic Word Lists, page 35
Grade Band	K–8
Length of Activity	This strategy is intended to be embedded throughout the day, not an explicit teaching activity.
Differentiation Ideas	**Striving Learners and English Learners:** Create a T-chart for students. One side should be labeled *Familiar Words*, and the other side *Academic Words*. When introducing academic words, use the left-hand side of the comment to provide a simpler term, a synonym in the student's native language, or an image to illustrate the concept.
Extension Ideas	• Create a word wall or picture dictionary containing routine-based vocabulary. Allow students to illustrate it. • Encourage students to use the word in their speaking and writing and to look for it in texts they read.

Academic Word Lists

Thinking and Problem-Solving Words	Digital and Research Skill Words	Partner or Group Work Words
categorize	access	collaborate
evaluate	cite	communicate
identify	curate	compromise
investigate	edit	contribute
justify	locate	cooperate
predict	navigate	delegate
prioritize	reference	discuss
rationalize	research	listen
reflect	retrieve	negotiate
synthesize	scan	participate

Speaking and Presentation Words	Reading and Writing Words	Classroom Responsibilities Words
articulate	analyze	assist
clarify	brainstorm	coordinate
describe	compare	delegate
emphasize	conclude	deliver
explain	connect	distribute
express	elaborate	maintain
persuade	infer	monitor
present	interpret	organize
rehearse	organize	oversee
respond	revise	record
state	summarize	update

Strategies for Developing a Curiosity About Words

LANGUAGE DOMAINS

Reading

Writing

Speaking

Listening

1.G Cloze Passages

Cloze passages provide valuable practice with sentence-level comprehension and vocabulary recognition. Have students work in pairs to read a paragraph aloud from one of the Cloze Passages Sets on pages 37–38, saying "blank" where words are missing. This first reading allows students to grasp the paragraph's overall meaning before selecting appropriate words. After that reading, have them revisit the passage to fill in the blanks, using words that begin with the first letters provided. Once students have filled in all the blanks, reread the paragraph as a class to discuss what students wrote and what word appeared in the original text. Allow for some flexibility in word choices, as long as they make sense within the passage.

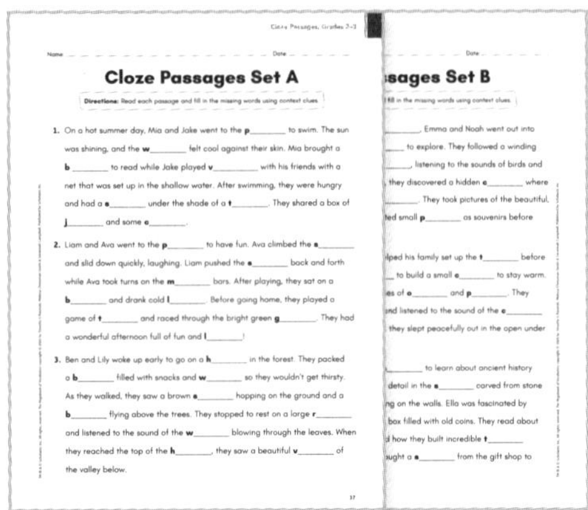

Cloze Passages, Grades 2–3

Name _______ Date _______

Cloze Passages Set A

Directions: Read each passage and fill in the missing words using context clues.

1. On a hot summer day, Mia and Jake went to the **p**_______ to swim. The sun was shining, and the **w**_______ felt cool against their skin. Mia brought a **b**_______ to read while Jake played **v**_______ with his friends with a net that was set up in the shallow water. After swimming, they were hungry and had a **s**_______ under the shade of a **t**_______. They shared a box of **j**_______ and some **c**_______.
2. Liam and Ava went to the **p**_______ to have fun. Ava climbed the **s**_______ and slid down quickly, laughing. Liam pushed the **s**_______ back and forth while Ava took turns on the **m**_______ bars. After playing, they sat on a **b**_______ and drank cold **l**_______. Before going home, they played a game of **t**_______ and raced through the bright green **g**_______. They had a wonderful afternoon full of fun and **l**_______!
3. Ben and Lily woke up early to go on a **h**_______ in the forest. They packed a **b**_______ filled with snacks and **w**_______ so they wouldn't get thirsty. As they walked, they saw a brown **s**_______ hopping on the ground and a **b**_______ flying above the trees. They stopped to rest on a large **r**_______ and listened to the sound of the **w**_______ blowing through the leaves. When they reached the top of the **h**_______, they saw a beautiful **v**_______ of the valley below.

37

Date _______

…sages Set B

…fill in the missing words using context clues.

_______. Emma and Noah went out into _______ to explore. They followed a winding _______, listening to the sounds of birds and … they discovered a hidden **c**_______ where _______. They took pictures of the beautiful, …ted small **p**_______ as souvenirs before

…lped his family set up the **t**_______ before _______ to build a small **c**_______ to stay warm. …es of **o**_______ and **p**_______. They …nd listened to the sound of the **c**_______ … they slept peacefully out in the open under

_______ to learn about ancient history … detail in the **s**_______ carved from stone …ng on the walls. Ella was fascinated by … box filled with old coins. They read about …d how they built incredible **t**_______ …ught a **s**_______ from the gift shop to

Materials	• Cloze Passages Set A, Grades 2–3, page 37 • Cloze Passages Set B, Grades 4–5, page 38
Grade Band	2–5
Length of Activity	15 minutes
Differentiation Ideas	• **Striving Learners:** Direct students to write their own paragraph, choose 5–6 words that have essential meaning for the passage, and change them to blank lines with the first letter provided. Students switch with a partner and complete. • **Striving Learners:** Create a paragraph with blanks for pre-selected words being studied in class. Provide enough context to help students infer the word, reinforcing their understanding of its meaning. • **Striving Learners and English Learners:** If the cloze sentences are too difficult, provide students with a choice of three possible words for each blank.
Extension Ideas	• Create a word wall or picture dictionary containing routine-based vocabulary. Allow students to illustrate it. • Encourage students to use the word in their speaking and writing, and to look for it in texts they read.
Answers	Correct answers will vary according to student interpretation of the context, but sample answers are provided below. **Set A: 1.** pool, water, book, volleyball, snack, tree, juice, chips **2.** playground, slide, swing, monkey, bench, lemonade, tag, grass, laughter **3.** hike, backpack, water, squirrel, bird, rock, wind, hill, view **Set B: 1.** summer, mountains, trail, forest, leaves, creek, rocks, waterfall, pebbles **2.** tent, wood, campfire, orange, purple, marshmallows, crickets, stars **3.** museum, sculptures, paintings, artifact, civilizations, temples, souvenir

Name: ________________ Date: ________

Cloze Passages Set A

Directions: Read each passage and fill in the missing words using context clues.

1. On a hot summer day, Mia and Jake went to the **p**________ to swim. The sun was shining, and the **w**________ felt cool against their skin. Mia brought a **b** ________ to read while Jake played **v**__________ with his friends with a net that was set up in the shallow water. After swimming, they were hungry and had a **s**________ under the shade of a **t**________. They shared a box of **j**________ and some **c**________.

2. Liam and Ava went to the **p**________ to have fun. Ava climbed the **s**________ and slid down quickly, laughing. Liam pushed the **s**________ back and forth while Ava took turns on the **m**________ bars. After playing, they sat on a **b**________ and drank cold **l**________. Before going home, they played a game of **t**________ and raced through the bright green **g**________. They had a wonderful afternoon full of fun and **l**________!

3. Ben and Lily woke up early to go on a **h**________ in the forest. They packed a **b**________ filled with snacks and **w**________ so they wouldn't get thirsty. As they walked, they saw a brown **s**________ hopping on the ground and a **b**________ flying above the trees. They stopped to rest on a large **r**________ and listened to the sound of the **w**________ blowing through the leaves. When they reached the top of the **h**________, they saw a beautiful **v**________ of the valley below.

Name: ______________________ Date: ______________

Cloze Passages Set B

Directions: Read each passage and fill in the missing words using context clues.

1. Once school was out during the **s**________, Emma and Noah went out into nature to the beautiful, tall **m**________ to explore. They followed a winding **t**________ through the dense **f**________, listening to the sounds of birds and rustling **l**________. Along the way, they discovered a hidden **c**________ where clear water flowed over smooth **r**________. They took pictures of the beautiful, cascading **w**________ and collected small **p**________ as souvenirs before heading back.

2. During the camping trip, Mateo helped his family set up the **t**________ before nightfall. They gathered **w**________ to build a small **c**________ to stay warm. As the sun set, the sky turned shades of **o**________ and **p**________. They roasted **m**________ over the fire and listened to the sound of the **c**________ singing in the distance. That night, they slept peacefully out in the open under the sparkling **s**________.

3. Ella and her dad visited the city **m**________ to learn about ancient history and see the art. They admired the detail in the **s**________ carved from stone and the colorful **p**________ hanging on the walls. Ella was fascinated by an ancient **a**________, a treasure box filled with old coins. They read about the lives of ancient **c**________ and how they built incredible **t**________ for worship. Before leaving, Ella bought a **s**________ from the gift shop to remember the day.

1.H Conversation Starters

This strategy provides students with a structured opportunity for modeling and practice of oral language skills through guided conversation. Copy, cut, and distribute the Conversation Starter Cards on pages 40–41 to partners or small groups. Have students take turns selecting a card and reading the prompt aloud. Begin by modeling strong listening behaviors (such as making eye contact, nodding to show understanding, and waiting your turn to speak) and clear speaking skills (such as using details and an appropriate volume). Encourage active listening and thoughtful responses to build confidence, fluency, and respectful communication. Have students take turns asking each other questions until the time is up or all cards have been used.

If you could live inside any board game or

If our class could go on a vacation anywhere in the world, where would you want to go, and what would we do there?

Materials	Conversation Starter Cards, pages 40–41
Grade Band	2–5
Length of Activity	Varies
Differentiation Ideas	• **Striving Learners and English Learners:** Before the whole-class activity, use the activity in a small-group setting to practice the task and preview the prompts so students can participate with confidence. • **Striving Learners and English Learners:** Provide sentence frames to students as a scaffold to promote complete sentences.
Extension Ideas	• Have students come up with their own Conversation Starter Cards for their peers. • Send this activity home for parents to use with their children as a way to support oral language development. • Copy all the cards, laminate them, and then place them on a ring. During activities such as transitions, lining up, and waiting in the hallway, ask students a question and have them whisper an answer to the person next to them.

Strategies for Developing a Curiosity About Words

LANGUAGE DOMAINS

Reading

Writing

Speaking

Listening

Conversation Starter Cards

If you could have any superpower for a day, what would you choose and why?

If you could live inside any board game or video game for a week, which one would you pick and why?

What's your idea of the perfect field trip? What would we do together?

What's the best prank you've ever played on someone (or want to play)?

If our class could go on a vacation anywhere in the world, where would you want to go, and what would we do there?

What's the funniest thing that has ever happened to you at school or with your friends?

If you could invent a new holiday, what would it celebrate, and how would we celebrate it?

If you could switch places with anyone in the school for a day, who would you choose, and what would you do?

If our class could have a theme song, what would it be?

If you could design your own dream house, what would it look like?

What's the silliest thing you've ever done that made everyone laugh?

Imagine we had a pet dragon! What would you name it, and what would it like to do?

If you could create your own ice cream flavor, what would it taste like, and what would you call it?	What's something you think our class should do together that we've never done before?	If you could turn into any animal for a day, what animal would you pick, and what would you do?
If you could meet any character from your favorite book or movie, who would it be, and what would you ask them?	If you had a magic wand, what's the first thing you would fix or change in the world?	What's the weirdest food you've ever tried, and would you eat it again?
What would you do if you found a hidden treasure chest in your backyard?	If you could have dinner with any famous person, dead or alive, who would you invite, and what would you ask them?	What's your favorite family tradition, and why do you think it's so special?
If you were a time traveler, what time period would you visit first and why?	If your family had to live in a tree house or a castle, which one would you choose, and what would it look like inside?	What's the coolest talent or skill you have that no one else knows about?

CHAPTER 1
Word Consciousness

Strategies for Developing a Curiosity About Words

LANGUAGE DOMAINS

Reading

Writing

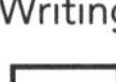

Speaking

Listening

1.1 Twenty Questions

Twenty Questions challenges students to draw upon their background knowledge and vocabulary to identify a secret word. Give a student a secret word by whispering it to them or writing it down. Then have the student call on classmates to ask yes-or-no questions to help determine the word. Classmates should listen carefully and track the answers to make increasingly targeted guesses. Instead of asking a question, a classmate may use their turn to guess the word. If guessed correctly, that classmate wins and takes the next turn with a new word. If no one guesses the word after 20 questions, reveal it and begin a new round.

Twenty Questions

Twenty Questions Ideas

Grades K-1	Grades 2-3	Grades 4-5	Grades 6-8
slide	bicycle	marathon	freedom
dog	octopus	scarecrow	container
ball	treasure	lava	justice
chair	airplane	tornado	whisper
sun	lighthouse	boomerang	truth
fish	penguin	fossil	sticky
car	cactus	puzzle	wisdom
tree	igloo	beekeeper	prey
cat	lantern	hoverboard	patience
cake	robot	balloon	perimeter
cow	waterfall	trampoline	courage
clock	snowman	anchor	marathon
train	castle	windmill	hope
bed	tornado	dome	doubt
frog	motorcycle	tugboat	collapse
duck	guitar	garden	imagination
boat	chocolate	basketball	creativity
drum	firetruck	bridge	perfume
chair	telescope	submarine	equality
sock	maze	jeans	beauty

43

Materials	Twenty Questions Ideas, page 43
Grade Band	2–5
Length of Activity	Varies
Differentiation Ideas	• **Striving Learners:** Model how to start with broad questions incorporating general categories or features, such as "Is it a living thing?" before narrowing it down with more specific questions. Or provide one starting clue, such as "This is a noun" or "This is something you might find on a beach." • **Thriving Learners:** Extend the activity by providing more challenging words, such as verbs instead of only nouns.
Extension Ideas	Play with a set of words from a text students are reading or a unit of study they're engaged in.

Twenty Questions Ideas

Grades K-1	Grades 2-3	Grades 4-5	Grades 6-8
slide	bicycle	marathon	freedom
dog	octopus	scarecrow	container
ball	treasure	lava	justice
chair	airplane	tornado	whisper
sun	lighthouse	boomerang	truth
fish	penguin	fossil	sticky
car	cactus	puzzle	wisdom
tree	igloo	beekeeper	prey
cat	lantern	hoverboard	patience
cake	robot	balloon	perimeter
cow	waterfall	trampoline	courage
clock	snowman	anchor	marathon
train	castle	windmill	hope
bed	tornado	dome	doubt
frog	motorcycle	tugboat	collapse
duck	guitar	garden	imagination
boat	chocolate	basketball	creativity
drum	firetruck	bridge	perfume
chair	telescope	submarine	equality
sock	maze	jeans	beauty

Strategies for Developing a Curiosity About Words

LANGUAGE DOMAINS

Reading

Writing

Speaking

Listening

1.J Vocabulary Parades

Vocabulary Parades, which are typically held one grade level at a time, give the entire school a chance to explore and celebrate words. Assign each student a vocabulary word to represent through creative costumes, props, or pictures. Then have all students walk down the hallways, displaying their words, costumes, props, and pictures proudly for the rest of the school to see. This strategy can take the better part of a school day, with students decorating signs to carry, gathering props, and donning costumes. Alternatively, you may have students prepare at home to allow families to contribute ideas.

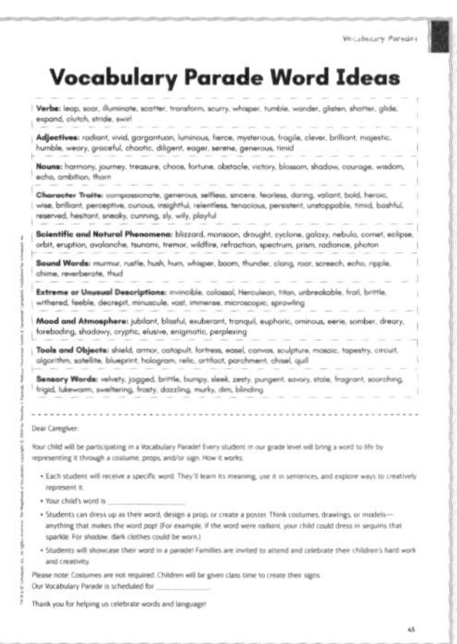

Vocabulary Parades

Vocabulary Parade Word Ideas

Verbs: leap, soar, illuminate, scatter, transform, scurry, whisper, tumble, wonder, glisten, shatter, glide, expand, clutch, stride, swirl

Adjectives: radiant, vivid, gargantuan, luminous, fierce, mysterious, fragile, clever, brilliant, majestic, humble, weary, graceful, chaotic, diligent, eager, serene, generous, timid

Nouns: harmony, journey, treasure, chaos, fortune, obstacle, victory, blossom, shadow, courage, wisdom, echo, ambition, thorn

Character Traits: compassionate, generous, selfless, sincere, fearless, daring, valiant, bold, heroic, wise, brilliant, perceptive, curious, insightful, relentless, tenacious, persistent, unstoppable, timid, bashful, reserved, hesitant, sneaky, cunning, sly, wily, playful

Scientific and Natural Phenomena: blizzard, monsoon, drought, cyclone, galaxy, nebula, comet, eclipse, orbit, eruption, avalanche, tsunami, tremor, wildfire, refraction, spectrum, prism, radiance, photon

Sound Words: murmur, rustle, hush, hum, whisper, boom, thunder, clang, roar, screech, echo, ripple, chime, reverberate, thud

Extreme or Unusual Descriptions: invincible, colossal, Herculean, titan, unbreakable, frail, brittle, withered, feeble, decrepit, minuscule, vast, immense, microscopic, sprawling

Mood and Atmosphere: jubilant, blissful, exuberant, tranquil, euphoric, ominous, eerie, somber, dreary, foreboding, shadowy, cryptic, elusive, enigmatic, perplexing

Tools and Objects: shield, armor, catapult, fortress, easel, canvas, sculpture, mosaic, tapestry, circuit, algorithm, satellite, blueprint, hologram, relic, artifact, parchment, chisel, quill

Sensory Words: velvety, jagged, brittle, bumpy, sleek, zesty, pungent, savory, stale, fragrant, scorching, frigid, lukewarm, sweltering, frosty, dazzling, murky, dim, blinding

Dear Caregiver:

Your child will be participating in a Vocabulary Parade! Every student in our grade level will bring a word to life by representing it through a costume, props, and/or sign. How it works:

- Each student will receive a specific word. They'll learn its meaning, use it in sentences, and explore ways to creatively represent it.
- Your child's word is ________________
- Students can dress up as their word, design a prop, or create a poster. Think costumes, drawings, or models—anything that makes the word pop! (For example, if the word were *radiant*, your child could dress in sequins that sparkle. For *shadow*, dark clothes could be worn.)
- Students will showcase their word in a parade! Families are invited to attend and celebrate their children's hard work and creativity.

Please note: Costumes are not required. Children will be given class time to create their signs.

Our Vocabulary Parade is scheduled for ____________

Thank you for helping us celebrate words and language!

45

Materials	• Vocabulary Parade Word Ideas and take-home letter, page 45 • cardstock and art supplies for creating signs
Grade Band	2–5
Length of Activity	Varies
Differentiation Ideas	• **Striving Learners and English Learners:** Instead of assigning a word, allow students to choose a word they are comfortable turning into a visual. Before allowing them to start, orally plan with students the representation they want to create. • **English Learners:** Display words in English and their native language.
Extension Ideas	Create a "Vocabulary Wall of Fame" featuring photos of students with their word representations and a description of the word.

Vocabulary Parade Word Ideas

Verbs: leap, soar, illuminate, scatter, transform, scurry, whisper, tumble, wander, glisten, shatter, glide, expand, clutch, stride, swirl
Adjectives: radiant, vivid, gargantuan, luminous, fierce, mysterious, fragile, clever, brilliant, majestic, humble, weary, graceful, chaotic, diligent, eager, serene, generous, timid
Nouns: harmony, journey, treasure, chaos, fortune, obstacle, victory, blossom, shadow, courage, wisdom, echo, ambition, thorn
Character Traits: compassionate, generous, selfless, sincere, fearless, daring, valiant, bold, heroic, wise, brilliant, perceptive, curious, insightful, relentless, tenacious, persistent, unstoppable, timid, bashful, reserved, hesitant, sneaky, cunning, sly, wily, playful
Scientific and Natural Phenomena: blizzard, monsoon, drought, cyclone, galaxy, nebula, comet, eclipse, orbit, eruption, avalanche, tsunami, tremor, wildfire, refraction, spectrum, prism, radiance, photon
Sound Words: murmur, rustle, hush, hum, whisper, boom, thunder, clang, roar, screech, echo, ripple, chime, reverberate, thud
Extreme or Unusual Descriptions: invincible, colossal, Herculean, titan, unbreakable, frail, brittle, withered, feeble, decrepit, minuscule, vast, immense, microscopic, sprawling
Mood and Atmosphere: jubilant, blissful, exuberant, tranquil, euphoric, ominous, eerie, somber, dreary, foreboding, shadowy, cryptic, elusive, enigmatic, perplexing
Tools and Objects: shield, armor, catapult, fortress, easel, canvas, sculpture, mosaic, tapestry, circuit, algorithm, satellite, blueprint, hologram, relic, artifact, parchment, chisel, quill
Sensory Words: velvety, jagged, brittle, bumpy, sleek, zesty, pungent, savory, stale, fragrant, scorching, frigid, lukewarm, sweltering, frosty, dazzling, murky, dim, blinding

---

Dear Caregiver:

Your child will be participating in a Vocabulary Parade! Every student in our grade level will bring a word to life by representing it through a costume, props, and/or sign. How it works:

- Each student will receive a specific word. They'll learn its meaning, use it in sentences, and explore ways to creatively represent it.
- Your child's word is ______________________.
- Students can dress up as their word, design a prop, or create a poster. Think costumes, drawings, or models—anything that makes the word *pop*! (For example, if the word were *radiant*, your child could dress in sequins that sparkle. For *shadow*, dark clothes could be worn.)
- Students will showcase their word in a parade! Families are invited to attend and celebrate their children's hard work and creativity.

Please note: Costumes are not required. Children will be given class time to create their signs.
Our Vocabulary Parade is scheduled for ______________.

Thank you for helping us celebrate words and language!

Strategies for Developing a Curiosity About Words

LANGUAGE DOMAINS

Reading

Writing

Speaking

Listening

1.K Vocabulary Theater

Vocabulary Theater provides students with an authentic way to practice words they are learning. Students work in small groups to write a script based on a selected scene from a class-shared text such as a literature study. As students write, they must thoughtfully incorporate designated vocabulary words from the shared text—and, in doing so, they reinforce the word meanings. Once the script is complete, each group creates simple character puppets to represent the characters from the shared text (using the Puppet Templates on page 47 or by creating original illustrations). Next, students rehearse their script, taking time to practice flow and expression, and gather simple props to support their story. Once ready, each group performs its vocabulary-infused play for the class or grade level.

Materials	• craft sticks • paper • colored pencils or markers • Puppet Templates, page 47
Grade Band	2–8
Length of Activity	Several class periods
Differentiation Ideas	• **Striving Learners and English Learners:** Allow students to look at the script while performing, instead of memorizing lines. • **Thriving Learners:** Give students more challenging, nuanced, or abstract vocabulary to incorporate into their script.
Extension Ideas	• Allow students to create simple backdrops for their plays. • Ask students to act as "reporters" who interview the cast members after the plays. Prompt them to ask questions such as "How did you decide what your character would say in the play?" or "What does the word ________ mean and how did you incorporate it into your play?"

Puppet Templates

CHAPTER 1
Word Consciousness

Strategies for Choosing the Right Expressive Words

LANGUAGE DOMAINS

Reading

Writing

Speaking

Listening

1.L Vocabulary Sentences

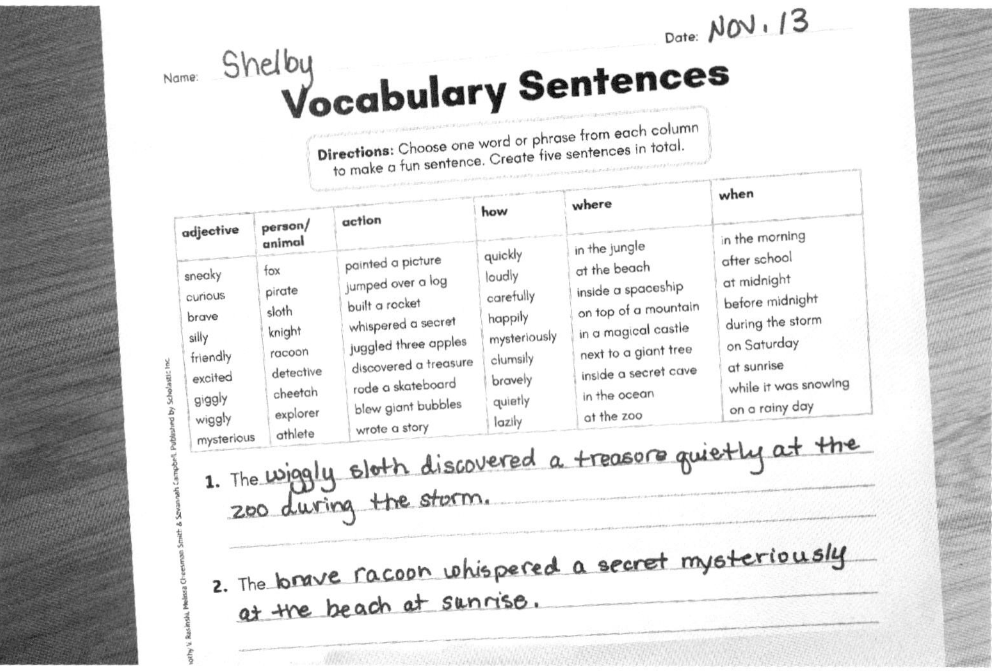

Date: NOV. 13

Name: Shelby

Vocabulary Sentences

Directions: Choose one word or phrase from each column to make a fun sentence. Create five sentences in total.

adjective	person/ animal	action	how	where	when
sneaky	fox	painted a picture	quickly	in the jungle	in the morning
curious	pirate	jumped over a log	loudly	at the beach	after school
brave	sloth	built a rocket	carefully	inside a spaceship	at midnight
silly	knight	whispered a secret	happily	on top of a mountain	before midnight
friendly	racoon	juggled three apples	mysteriously	in a magical castle	during the storm
excited	detective	discovered a treasure	clumsily	next to a giant tree	on Saturday
giggly	cheetah	rode a skateboard	bravely	inside a secret cave	at sunrise
wiggly	explorer	blew giant bubbles	quietly	in the ocean	while it was snowing
mysterious	athlete	wrote a story	lazily	at the zoo	on a rainy day

1. The wiggly sloth discovered a treasore quietly at the zoo during the storm.

2. The brave racoon whispered a secret mysteriously at the beach at sunrise.

Display Vocabulary Sentences on page 49 for students. Have students choose one word/phrase from each column to create new sentences, writing on the provided lines. This helps students be exposed to underutilized words and to try new vocabulary in their writing. Students can share sentences orally with a partner or the whole class.

Materials	Vocabulary Sentences, page 49
Grade Band	2–3
Length of Activity	20 minutes
Differentiation Ideas	• **Striving Learners and English Learners:** Cross out one or two columns to scaffold the process until students are ready for the content of all columns.
Extension Ideas	• Challenge students to rearrange the sentence and put the words and phrases in a different order, starting with either the where or when. Explain to them that the subject doesn't always have to be first and that this will help make their writing more interesting. • Have students make up their own words and phrases for each column. Then combine their great ideas and repeat the activity. • Allow students to create illustrations for each sentence.

Name: ______________________ Date: ____________

Vocabulary Sentences

Directions: Choose one word or phrase from each column to make a fun sentence. Create five sentences in total.

adjective	person/ animal	action	how	where	when
sneaky	fox	painted a picture	quickly	in the jungle	in the morning
curious	pirate	jumped over a log	loudly	at the beach	after school
brave	sloth	built a rocket	carefully	inside a spaceship	at midnight
silly	knight	whispered a secret	happily	on top of a mountain	before midnight
friendly	raccoon	juggled three apples	mysteriously	in a magical castle	during the storm
excited	detective	discovered a treasure	clumsily	next to a giant tree	on Saturday
giggly	cheetah	rode a skateboard	bravely	inside a secret cave	at sunrise
wiggly	explorer	blew giant bubbles	quietly	in the ocean	while it was snowing
mysterious	athlete	wrote a story	lazily	at the zoo	on a rainy day

1. The ______________________

2. The ______________________

3. The ______________________

4. The ______________________

5. The ______________________

LANGUAGE DOMAINS

Reading

Writing

Speaking

Listening

1.M **Word-Swap Sentences: Using a Thesaurus**

For this strategy, students use a thesaurus to find precise and interesting words. Distribute Word-Swap Sentences on page 51 to each student. Model for students the purpose and steps for taking a sentence with a basic word, such as "The sun was *bright* in the sky," and have them begin by looking up the indicated word, *bright*, in a print or digital thesaurus. Students may find these synonyms: *shiny*, *sparkling*, and *blazing*. Focus on the sentence context to choose the best word. For example, in the example sentence, *blazing* fits best, as the sun is not typically described as *shiny* or *sparkling*. Then have student pairs read the other sentences on the page and use a thesaurus to swap the boldfaced words for better ones. Upon completion, ask partners to choose their favorite sentence to share with the class.

Materials	• Word-Swap Sentences, page 51 • print or digital thesauruses
Grade Band	2–5
Length of Activity	15 minutes per session
Differentiation Ideas	• **Striving Learners and English Learners:** Provide additional support in small groups by talking through various choices to help students see if the replacement word makes sense in the sentence. • **English Learners:** For English Learners with bilingual dictionaries, use this strategy as an additional time to show students how to use their bilingual dictionaries to understand words.
Extension Ideas	• During writing time, ask students to use this strategy with at least one word in their own writing. • Encourage students to focus specifically on adding interesting adjectives or adverbs to the sentences.

Name: ______________________________ Date: ______________

Word-Swap Sentences

Directions: Use a physical or digital thesaurus to swap out the given word for a word that fits the situation in an interesting way.

1. The ______________________ dog ran across the yard.
big

2. She was ______________________ to see her friend after being away.
happy

3. The bird ______________________ quickly away from the tree.
flew

4. The soup was ______________________ and smelled delicious.
hot

5. The baby was ______________________ and started to cry.
tired

6. He gave me a ______________________ present for my birthday.
nice

7. The hungry children ______________________ all their lunch before going outside.
ate

8. The cake was ______________________, but I wanted more frosting.
good

9. She ______________________ "Thank you" after getting the gift.
said

10. It was a ______________________ day, so we wore jackets.
cold

11. The movie was ______________________ and made us laugh.
funny

12. My backpack is ______________________ with all my books.
heavy

13. We ______________________ a big sandcastle on the beach today.
made

14. The teacher gave us a ______________________ test.
hard

15. She was ______________________ when her balloon floated away.
sad

16. He ______________________ slowly across the finish line.
walked

17. The kitten was ______________________ and fluffy.
small

18. He is a ______________________ runner and won the race.
fast

19. The book was ______________________, so I read it in one day.
interesting

20. The music was ______________________ at the party.
loud

LANGUAGE DOMAINS

Reading

Writing

Speaking

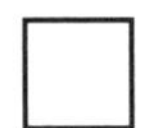

Listening

1.N Expanding Sentences

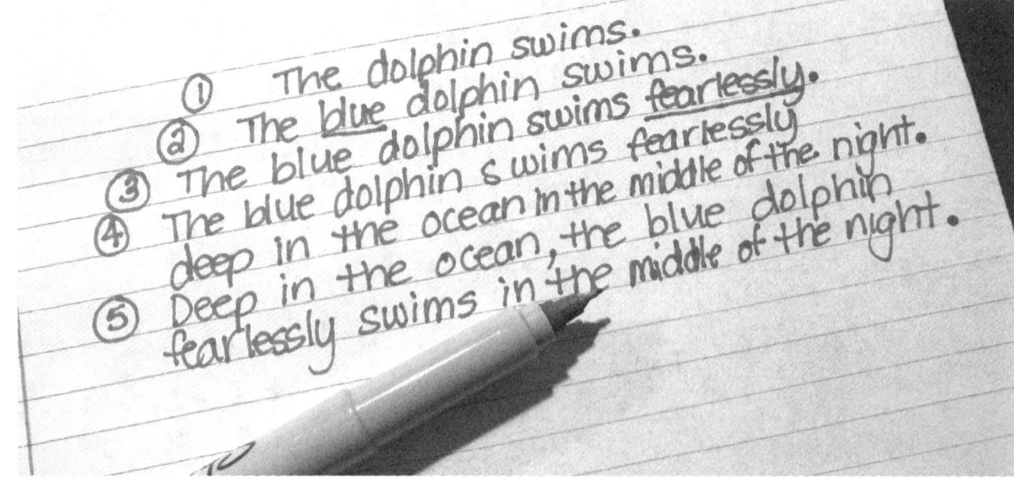

Students often write simple sentences and need to be explicitly taught how to expand them to be more descriptive writers. In this strategy, you show students step by step, how to add details to a sentence, a process they will be able to replicate on their own through practice. Use the Teacher Directions for Expanding Sentences on page 53 to lead students through this strategy. Students will need the *How* Adverbs Ending in *-ly* on page 54 for step 3 of the activity, so this can be copied or projected.

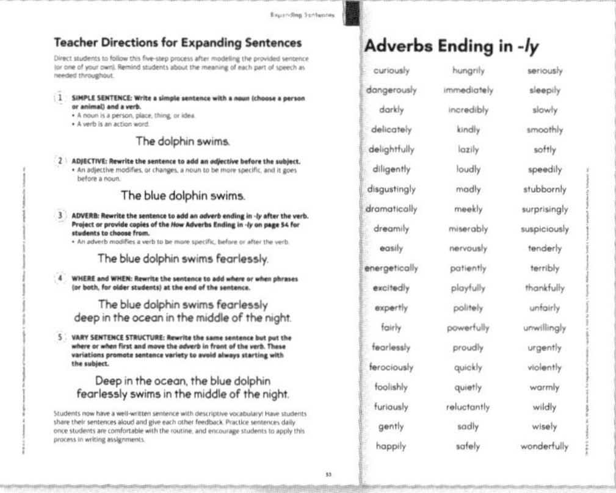

Expanding Sentences

Teacher Directions for Expanding Sentences

Direct students to follow this five-step process after modeling the provided sentence (or one of your own). Remind students about the meaning of each part of speech as needed throughout.

1 **SIMPLE SENTENCE: Write a simple sentence with a *noun* (choose a person or animal) and a verb.**
- A noun is a person, place, thing, or idea.
- A verb is an action word.

The dolphin swims.

2 **ADJECTIVE: Rewrite the sentence to add an *adjective* before the subject.**
- An adjective modifies, or changes, a noun to be more specific, and it goes before a noun.

The blue dolphin swims.

3 **ADVERB: Rewrite the sentence to add an *adverb* ending in *-ly* after the verb. Project or provide copies of the *How* Adverbs Ending in *-ly* on page 54 for students to choose from.**
- An adverb modifies a verb to be more specific, before or after the verb.

The blue dolphin swims fearlessly.

4 **WHERE and WHEN: Rewrite the sentence to add *where* or *when* phrases (or both, for older students) at the end of the sentence.**

The blue dolphin swims fearlessly deep in the ocean in the middle of the night.

5 **VARY SENTENCE STRUCTURE: Rewrite the same sentence but put the *where* or *when* first and move the *adverb* in front of the verb. These variations promote sentence variety to avoid always starting with the subject.**

Deep in the ocean, the blue dolphin fearlessly swims in the middle of the night.

Students now have a well-written sentence with descriptive vocabulary! Have students share their sentences aloud and give each other feedback. Practice sentences daily once students are comfortable with the routine, and encourage students to apply this process in writing assignments.

53

Adverbs Ending in *-ly*

curiously	hungrily	seriously
dangerously	immediately	sleepily
darkly	incredibly	slowly
delicately	kindly	smoothly
delightfully	lazily	softly
diligently	loudly	speedily
disgustingly	madly	stubbornly
dramatically	meekly	surprisingly
dreamily	miserably	suspiciously
easily	nervously	tenderly
energetically	patiently	terribly
excitedly	playfully	thankfully
expertly	politely	unfairly
fairly	powerfully	unwillingly
fearlessly	proudly	urgently
ferociously	quickly	violently
foolishly	quietly	warmly
furiously	reluctantly	wildly
gently	sadly	wisely
happily	safely	wonderfully

Materials	• Teacher Directions for Expanding Sentences, page 53 • *How* Adverbs Ending in *-ly*, page 54 • lined or blank sheet of paper
Grade Band	2–8
Length of Activity	60 minutes
Differentiation Ideas	**Striving Learners and English Learners:** Check in on each step for understanding or complete this strategy in a small group first.
Extension Ideas	• Allow students to add in as many adjectives or adverbs as the sentence will allow, to create creative sentences. • Glue the *How* Adverbs Ending in *-ly* in the students' notebooks for future reference. • Give students a picture that they should use to write another sentence. Pictures can be swapped the next day to practice again. Continue until students are comfortable with this strategy.

Teacher Directions for Expanding Sentences

Direct students to follow this five-step process after modeling the provided sentence (or one of your own). Remind students about the meaning of each part of speech as needed throughout.

1. **SIMPLE SENTENCE: Write a simple sentence with a *noun* (choose a person or animal) and a *verb*.**
   - A noun is a person, place, thing, or idea.
   - A verb is an action word.

   The dolphin swims.

2. **ADJECTIVE: Rewrite the sentence to add an *adjective* before the subject.**
   - An adjective modifies, or changes, a noun to be more specific, and it goes before a noun.

   The blue dolphin swims.

3. **ADVERB: Rewrite the sentence to add an *adverb* ending in -*ly* after the verb. Project or provide copies of the *How* Adverbs Ending in -*ly* on page 54 for students to choose from.**
   - An adverb modifies a verb to be more specific, before or after the verb.

   The blue dolphin swims fearlessly.

4. **WHERE and WHEN: Rewrite the sentence to add *where* or *when* phrases (or both, for older students) at the end of the sentence.**

   The blue dolphin swims fearlessly deep in the ocean in the middle of the night.

5. **VARY SENTENCE STRUCTURE: Rewrite the same sentence but put the *where* or *when* first and move the *adverb* in front of the *verb*. These variations promote sentence variety to avoid always starting with the subject.**

   Deep in the ocean, the blue dolphin fearlessly swims in the middle of the night.

Students now have a well-written sentence with descriptive vocabulary! Have students share their sentences aloud and give each other feedback. Practice sentences daily once students are comfortable with the routine, and encourage students to apply this process in writing assignments.

How Adverbs Ending in *-ly*

abruptly
amazingly
angrily
anxiously
arrogantly
awkwardly
bashfully
beautifully
bitterly
boldly
bravely
breathlessly
briskly
calmly
carefully
carelessly
casually
cheerfully
cleverly
compassionately
curiously
dangerously
darkly
delicately
delightfully
diligently
disgustingly
dramatically
dreamily
easily
energetically
excitedly
expertly
fairly
fearlessly
ferociously
foolishly
furiously
gently
happily
hungrily
immediately
incredibly
kindly
lazily
loudly
madly
meekly
miserably
nervously
patiently
playfully
politely
powerfully
proudly
quickly
quietly
reluctantly
sadly
safely
seriously
sleepily
slowly
smoothly
softly
speedily
stubbornly
surprisingly
suspiciously
tenderly
terribly
thankfully
unfairly
unwillingly
urgently
violently
warmly
wildly
wisely
wonderfully

1.0 Show, Don't Tell

This strategy allows you to introduce the difference between *telling* about an experience and *showing* an experience, using details to create vivid images for readers. For example, instead of writing, *I was nervous*, the student may say, *My hands trembled as I stared at the paper*, or *My heart was beating so loudly, I was sure everyone could hear it.* There are six common strategies to *show* in writing: physical details, figurative language, actions, dialogue, five senses, and feelings. Reveal and explain each technique by copying the Show, Don't Tell Teacher Cards from page 56 on the corresponding colored paper, or color them in with colored pencils. Distribute Show, Don't Tell Underlining on page 57, and have students read each paragraph and underline each technique with the corresponding colored pencil. Then students can practice writing their own with Show, Don't Tell "My Try" on page 58 and underline in the color of the strategies they used.

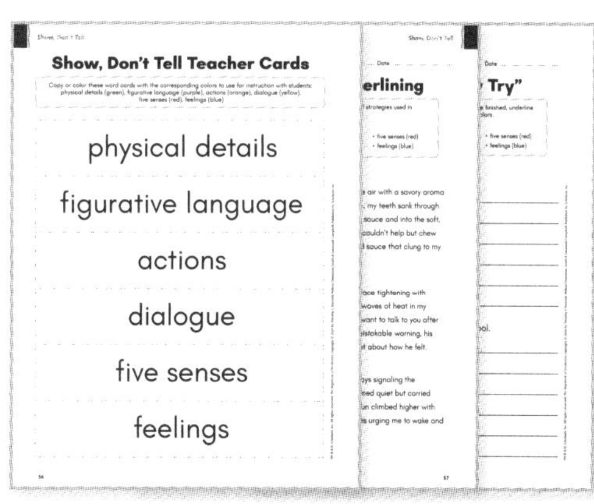

Materials	• Show, Don't Tell Teacher Cards, page 56 • Show, Don't Tell Underlining, page 57 • Show, Don't Tell "My Try," page 58 • colored pencils or crayons
Grade Band	2–8
Length of Activity	Two 30-minute sessions
Differentiation Ideas	• **Striving Learners:** Work with students to brainstorm a few Show, Don't Tell words and ideas for the "My Try" writing prompts so they have a starting point. • **English Learners:** Create a small sketch of each sentence on the "My Try" page to make sure the student understands the meaning of the original sentence to be changed.
Extension Ideas	• Encourage students to apply these strategies in future writing projects. • Ask students to find a sentence in their own writing that needs revision to be more descriptive, using one of the strategies.

LANGUAGE DOMAINS

Reading

Writing

Speaking

Listening

Show, Don't Tell Teacher Cards

Copy or color these word cards with the corresponding colors to use for instruction with students: physical details (green), figurative language (purple), actions (orange), dialogue (yellow), five senses (red), feelings (blue)

physical details

figurative language

actions

dialogue

five senses

feelings

Name: ______________________ Date: ____________

Show, Don't Tell Underlining

Directions: Use colored pencils to underline the Show, Don't Tell strategies used in each paragraph.

SHOW, DON'T TELL STRATEGIES:

- physical details (green)
- figurative language (purple)
- actions (orange)
- dialogue (yellow)
- five senses (red)
- feelings (blue)

The pizza was good.

Steam swirled up from the gooey, melted cheese, filling the air with a savory aroma that instantly made my mouth water. As I took the first bite, my teeth sank through the smooth, warm cheese, cutting through the rich tomato sauce and into the soft, buttery crust. The flavors melded together perfectly, and I couldn't help but chew quickly, eager to savor every moment. Even the cheese and sauce that clung to my fingertips seemed to beg for a taste.

He is mad.

Sitting at his desk, he clenched his jaw, the muscles in his face tightening with irritation. His eyes, burning with intensity, seemed to shoot waves of heat in my direction. The words burst from his lips, sharp and cold, "I want to talk to you after class." The final hiss that escaped his voice carried an unmistakable warning, his anger simmering just beneath the surface, leaving no doubt about how he felt.

The morning was nice.

Beyond the mountains, the sun slowly emerged, its bright rays signaling the beginning of a new day. The sky, a soft shade of blue, seemed quiet but carried a hint of sorrow. A gentle breeze stirred the trees, as the sun climbed higher with warmth. Birds sang softly outside my window, their melodies urging me to wake and join the day.

Name: ______________________ Date: __________

Show, Don't Tell "My Try"

Directions: Write your own Show, Don't Tell paragraphs. When you're finished, underline the type of Show, Don't Tell strategies you used in the appropriate colors.

SHOW, DON'T TELL STRATEGIES:

- physical details (green)
- figurative language (purple)
- actions (orange)
- dialogue (yellow)
- five senses (red)
- feelings (blue)

The puppy was a terror.

____

____

____

____

____

____

Alex was nervous the night before the first day of school.

____

____

____

____

____

____

1.P Word Choice Reference Sheets

Choosing a precise word to express an idea does not always come easily to students. With this strategy, students get a variety of words to use in their writing. Select a Word Choice Reference Sheet on pages 60–65, copy or download it, and distribute it to help students make their writing more precise and engaging.

Onomatopoeia: Have students come up with situations in which they would use certain onomatopoeia words. For example, *hoot* could be used for an owl in a tree in the middle of the forest or as the sound a fan makes at a hockey game. Students can then write a situation and the class guesses which onomatopoeia it is.

Words to Use Instead of *Said*: Take a chapter book or narrative writing the students have done and look for character dialogue. Have students practice changing the word *said* to something that describes the situation better or that will make the writing more interesting.

Positive and Negative Character Traits: Use these lists when students are writing a narrative as a way to design their character and what traits they would like them to have, or to list traits of main characters in a story or book they are reading.

Five-Senses Words: Have students think of a scene and use the lists to describe it using all five senses. Students can use an online dictionary if they need to double-check the meaning of a word on the list.

Color Words: Dramatically describe objects in the classroom using the color words provided to create a sentence. For example, "The strawberry-red marker showed brightly on the snowy-colored board." The goal is to get students practicing more descriptive language in a playful way.

Encourage students to apply the strategies in future writing assignments and discussions to ensure ongoing growth.

Materials	Word Choice Reference Sheets: • Onomatopoeia, page 60 • Words to Use Instead of *Said*, page 61 • Positive Character Traits, page 62 • Negative Character Traits, page 63 • Five-Senses Words, page 64 • Color Words, page 65
Grade Band	2–8
Differentiation Ideas	**Striving Learners and English Learners:** For any upcoming writing assignment, limit the choices for the words by drawing a star next to two or three words that you want students to use.
Extension Ideas	Have students glue Reference Sheets into a writing notebook for use during writing lessons and activities.

Strategies for Choosing the Right Expressive Words

LANGUAGE DOMAINS

Reading

Writing

Speaking

Listening

Onomatopoeia

bang
bark
beep
bloop
boing
boo
boom
bowwow
brr
burp
buzz
chirp
chomp
chug
clack
clang
clap
clash
clatter
click
clink
clip-clop
clomp
cluck
clunk
coo
crack
crackle
crash
creak
crinkle
croak
crunch
ding-dong
drip
fizz
glug
gong
grate
grind
groan
grunt
gurgle
hiss
honk
hoot
howl
hum
jingle
kaboom
kerplunk
knock
meow
moan
moo
neigh
patter
ping
plop
poof
pop
pow
puff
purr
quack
rap
rattle
rev
ring
roar
rumble
rustle
screech
shriek
sigh
sizzle
slurp
smack
snort
splash
squeak
squeal
squish
swish
swoosh
tap
thud
thump
tick
tinkle
twang
vroom
whack
whiz
whoop
whoosh
yap
yowl
zip
zoom

Words to Use Instead of *Said*

In a Happy Way:
beamed, chirped, chuckled, giggled, joked, laughed, rejoiced, sang out

In a Sad Way:
agonized, bawled, blubbered, cried, groaned, moaned, mourned, pouted, sighed, sniveled, sobbed, wept, whimpered, whined

In a Frightened Way:
gasped, quaked, quivered, shuddered, stammered, trembled, whispered, yelped

In an Angry Way:
barked, blurted, fumed, grumbled, hissed, miffed, raged, retorted, screamed, scolded, seethed, snarled, snapped, thundered

In a Confused Way:
doubted, muttered, puzzled, questioned, wondered

In a Pained Way:
bellowed, cried, cried out, grieved, howled, roared, shrieked, wailed, winced, yelped

In an Excited Way:
boomed, cheered, exclaimed, gushed, squealed, whooped

In a Tired/Sleepy Way:
droned, mumbled, muttered, yawned

In an Understanding Way:
acknowledged, agreed, comforted, consoled, empathized, reassured, sympathized

In a Bossy Way:
begged, bossed, demanded, dictated, implored, insisted, ordered, preached, pleaded

In a Quiet/Soft Way:
breathed, coaxed, crept, murmured, uttered, whispered

In a Loud/Strong Way:
announced, declared, proclaimed, projected, resounded, shouted, thundered

In a Reflective Way:
considered, contemplated, debated, pondered, revealed, vented, vocalized

Positive Character Traits

ambitious
adventurous
bold
brave
calm
careful
caring
cheerful
confident
considerate
cooperative
courageous
courteous
creative
curious
dependable
determined
energetic
enthusiastic
fair

forgiving
friendly
funny
generous
gentle
grateful
hardworking
helpful
honest
humble
independent
intelligent
joyful
kind
kindhearted
loving
loyal
open-minded
optimistic
outgoing

patient
peaceful
persistent
playful
polite
responsible
respectful
resourceful
selfless
silly
sincere
smart
spunky
strong
supportive
thoughtful
trusting
trustworthy
understanding
wise

Negative Character Traits

aggressive
arrogant
bossy
careless
childish
clumsy
conceited
cowardly
cruel
deceitful
demanding
dishonest
disloyal
disobedient
disrespectful
disorganized
distant
egotistical
evil
foolish
forgetful
greedy

grumpy
harsh
hateful
impatient
impulsive
inconsiderate
irresponsible
jealous
lazy
loud
manipulative
mean
messy
moody
obnoxious
overconfident
pessimistic
petty
possessive
reckless
rude
ruthless

sarcastic
secretive
selfish
sneaky
spoiled
stubborn
suspicious
thoughtless
tricky
unappreciative
uncooperative
ungrateful
unhelpful
unkind
unreliable
untrustworthy
vain
vindictive
weak
wasteful
whiny
wild

Five-Senses Words

Sight: blazing, bright, blurry, bold, colorful, dark, dazzling, dim, distinct, drab, faint, flashy, flickering, foggy, gleaming, glimmering, glittering, gloomy, glowing, hazy, illuminated, light, misty, murky, pale, radiant, reflective, shadowy, shiny, shimmering, smoky, sparkling, speckled, spotted, streaked, transparent, twinkling, vibrant, vivid, wispy

Sound: banging, beeping, booming, bubbling, buzzing, chattering, chirping, clicking, clunking, crackling, creaking, croaking, crunching, deafening, drumming, echoing, faint, giggling, grumbling, growling, gurgling, hissing, honking, humming, jingling, melodic, muffled, noisy, pattering, pounding, rattling, roaring, rustling, screeching, silent, sizzling, splashing, thudding, whistling, yelling

Touch: abrasive, bumpy, chilly, clammy, coarse, cool, damp, dry, feathery, fluffy, fuzzy, gooey, grainy, greasy, gritty, hard, hot, icy, itchy, jagged, lumpy, moist, mushy, plush, powdery, prickly, rigid, rough, rubbery, scratchy, silky, slimy, slippery, smooth, soft, spiky, sticky, velvety, warm, wet

Taste: acidic, bitter, bland, buttery, charred, cheesy, chocolaty, citrusy, cold, cool, creamy, crispy, crunchy, dry, earthy, fizzy, flavorful, fresh, fruity, garlicky, gooey, hearty, minty, mushy, nutty, peppery, salty, savory, sour, spicy, sugary, sweet, tangy, toasty, zesty

Smell: airy, aromatic, bitter, burnt, citrusy, clean, damp, dank, earthy, faint, fishy, floral, flowery, fragrant, fresh, fruity, garlicky, grassy, humid, mildewy, minty, moldy, musty, peppery, perfumed, piney, pungent, putrid, rancid, rotten, salty, smoky, sour, spicy, stinky, strong, sweet, woody

Color Words

red shades: crimson, scarlet, ruby, cherry, maroon, rose, brick, vermilion, tomato, blush

orange shades: amber, apricot, bronze, carrot, copper, coral, peach, pumpkin, tangerine, rust

yellow shades: gold, lemon, canary, butter, blond, mustard, dandelion, sunflower, honey, goldenrod

green shades: emerald, lime, olive, forest, jade, mint, sage, kelly, turquoise, clover, fern

blue shades: sky, cobalt, navy, teal, turquoise, aqua, cerulean, sapphire, denim, azure

purple shades: lavender, violet, amethyst, plum, lilac, grape, orchid, magenta

pink shades: bubblegum, fuchsia, carnation, blush, rose, salmon, watermelon, peony, cotton candy, hot pink

brown shades: chocolate, coffee, chestnut, mahogany, cinnamon, tan, beige, mocha, copper, walnut, hazelnut

black shades: jet, onyx, ebony, charcoal, ink, midnight, obsidian, soot, raven, coal

white shades: ivory, snow, pearl, frost, milky, alabaster, chalk, cream, eggshell, cloudy

gray shades: silver, smoke, ash, slate, dove, graphite, charcoal, pewter, steel, cloudy

Strategies for Choosing the Right Expressive Words

LANGUAGE DOMAINS

Reading

Writing

Speaking

Listening

1.Q What's the Best Word?

Read aloud to the class a scenario from one of the Scenario Cards on pages 67–68. Then have students brainstorm words with a partner that best fit the scenario and ask students to share their words while you write them on the board. The class can vote on which word best fits the scenario. This process encourages students to think beyond their usual vocabularies, learn new words, and expand their language through context to be more precise. While we list words as suggestions, depending on the grade, students may use simpler or more advanced words. These suggestions can be shared with students to expose them to new vocabulary after they've shared their own ideas.

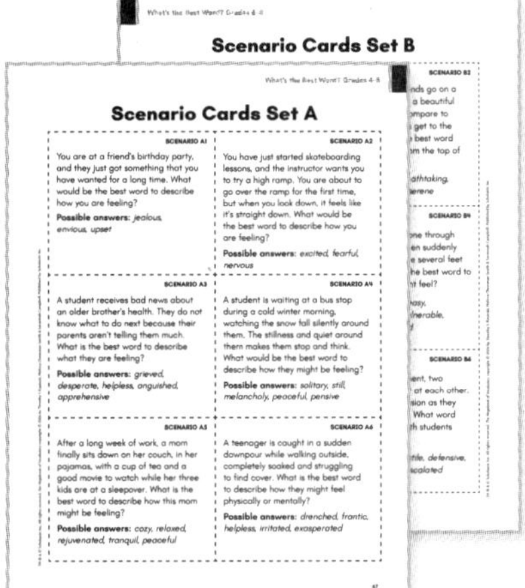

Scenario Cards Set B

What's the Best Word? Grades 4–5

Scenario Cards Set A

SCENARIO A1
You are at a friend's birthday party, and they just got something that you have wanted for a long time. What would be the best word to describe how you are feeling?
Possible answers: *jealous, envious, upset*

SCENARIO A2
You have just started skateboarding lessons, and the instructor wants you to try a high ramp. You are about to go over the ramp for the first time, but when you look down, it feels like it's straight down. What would be the best word to describe how you are feeling?
Possible answers: *excited, fearful, nervous*

SCENARIO A3
A student receives bad news about an older brother's health. They do not know what to do next because their parents aren't telling them much. What is the best word to describe what they are feeling?
Possible answers: *grieved, desperate, helpless, anguished, apprehensive*

SCENARIO A4
A student is waiting at a bus stop during a cold winter morning, watching the snow fall silently around them. The stillness and quiet around them makes them stop and think. What would be the best word to describe how they might be feeling?
Possible answers: *solitary, still, melancholy, peaceful, pensive*

SCENARIO A5
After a long week of work, a mom finally sits down on her couch, in her pajamas, with a cup of tea and a good movie to watch while her three kids are at a sleepover. What is the best word to describe how this mom might be feeling?
Possible answers: *cozy, relaxed, rejuvenated, tranquil, peaceful*

SCENARIO A6
A teenager is caught in a sudden downpour while walking outside, completely soaked and struggling to find cover. What is the best word to describe how they might feel physically or mentally?
Possible answers: *drenched, frantic, helpless, irritated, exasperated*

67

Materials	• Scenario Cards Set A, Grades 4–5, page 67 • Scenario Cards Set B, Grades 6–8, page 68
Grade Band	4–8
Length of Activity	Varies
Differentiation Ideas	**Striving Learners and English Learners:** If students tend to use more common words to describe the feelings in the scenarios, such as *happy*, then encourage them to look up the word in a thesaurus for ideas, or provide two words from the possible answers to have them choose which would fit best.
Extension Ideas	Encourage students to make up their own scenarios for a certain type of word they have in mind, then read it to the class to have the class find a great word.
Answers	Answers integrated into Scenario Cards Sets, pages 67–68

Scenario Cards Set A

SCENARIO A1

You are at a friend's birthday party, and they just got something that you have wanted for a long time. What would be the best word to describe how you are feeling?

Possible answers: *jealous, envious, upset*

SCENARIO A2

You have just started skateboarding lessons, and the instructor wants you to try a high ramp. You are about to go over the ramp for the first time, but when you look down, it feels like it's straight down. What would be the best word to describe how you are feeling?

Possible answers: *excited, fearful, nervous*

SCENARIO A3

A student receives bad news about an older brother's health. They do not know what to do next because their parents aren't telling them much. What is the best word to describe what they are feeling?

Possible answers: *grieved, desperate, helpless, anguished, apprehensive*

SCENARIO A4

A student is waiting at a bus stop during a cold winter morning, watching the snow fall silently around them. The stillness and quiet around them makes them stop and think. What would be the best word to describe how they might be feeling?

Possible answers: *solitary, still, melancholy, peaceful, pensive*

SCENARIO A5

After a long week of work, a mom finally sits down on her couch, in her pajamas, with a cup of tea and a good movie to watch while her three kids are at a sleepover. What is the best word to describe how this mom might be feeling?

Possible answers: *cozy, relaxed, rejuvenated, tranquil, peaceful*

SCENARIO A6

A teenager is caught in a sudden downpour while walking outside, completely soaked and struggling to find cover. What is the best word to describe how they might feel physically or mentally?

Possible answers: *drenched, frantic, helpless, irritated, exasperated*

Scenario Cards Set B

SCENARIO B1

A student gave a great performance in the school play and just finished their last performance. What would be the best word to describe how they might feel later that night at home?

Possible answers: *relieved, exhausted, proud*

SCENARIO B2

You and a group of friends go on a hike up a mountain. It's a beautiful day, but that doesn't compare to what you see when you get to the top. What would be the best word to describe the view from the top of the mountain?

Possible answers: *breathtaking, stunning, picturesque, serene*

SCENARIO B3

A student receives an unexpected award during a school assembly for academic success and they notice their parents in the audience to support them. What would be the best word to describe their feelings?

Possible answers: *elated, astonished, exhilarated, grateful, flattered, proud*

SCENARIO B4

A student is walking alone through a dark alley at night, then suddenly hears some leaves rustle several feet away. What would be the best word to describe how they might feel?

Possible answers: *uneasy, apprehensive, eerie, vulnerable, trepidatious, frightened*

SCENARIO B5

A student received a compliment from a teacher about something kind they saw them do at school. What would be the best word to describe how that student might feel?

Possible answers: *flattered, validated, worthy, empowered, grateful*

SCENARIO B6

During a heated argument, two students begin to shout at each other. The air is thick with tension as they exchange harsh words. What word might describe how both students are feeling?

Possible answers: *hostile, defensive, furious, antagonistic, escalated*

1.R Word Wars

For this strategy, students engage in mini-debates with classmates to practice using precise language. Give each student a Word Wars Topic Card on page 71 and access to the Debate Sentence Starters on page 70, which you can project on the screen or distribute a copy of to each student. Give students several minutes to prepare before the debate begins. During the debate, allow each student to speak for 10 seconds, alternating arguments three times. Modify times as needed. The goal is for students to incorporate at least six of the vocabulary words into their argument. The debates can be held in front of the class, one group at a time, or simultaneously with students paired up around the room while you circulate. Encourage students to listen carefully to the other side so they can respond thoughtfully and counter-argue. This strategy helps students use more formal language, expanding their expressive vocabularies for future conversations.

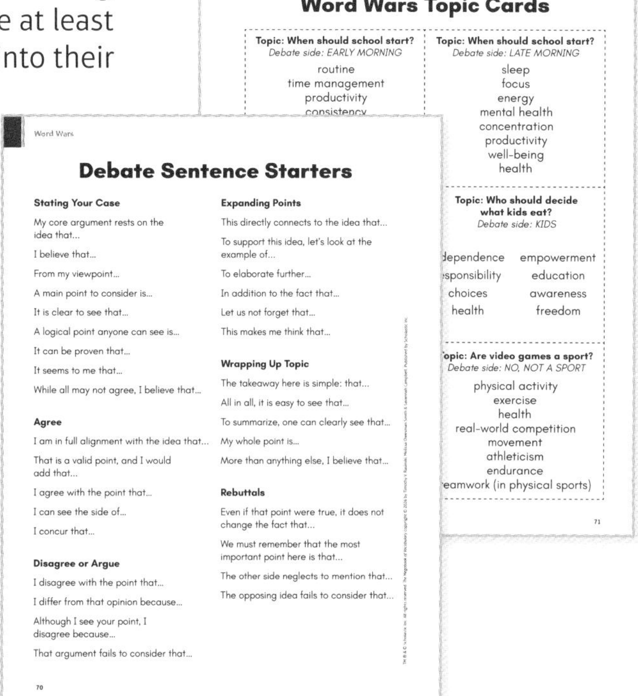

Word Wars

Word Wars Topic Cards

Topic: When should school start?
Debate side: EARLY MORNING
routine
time management
productivity
consistency

Topic: When should school start?
Debate side: LATE MORNING
sleep
focus
energy
mental health
concentration
productivity
well-being
health

Topic: Who should decide what kids eat?
Debate side: KIDS
dependence | empowerment
sponsibility | education
choices | awareness
health | freedom

opic: Are video games a sport?
Debate side: NO, NOT A SPORT
physical activity
exercise
health
real-world competition
movement
athleticism
endurance
eamwork (in physical sports)

71

Word Wars

Debate Sentence Starters

Stating Your Case
My core argument rests on the idea that...
I believe that...
From my viewpoint...
A main point to consider is...
It is clear to see that...
A logical point anyone can see is...
It can be proven that...
It seems to me that...
While all may not agree, I believe that...

Agree
I am in full alignment with the idea that...
That is a valid point, and I would add that...
I agree with the point that...
I can see the side of...
I concur that...

Disagree or Argue
I disagree with the point that...
I differ from that opinion because...
Although I see your point, I disagree because...
That argument fails to consider that...

Expanding Points
This directly connects to the idea that...
To support this idea, let's look at the example of...
To elaborate further...
In addition to the fact that...
Let us not forget that...
This makes me think that...

Wrapping Up Topic
The takeaway here is simple: that...
All in all, it is easy to see that...
To summarize, one can clearly see that...
My whole point is...
More than anything else, I believe that...

Rebuttals
Even if that point were true, it does not change the fact that...
We must remember that the most important point here is that...
The other side neglects to mention that...
The opposing idea fails to consider that...

70

Materials	• Debate Sentence Starters, page 70 • Word Wars Topic Cards, page 71
Grade Band	4–8
Length of Activity	10 minutes
Differentiation Ideas	**Striving Learners and English Learners:** Read each vocabulary word aloud to support oral language development and troubleshoot any pronunciation or comprehension issues.
Extension Ideas	• Create debates with topics being studied in class (two sides of a historical debate) with a list of words for students to use. • Have students write a paragraph that solidifies their ideas using all the vocabulary words.

LANGUAGE DOMAINS

Reading

Writing

Speaking

Listening

Debate Sentence Starters

Stating Your Case

My core argument rests on the idea that...

I believe that...

From my viewpoint...

A main point to consider is...

It is clear to see that...

A logical point anyone can see is...

It can be proven that...

It seems to me that...

While all may not agree, I believe that...

Agree

I am in full alignment with the idea that...

That is a valid point, and I would add that...

I agree with the point that...

I can see the side of...

I concur that...

Disagree or Argue

I disagree with the point that...

I differ from that opinion because...

Although I see your point, I disagree because...

That argument fails to consider that...

Expanding Points

This directly connects to the idea that...

To support this idea, let's look at the example of...

To elaborate further...

In addition to the fact that...

Let us not forget that...

This makes me think that...

Wrapping Up Topic

The takeaway here is simple: that...

All in all, it is easy to see that...

To summarize, one can clearly see that...

My whole point is...

More than anything else, I believe that...

Rebuttals

Even if that point were true, it does not change the fact that...

We must remember that the most important point here is that...

The other side neglects to mention that...

The opposing idea fails to consider that...

Word Wars Topic Cards

Topic: When should school start?
Debate side: EARLY MORNING

routine
time management
productivity
consistency
preparation
efficiency
balance
organization

Topic: When should school start?
Debate side: LATE MORNING

sleep
focus
energy
mental health
concentration
productivity
well-being
health

Topic: Who should decide what kids eat?
Debate side: PARENTS / ADULTS

nutrition
health
control
protection
guidance
habit
balance
safety

Topic: Who should decide what kids eat?
Debate side: KIDS

independence
responsibility
choices
health
empowerment
education
awareness
freedom

Topic: Are video games a sport?
Debate side: YES, A SPORT

strategy
teamwork
skill
competition
coordination
training
focus
reflexes

Topic: Are video games a sport?
Debate side: NO, NOT A SPORT

physical activity
exercise
health
real-world competition
movement
athleticism
endurance
teamwork (in physical sports)

Strategies for Learning Words You Provide, pages 74–96

Strategies for Learning Words We Provide, pages 97–163

Chapter 2 downloadables are available here.

CHAPTER 2

Individual-Word Learning

"I know nothing in the world that has as much power as a word. Sometimes I write one, and I look at it until it begins to shine."

—Emily Dickinson

Given that students are expected to learn around 3,000 new words annually once formal schooling begins (Graves, 2016), it is clear that vocabulary instruction is a massive undertaking. It is important to select words for instruction strategically, ensuring that the words are ones that students are likely to encounter in multiple contexts (Snow, 2010). And while we cannot possibly teach all the words students need to learn in a year, it is still crucial to teach as many individual words as possible.

Knowing students are less likely to encounter academic words *incidentally* in everyday experiences, it is essential to target those words *intentionally* in instruction (McKeown, 2019). Explicit instruction is a necessity for students to acquire deep knowledge of words. Graves states, "Vocabulary instruction is most effective when learners are given both definitional and contextual information, when learners actively process the new word meanings, and when they experience multiple encounters with the word. Said somewhat differently, vocabulary instruction is most effective, and is most likely to influence students' comprehension, when it is rich, deep, and extended" (2016). While supplying definitional and contextual information is an established practice by most teachers, you can enrich instruction by incorporating engaging experiences that help students deepen their understanding of word meanings, which is what this chapter is all about.

Because teaching individual words from an early age is crucial for fostering long-term success in reading and writing, it is our duty to expose kids to new words and their meanings. As Lily Howard Scott states in *The Words That Shape Us*, after a young child hears some advice from his mother about listening to his inner voice when making decisions in difficult situations, that phrase, *inner voice*, had "nestled inside of him" (Scott, 2025). How do we help students "nestle" words inside themselves? How do we make those words stick? Just as most learning sticks: through intentional practice. By providing explicit instruction and then multiple contextualized exposures to selected words, we can facilitate deeper understanding and ensure retention to support students as effective comprehenders.

Three Keys to Teaching Individual Words

1. Student-Friendly Definition

After pronouncing the word, have students chorally repeat it several times to solidify pronunciation. Then provide them with a student-friendly definition made of words that are already in a student's vocabulary to help them access the meaning quickly and accurately.

turbulent
wild and full of movement

2. Contextual Examples

Include a variety of contextual examples to solidify meaning and create rich, nuanced, receptive understanding.

The **turbulent** waves slammed against the hull, each one erasing any illusion of control the crew still had.	The **turbulent** sky churned with dark clouds and jagged lightning, mirroring the tension building inside the home.	Maya tried to stay calm as she waited for her final grade, but her **turbulent** thoughts made peace impossible.	Even though we won the championship, the season had been **turbulent**, filled with injuries and tough losses.	The **turbulent** crowd scattered in all directions, panic overtaking any sense of order.

3. Multiple Exposures

Provide multiple encounters for application across various settings to cement the expressive, permanent use of the word in their vocabulary bank.

Answering a Question	Completing a Sentence	Listing Examples and Nonexamples	Using the Word in Revision	Encouraging Its Use in Everyday Speech	Creating Visuals
What might cause people at a concert to become **turbulent**?	The **turbulent** lake made it difficult for the boat to ___________.	Example: stormy sky Nonexample: newly paved road	"During Sarah's vacation, the **turbulent** weather caused a change of plans."	My sleep was so **turbulent** last night, I just couldn't rest!	

Strategies for Learning Words You Provide

LANGUAGE DOMAINS

Reading

Writing
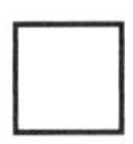

Speaking

Listening

2.A **Picture Walks During Read-Alouds**

Quality read-alouds are essential to developing vocabulary that students may not be able to read independently. When you utilize the "See It, Say It, Read It, Show It" protocol, you enhance both vocabulary and reading comprehension. Here's how:

Choose 3–5 target Tier 2 words from the picture book that are essential to the story.

1. **See It:** ***See the illustration*** Take students on a picture walk by pointing to an illustration in the book that can help them understand one of your target words. Then ask them to look at the picture and share what they see happening.
2. **Say It:** ***Say the definition*** Ask students to repeat the target word and give them a student-friendly definition; then repeat steps 1 and 2 for the remaining chosen words.
3. **Read It:** ***Read the book*** Read the book aloud, stopping when you reach a target word. Then ask students to repeat the word and think about how the pictures and words work together to help them understand that word's meaning.
4. **Show It:** ***Show the learning*** After reading the text, return to the list of target words and ask students to show the meaning of each target word by acting it out, drawing it, or turning and talking to give their partners a definition of the word.

Materials	picture book to read aloud
Grade Band	K–3
Length of Activity	20 minutes
Differentiation Ideas	**Striving Learners and English Learners:** Provide a matching visual for support during Show It that displays the meaning of the target vocabulary words.
Extension Ideas	Ask open-ended questions about the words, such as "What might happen if someone is feeling ____?" or "Where else might you see something that is ______?"

2.B Vocabulary Structures

barrier

erupt

To master new vocabulary words, students need repeated and varied exposures to them. Vocabulary Structures ensures that. Display learned vocabulary words on the board or an anchor chart. Then have each student create a visual representation of one of the words using modeling clay. After, invite students to walk around the room or get into groups to guess which word each classmate created. Students may offer clues to describe their representation, being careful not to mention the target word directly. For example, if the word is *parched*, the student may explain that their representation is of a person who needs water, but they may not use the word *parched*. This encourages creative thinking and reinforces the connection between words and their meanings.

Materials	modeling clay
Grade Band	K–8
Length of Activity	10–20 minutes
Differentiation Ideas	**Striving Learners:** Provide words that are more concrete, such as nouns, instead of abstract ideas that may be difficult to represent.
Extension Ideas	Have students vote on their favorite representations for key vocabulary words. The winner can be left to air-dry and then displayed.

LANGUAGE DOMAINS

Reading

Writing

Speaking

Listening

CHAPTER 2
Individual-Word Learning

Strategies for Learning Words You Provide

LANGUAGE DOMAINS

Reading

Writing

Speaking

Listening

2.C **Plot the Vocabulary With Literary Text**

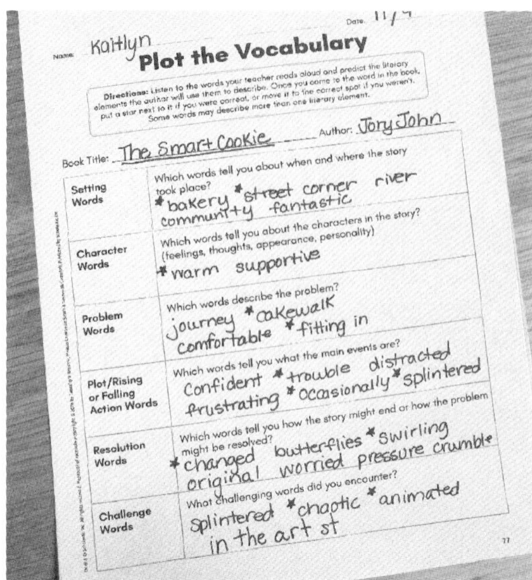

Name: Kaitlyn Date: 11/4

Plot the Vocabulary

Directions: Listen to the words your teacher reads aloud and predict the literary elements the author will use them to describe. Once you come to the word in the book, put a star next to it if you were correct, or move it to the correct spot if you weren't. Some words may describe more than one literary element.

Book Title: The Smart Cookie Author: Jory John

Setting Words	Which words tell you about when and where the story took place? *bakery *street corner river community fantastic
Character Words	Which words tell you about the characters in the story? (feelings, thoughts, appearance, personality) *warm supportive
Problem Words	Which words describe the problem? journey *cakewalk comfortable *fitting in
Plot/Rising or Falling Action Words	Which words tell you what the main events are? Confident *trouble distracted frustrating *occasionally *splintered
Resolution Words	Which words tell you how the story might end or how the problem might be resolved? *changed butterflies *swirling original worried pressure crumble
Challenge Words	What challenging words did you encounter? Splintered *chaotic *animated in the art st

77

Plot the Vocabulary assists students in recognizing how words connect to specific narrative elements, such as setting, character, and plot. Before reading a picture or chapter book, preselect vocabulary words from the story, categorizing them into narrative elements, such as *mountainous* for setting words, *adventure* for problem words, and *nervous* for character words. Read the words aloud one at a time to students, and have them predict which narrative element each word connects to and write it in the corresponding box on Plot the Vocabulary on page 77. Include some challenging words that could connect to multiple elements to elicit discussion. As you read the book aloud or as the students read the book silently, refer back to the students' filled-in Plot the Vocabulary sheets to see if their predictions were correct. If they were, mark with a star.

Materials	• narrative picture book to read aloud • Plot the Vocabulary, page 77
Grade Band	2–8
Length of Activity	Varies depending on length of the book you choose
Differentiation Ideas	**Striving Learners and English Learners:** Write the words on the classroom screen or board for students to add to their Plot the Vocabulary chart to help with spelling.
Extension Ideas	Encourage students to find more key words for each narrative element during class reading time.

Name: ______________________ Date: ____________

Plot the Vocabulary

Directions: Listen to the words your teacher has selected from the book. Make a prediction about which literary element the author will use each word for and write that word in the corresponding box below. When you hear the word in the book, put a star next to it if you were correct, or move it to the correct spot if you weren't. (Note that some words may be used for more than one literary element.)

Book Title: ______________________ Author: ______________

Setting Words	Which words tell you about when and where the story took place?
Character Words	Which words tell you about the characters in the story? (feelings, thoughts, appearance, personality)
Problem Words	Which words describe the problem?
Plot Words	Which words tell you what the main events are?
Resolution Words	Which words tell you how the story might end or how the problem might be resolved?
Challenge Words	What challenging words did you encounter?

Strategies for Learning Words You Provide

LANGUAGE DOMAINS

Reading

Writing

Speaking

Listening

2.D Conditional Sentences

The mischievous wind blew my hat right into a puddle.

Must contain the word: mischevious

# of words in sentence: 10

Must include a weather-related word

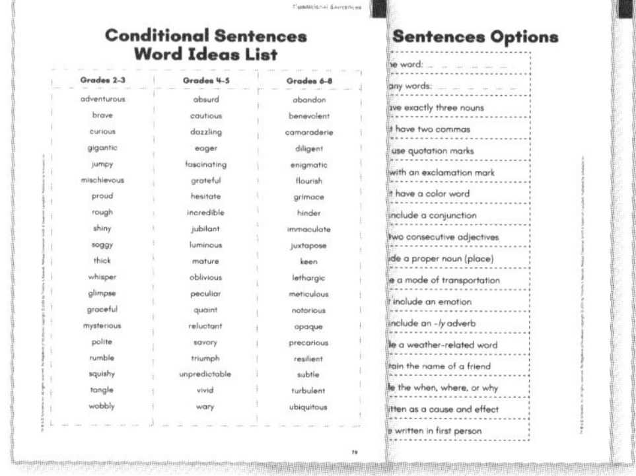

Conditional Sentences

Conditional Sentences Word Ideas List

Grades 2–3	Grades 4–5	Grades 6–8
adventurous	absurd	abandon
brave	cautious	benevolent
curious	dazzling	camaraderie
gigantic	eager	diligent
jumpy	fascinating	enigmatic
mischievous	grateful	flourish
proud	hesitate	grimace
rough	incredible	hinder
shiny	jubilant	immaculate
soggy	luminous	juxtapose
thick	mature	keen
whisper	oblivious	lethargic
glimpse	peculiar	meticulous
graceful	quaint	notorious
mysterious	reluctant	opaque
polite	savory	precarious
rumble	triumph	resilient
squishy	unpredictable	subtle
tangle	vivid	turbulent
wobbly	wary	ubiquitous

79

Sentences Options

e word:
any words:
ave exactly three nouns
t have two commas
use quotation marks
with an exclamation mark
t have a color word
include a conjunction
two consecutive adjectives
ide a proper noun (place)
e a mode of transportation
t include an emotion
include an *-ly* adverb
le a weather-related word
tain the name of a friend
le the when, where, or why
itten as a cause and effect
e written in first person

Conditional sentences stretch students' vocabulary and writing skills by requiring them to follow specific written requirements, such as using a certain number of words in their sentence, a particular part of speech, or a specific verb tense. Choose a word from a class text, unit of study, or the Conditional Sentences Word Ideas List on page 79, and provide a basic definition of the word. Then select any number of options from the Conditional Sentences Options on pages 80–81, or copy and cut apart the strips, and have students randomly draw them from a bowl to establish the sentence requirements. Read the conditions aloud or project them on a screen. Pass out index cards or lined paper to individual students or pairs of students and have them create a sentence that meets the conditions. Then have them share their sentences. Repeat this process with as many words as time allows. Increase the number of options as students become more experienced with this strategy.

Example: Using the word *mischievous*, write a 10-word sentence that also includes a weather-related word. For example, "The mischievous wind blew my hat right into a puddle."

Materials	• Conditional Sentences Word Ideas List, page 79 • Conditional Sentences Options, pages 80–81 • index cards or lined paper
Grade Band	2–8
Length of Activity	5 minutes per word
Differentiation Ideas	• **Striving Learners and English Learners:** Limit conditions to one requirement. • **Thriving Learners:** Encourage them to create their own challenging conditions to share with peers.
Extension Ideas	Create new conditions based on content studied in class, such as "Must use a future tense verb" or "Must use the word *ecosystem*."

Conditional Sentences Word Ideas List

Grades 2-3	Grades 4-5	Grades 6-8
adventurous	absurd	abandon
brave	cautious	benevolent
curious	dazzling	camaraderie
gigantic	eager	diligent
jumpy	fascinating	enigmatic
mischievous	grateful	flourish
proud	hesitate	grimace
rough	incredible	hinder
shiny	jubilant	immaculate
soggy	luminous	juxtapose
thick	mature	keen
whisper	oblivious	lethargic
glimpse	peculiar	meticulous
graceful	quaint	notorious
mysterious	reluctant	opaque
polite	savory	precarious
rumble	triumph	resilient
squishy	unpredictable	subtle
tangle	vivid	turbulent
wobbly	wary	ubiquitous

Conditional Sentences Options

Must contain the word: ____________

Must have this many words: ____________

Must have exactly three nouns

Must have two commas

Must use quotation marks

Must end with an exclamation mark

Must have a color word

Must include a conjunction

Must have two consecutive adjectives

Must include a proper noun (place)

Must include a mode of transportation

Must include an emotion

Must include an -*ly* adverb

Must include a weather-related word

Must contain the name of a friend

Must include the when, where, or why

Must be written as a cause and effect

Must be written in first person

Must be written in third person
Must include a season
Must include a measurement of time
Must include a musical instrument
Must include onomatopoeia
Must include a simile or metaphor
Must be an opinion
Must be a fact
Must include a mythical creature
Must include a superhero
Must include a wild animal
Must include a career
Must include a word about space
Must be an odd number of words
Must be an even number of words
Must be in past tense
Must be in future tense
Must include a number

LANGUAGE DOMAINS

Reading

Writing

Speaking

Listening

2.E Word Box Graphic Organizers

Graphic organizers provide an opportunity to process a word's meaning and practice using unfamiliar words—essential steps in coming to know a word (Graves, 2016). This collection of graphic organizers enables students to work directly with a word's meaning to anchor it and explore its relationship to other words. Select key vocabulary words from a story or unit of study, then have students explore their meanings by completing one of the Word Boxes Graphic Organizers on pages 83–87. Choose the organizer that best fits the needs of your students. Provide scaffolding and examples as needed. For example, for Word Boxes A, using the word *glimpse*, discuss with students that the word *glimpse* IS looking at something quickly and then looking away, and IS NOT looking at something over time through a magnifying glass.

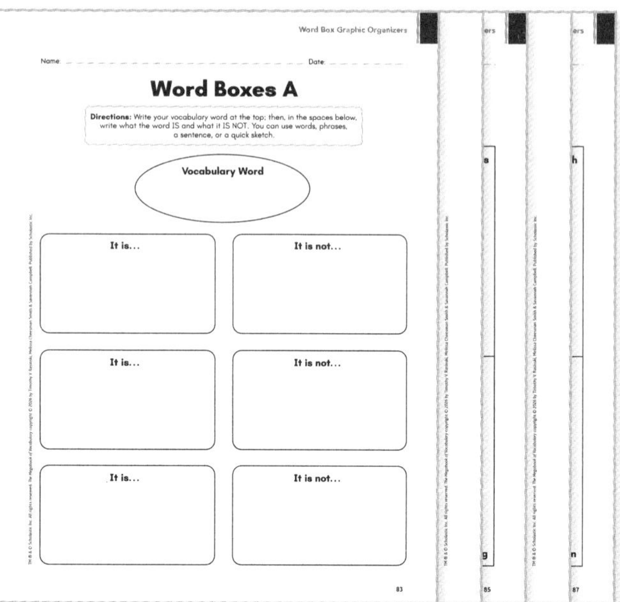

Materials	• Word Boxes A, page 83 • Word Boxes B, page 84 • Word Boxes C, page 85 • Word Boxes D, page 86 • Word Boxes E, page 87
Grade Band	2–8
Length of Activity	Varies
Differentiation Ideas	**Striving Learners and English Learners:** Model examples of each part of the graphic organizer to the whole class or in small groups multiple times to ensure understanding of the structure and expectations.
Extension Ideas	Have students create their own Word Boxes by giving them a blank sheet of paper and having them fold it into four parts. Students then write the word in the middle of the page and circle it. They can choose any four ways they want to show the topic, with ideas from the other four Word Boxes as examples.

Name: ______________________ Date: ____________

Word Boxes A

Directions: Write your vocabulary word at the top; then, in the spaces below, write what the word IS and what it IS NOT. You can use words, phrases, a sentence, or a quick sketch.

Vocabulary Word

It is...	It is not...

It is...	It is not...

It is...	It is not...

Name: ______________________________ Date: ______________

Word Boxes B

Directions: Write your vocabulary word in the middle; then fill out each space with details about it.

Dictionary Definition	**Illustration**
My Definition	
Vocabulary Word	
Example	**Nonexample**

Name: ____________________ Date: __________

Word Boxes C

Directions: Write your vocabulary word in the middle; then fill out each space with details about it.

Definition	**Characteristics**
Vocabulary Word	
Example / Nonexample	**Drawing**

Name: ________________________________ Date: ____________

Word Boxes D

Directions: Write your vocabulary word in the middle; then fill out each space with details about it.

Explanation	**Related Terms**
Vocabulary Word	
Misunderstanding	**Used in a Sentence**

Name: ______________________ Date: ______________

Word Boxes E

Directions: Write your vocabulary word in the middle; then fill out each space with details about it.

Dictionary Definition	**Part of Speech**
Divided Into Syllables	**Illustration**

Vocabulary Word

Strategies for Learning Words You Provide

LANGUAGE DOMAINS

Reading

Writing

Speaking

Listening

2.F Knowledge Rating Charts

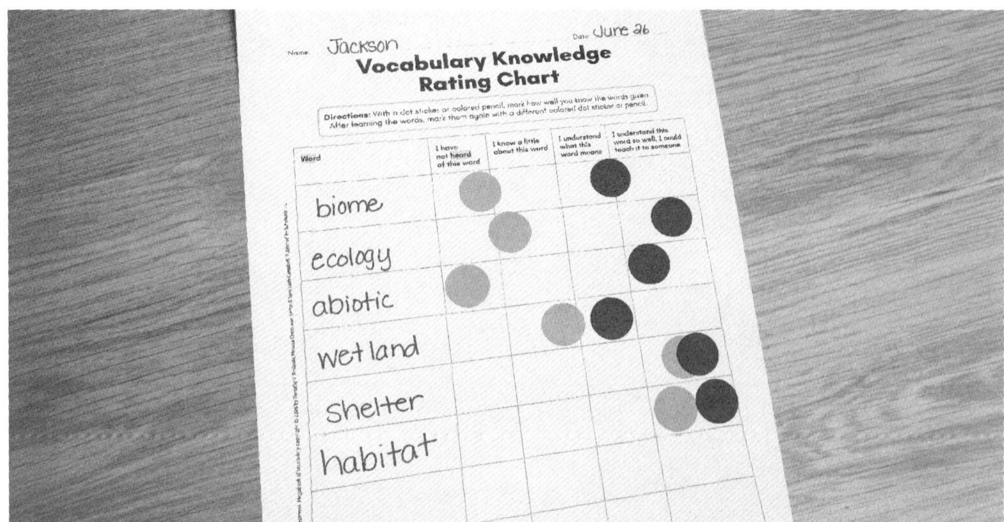

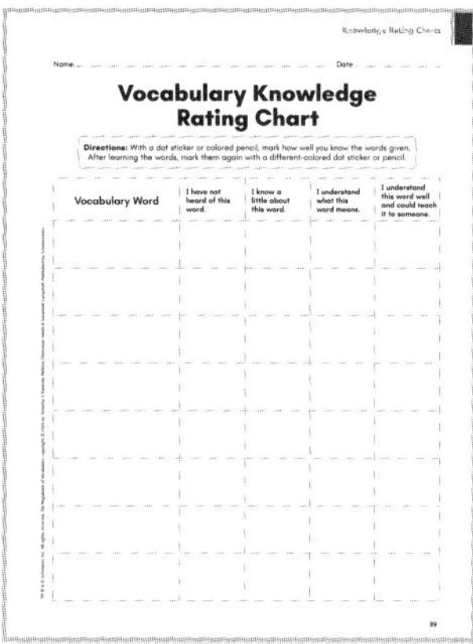

Vocabulary Knowledge Rating Chart

Vocabulary Word	I have not heard of this word.	I know a little about this word.	I understand what this word means.	I understand this word well and could teach it to someone.

Knowing a word is not an all-or-nothing proposition. There is a continuum of knowledge, from never having heard of it to having a "rich, decontextualized knowledge of a word's meaning, its relationships to other words, and its extensions to metaphorical uses" (Graves, 2016). This strategy asks students to rate how well they know pre-selected words. Students use the Vocabulary Knowledge Rating Chart on page 89 to rate how well they know the given vocabulary words before starting a new content unit. Have them write the words in the chart as you pronounce and spell them. Then have them use colored dot stickers or colored pencils to rate their knowledge of each word. At the end of the unit, have students use different-colored dots or pencils to rate their knowledge of each word and gauge their own word-learning progress. Collect papers to find patterns of words students still seem to struggle with, guiding your further instruction of the words.

Materials	• Vocabulary Knowledge Rating Chart, page 89 • colored dot stickers or colored pencils
Grade Band	2–8
Length of Activity	5 minutes, once before a unit of study and once after
Differentiation Ideas	This strategy does not need to be differentiated because all students can rate their knowledge, regardless of where they are developmentally.
Extension Ideas	• Use preselected words from a literature study to expose students to the words before reading. • Repeat the strategy as a checkpoint in the middle of the unit. • Have students use the words to write one paragraph that summarizes a unit of study.

Name: ______________________ Date: ______________

Vocabulary Knowledge Rating Chart

Directions: With a dot sticker or colored pencil, mark how well you know the words given. After learning the words, mark them again with a different-colored dot sticker or pencil.

Vocabulary Word	I have not heard of this word.	I know a little about this word.	I understand what this word means.	I understand this word well and could teach it to someone.

CHAPTER 2
Individual-Word Learning

Strategies for Learning Words You Provide

LANGUAGE DOMAINS

Reading

Writing

Speaking

Listening

2.G Choice Boards

Select vocabulary words from a unit of study or shared text, such as a literature study. Distribute the chosen Choice Board on pages 91–93. Begin by having students write the preselected words and definitions in the blanks provided at the top of the Choice Board sheet to ensure they know the correct definitions. Then have students choose three activities to complete from the Choice Board to make a line across, down, or diagonally. As students complete each activity, have them mark it on their Choice Board with a stamp, sticker, or initials and staple all completed activities to it. Then have students discuss the activities in small groups and turn in their Choice Boards for review.

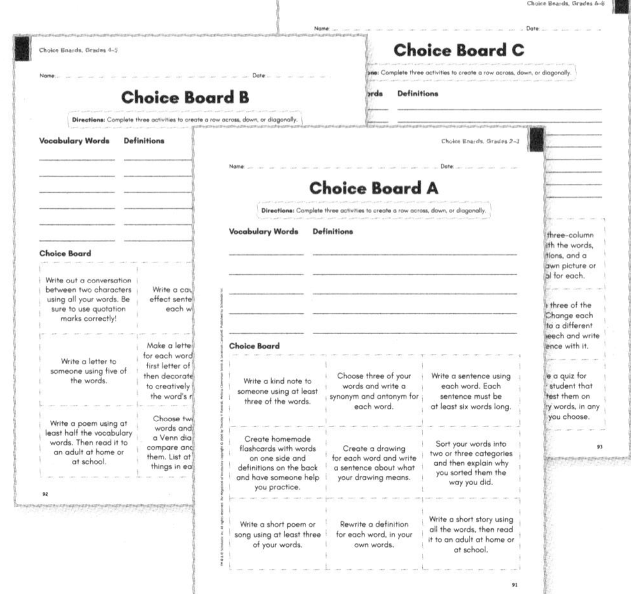

Choice Boards, Grades 2–3

Name: Date:

Choice Board A

Directions: Complete three activities to create a row across, down, or diagonally.

Vocabulary Words **Definitions**

Choice Board

Write a kind note to someone using at least three of the words.	Choose three of your words and write a synonym and antonym for each word.	Write a sentence using each word. Each sentence must be at least six words long.
Create homemade flashcards with words on one side and definitions on the back and have someone help you practice.	Create a drawing for each word and write a sentence about what your drawing means.	Sort your words into two or three categories and then explain why you sorted them the way you did.
Write a short poem or song using at least three of your words.	Rewrite a definition for each word, in your own words.	Write a short story using all the words, then read it to an adult at home or at school.

91

Choice Boards, Grades 4–5

Choice Board B

Directions: Complete three activities to create a row across, down, or diagonally.

Vocabulary Words **Definitions**

Choice Board

Write out a conversation between two characters using all your words. Be sure to use quotation marks correctly!

Write a letter to someone using five of the words.

Write a poem using at least half the vocabulary words. Then read it to an adult at home or at school.

Choice Boards, Grades 6–8

Choice Board C

Materials	• Choice Board A, Grades 2–3, page 91 • Choice Board B, Grades 4–5, page 92 • Choice Board C, Grades 6–8, page 93
Grade Band	2–8
Length of Activity	1–2 class periods
Differentiation Ideas	**Striving Learners and English Learners:** Have students complete the activities in pairs to increase expressive oral use of the words.
Extension Ideas	Make one box a *free choice* box to let students create their own activity to practice vocabulary words.

Name: ______________________ Date: ____________

Choice Board A

Directions: Complete three activities to create a row across, down, or diagonally.

Vocabulary Words / Definitions

Vocabulary Words	Definitions
____________	______________________
____________	______________________
____________	______________________
____________	______________________
____________	______________________

Choice Board

Write a kind note to someone using at least three of the words.	Choose three of your words and write a synonym and antonym for each word.	Write a sentence using each word. Each sentence must be at least six words long.
Create homemade flashcards with words on one side and definitions on the back and have someone help you practice.	Create a drawing for each word and write a sentence about what your drawing means.	Sort your words into two or three categories and then explain why you sorted them the way you did.
Write a short poem or song using at least three of your words.	Rewrite a definition for each word, in your own words.	Write a short story using all the words, then read it to an adult at home or at school.

Name: ______________________ Date: ______________

Choice Board B

Directions: Complete three activities to create a row across, down, or diagonally.

Vocabulary Words	Definitions

Choice Board

Write out a conversation between two characters using all your words. Be sure to use quotation marks correctly!	Write a cause-and-effect sentence with each word.	Make a three-column chart with the words, definitions, and a drawn symbol or picture for each.
Write a letter to someone using five of the words.	Make a letter drawing for each word: Write the first letter of the word, then decorate the letter to creatively represent the word's meaning.	Make a list of three synonyms for four of your words.
Write a poem using at least half the vocabulary words. Then read it to an adult at home or at school.	Choose two of the words and create a Venn diagram to compare and contrast them. List at least two things in each area.	Sort the words into two or three categories, then describe how you sorted them.

Name: ______________________ Date: ______________

Choice Board C

Directions: Complete three activities to create a row across, down, or diagonally.

Vocabulary Words	Definitions

Choice Board

Create a crossword puzzle using all the vocabulary words, rewriting the clues in a creative way.	Create a short comic strip using each of the words once.	Make a three-column chart with the words, definitions, and a hand-drawn picture or symbol for each.
Write a note of apology to someone using five of the words.	Create a word cluster for three of the words by writing each word in the middle, then at least six related words or phrases around it.	Choose three of the words. Change each word into a different part of speech and write a sentence with it.
Find a way the words fit together in a group, even if it is in a random way. Write out your connections.	Choose two of the words and create a Venn diagram to compare and contrast them. List at least two things in each area.	Create a quiz for another student that would test them on vocabulary words, in any format you choose.

CHAPTER 2
Individual-Word Learning

Strategies for Learning Words You Provide

LANGUAGE DOMAINS

Reading
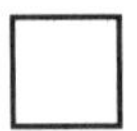

Writing

Speaking

Listening

2.H Create a Comic Strip

Introduce a new vocabulary word to students with a kid-friendly definition and sentences containing the word. Then have students work in pairs to fill in a Comic Strip Template on pages 95–96, which must include the word in context. Make sure students plan ahead how the word will be used in the comic strip. They should plan out each box before using the template to make sure their ideas will fit in the space. When they are finished, have students share their comic strips with the class.

Materials	• Comic Strip Template A, Grades 2–3, page 95 • Comic Strip Template B, Grades 4–8, page 96
Grade Band	2–8
Length of Activity	30–45 minutes
Differentiation Ideas	**Striving Learners and English Learners:** Model the first one or two boxes to get them going, then orally discuss some ideas before independent practice.
Extension Ideas	Allow students to create their own template.

Name: ______________________ Date: __________

Comic Strip Template A

Directions: Fill in the speech bubbles to create a short conversation between the two characters. Be sure to use the vocabulary word. Then color the pictures.

Vocabulary Word: ______________________

Name: ____________________ Date: __________

Comic Strip Template B

Directions: Create drawings and fill in the speech bubbles to create a comic strip. Be sure to use the vocabulary word. Then color the pictures.

Vocabulary Word: ______________________

2.1 Yes-or-No Questions

When teaching a new vocabulary word, invite students to actively engage with it using a simple yes-or-no questioning strategy, a low-risk way to explore meaning and check for understanding. For example, the word *unruly* could inspire questions such as: *Was the class unruly on the field trip?* or *Do you have unruly hair in the mornings?* Then have students respond with a thumbs-up or thumbs-down to answer the question and demonstrate understanding or lack thereof. Some questions may invite different responses based on personal opinion or background knowledge, which encourages deeper thinking about the word's use.

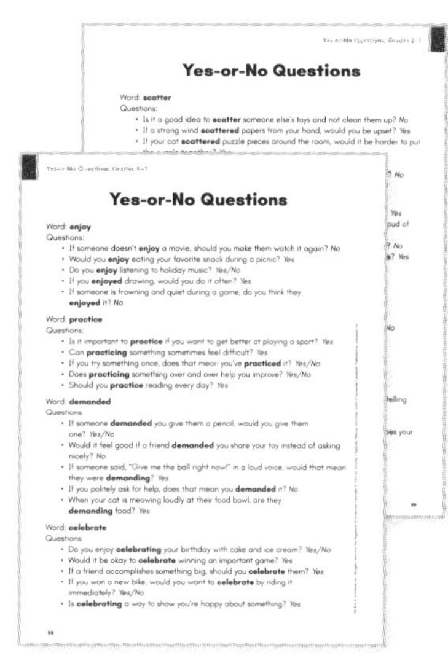

Yes-or-No Questions

Word: **scatter**

Questions:

- Is it a good idea to **scatter** someone else's toys and not clean them up? *No*
- If a strong wind **scattered** papers from your hand, would you be upset? *Yes*
- If your cat **scattered** puzzle pieces around the room, would it be harder to put

Yes-or-No Questions, Grades K–1

Yes-or-No Questions

Word: **enjoy**

Questions:

- If someone doesn't **enjoy** a movie, should you make them watch it again? *No*
- Would you **enjoy** eating your favorite snack during a picnic? *Yes*
- Do you **enjoy** listening to holiday music? *Yes/No*
- If you **enjoyed** drawing, would you do it often? *Yes*
- If someone is frowning and quiet during a game, do you think they **enjoyed** it? *No*

Word: **practice**

Questions:

- Is it important to **practice** if you want to get better at playing a sport? *Yes*
- Can **practicing** something sometimes feel difficult? *Yes*
- If you try something once, does that mean you've **practiced** it? *Yes/No*
- Does **practicing** something over and over help you improve? *Yes/No*
- Should you **practice** reading every day? *Yes*

Word: **demanded**

Questions:

- If someone **demanded** you give them a pencil, would you give them one? *Yes/No*
- Would it feel good if a friend **demanded** you share your toy instead of asking nicely? *No*
- If someone said, "Give me the ball right now!" in a loud voice, would that mean they were **demanding**? *Yes*
- If you politely ask for help, does that mean you **demanded** it? *No*
- When your cat is meowing loudly at their food bowl, are they **demanding** food? *Yes*

Word: **celebrate**

Questions:

- Do you enjoy **celebrating** your birthday with cake and ice cream? *Yes/No*
- Would it be okay to **celebrate** winning an important game? *Yes*
- If a friend accomplishes something big, should you **celebrate** them? *Yes*
- If you won a new bike, would you want to **celebrate** by riding it immediately? *Yes/No*
- Is **celebrating** a way to show you're happy about something? *Yes*

98

Materials	• Yes-or-No Questions, Grades K–1, page 98 • Yes-or-No Questions, Grades 2–3, page 99
Grade Band	K–3
Length of Activity	5–7 minutes
Differentiation Ideas	**Striving Learners and English Learners:** Front-load the content by introducing the vocabulary word in small groups. Provide visuals to illustrate the vocabulary word's meaning.
Extension Ideas	After providing yes-or-no questions, ask students to elaborate by saying "Yes/No, because..." or give students open-ended questions to ask and respond to with a partner. This not only strengthens critical thinking skills but also helps students use more complex sentences to explain their reasoning and express their ideas clearly.
Answers	Answers integrated in Yes-or-No Questions, pages 98–99

Strategies for Learning Words We Provide

LANGUAGE DOMAINS

Reading

Writing

Speaking

Listening

Yes-or-No Questions

Word: **enjoy**
Questions:

- If someone doesn't **enjoy** a movie, should you make them watch it again? *No*
- Would you **enjoy** eating your favorite snack during a picnic? *Yes*
- Do you **enjoy** listening to holiday music? *Yes/No*
- If you **enjoyed** drawing, would you do it often? *Yes*
- If someone is frowning and quiet during a game, do you think they **enjoyed** it? *No*

Word: **practice**
Questions:

- Is it important to **practice** if you want to get better at playing a sport? *Yes*
- Can **practicing** something sometimes feel difficult? *Yes*
- If you try something once, does that mean you've **practiced** it? *Yes/No*
- Does **practicing** something over and over help you improve? *Yes/No*
- Should you **practice** reading every day? *Yes*

Word: **demanded**
Questions:

- If someone **demanded** you give them a pencil, would you give them one? *Yes/No*
- Would it feel good if a friend **demanded** you share your toy instead of asking nicely? *No*
- If someone said, "Give me the ball right now!" in a loud voice, would that mean they were **demanding**? *Yes*
- If you politely ask for help, does that mean you **demanded** it? *No*
- When your cat is meowing loudly at their food bowl, are they **demanding** food? *Yes*

Word: **celebrate**
Questions:

- Do you enjoy **celebrating** your birthday with cake and ice cream? *Yes/No*
- Would it be okay to **celebrate** winning an important game? *Yes*
- If a friend accomplishes something big, should you **celebrate** them? *Yes*
- If you won a new bike, would you want to **celebrate** by riding it immediately? *Yes/No*
- Is **celebrating** a way to show you're happy about something? *Yes*

Yes-or-No Questions

Word: **scatter**
Questions:

- Is it a good idea to **scatter** someone else's toys and not clean them up? *No*
- If a strong wind **scattered** papers from your hand, would you be upset? *Yes*
- If your cat **scattered** puzzle pieces around the room, would it be harder to put the puzzle together? *Yes*
- If you put all your toys neatly in a box, are they **scattered**? *No*
- If all the kids are sitting close together in a circle, are they **scattered**? *No*

Word: **success**
Questions:

- Does **success** sometimes take time and patience in order to happen? *Yes*
- If someone tries their best but doesn't win a race, can they still feel proud of their **success**? *Yes*
- If you stop working toward your goal, will it be easy to reach **success**? *No*
- If you practice tying your shoes and you finally get it, is that a **success**? *Yes*
- Can you be **successful** even if you are not perfect? *Yes*

Word: **queasy**
Questions:

- If your stomach hurts after eating too much candy, could you feel **queasy**? *Yes/No*
- Would you feel **queasy** if you were asked to go speak on stage? *Yes/No*
- Do you ever feel **queasy** riding in a car? *Yes/No*
- Do roller coasters make you feel **queasy**? *Yes/No*
- If you feel **queasy**, should you eat a big meal? *No*

Word: **suggested**
Questions:

- If you are **suggesting** something to someone, does that mean you're telling them what to do? *No*
- Can a **suggestion** be helpful if someone is stuck on what to do? *Yes*
- If you **suggested** to your friend that you both go to the water park, does your friend have to agree to it? *No*
- Do you always have to follow someone's **suggestion**? *No*
- If I said, "How about we eat chicken nuggets for lunch?," is that a **suggestion**? *Yes*

CHAPTER 2

Individual-Word Learning

Strategies for Learning Words We Provide

LANGUAGE DOMAINS

Reading

Writing

Speaking ✓

Listening ✓

2.J Body Vocabulary

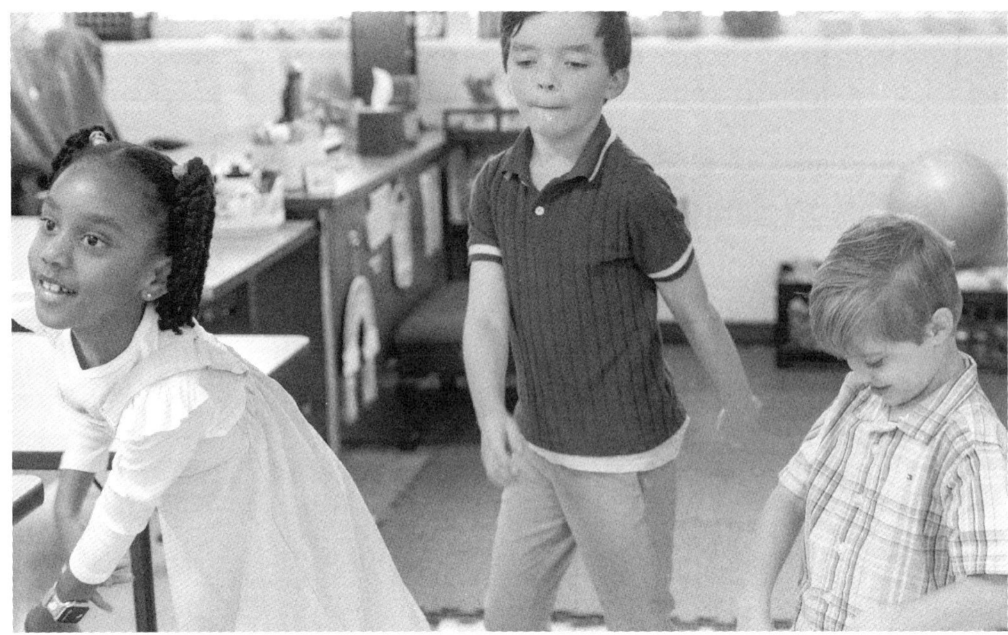

This strategy provides a concrete way of learning a word's meaning through movement. Call out a word from the Body Vocabulary Words on page 101 and have students repeat it, then have them mimic the movement or gesture associated with it, modeling for them as necessary. This strategy allows students to hear the word multiple times while actively engaging with it through movement. Ask children who resist movement or struggle with it to simply to repeat the word.

Body Vocabulary

Body Vocabulary Words

My body can...

sway wiggle gallop prance bounce whirl stretch
slouch hustle amble drag trudge saunter

My legs and feet can...

kick tap skip dance slip leap
scuff drag tiptoe stumble trample shuffle

My arms and hands can...

grab clasp squeeze knead snatch pinch flail
wring clench beckon clutch weave thrust fling

My face can...

frown grimace smile pout yawn stare
scowl sneer leer gape glare squint

My shoulders can...

shrug slouch droop roll

My torso can...

arch slump hunch lean twist shake jiggle

101

Materials	Body Vocabulary Words, page 101
Grade Band	K–3
Length of Activity	10 minutes
Differentiation Ideas	**Striving Learners and English Learners:** Write the word on the board so students are seeing the word in print.
Extension Ideas	• Ask students to come up with their own words to have the class act out with gestures or creative movement. • Have students choose a body part (shoulders, legs, arms, etc.) and draw illustrations of related words from the Body Vocabulary Words page. Students must think critically about how words like *tap*, *drag*, and *slip* can be illustrated to show their differences.

Body Vocabulary Words

My body can...

sway wiggle gallop prance bounce whirl stretch
slouch hustle amble drag trudge saunter

My legs and feet can...

kick tap skip dance slip leap
scuff drag tiptoe stumble trample shuffle

My arms and hands can...

grab clasp squeeze knead snatch pinch flail
wring clench beckon clutch weave thrust fling

My face can...

frown grimace smile pout yawn stare
scowl sneer leer gape glare squint

My shoulders can...

shrug slouch droop roll

My torso can...

arch slump hunch lean twist shake jiggle

CHAPTER 2
Individual-Word Learning

Strategies for Learning Words We Provide

LANGUAGE DOMAINS

Reading

Writing
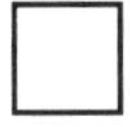

Speaking

Listening

2.K Picture-Powered Vocabulary

Help students acquire vocabulary by front-loading an upcoming concept to be learned with images to help students visualize that concept. For example, for a unit on habitats, gather pictures of different animal habitats. Another option is to use one of the Picture Preview sheets on pages 103–106. After presenting the images, invite students to discuss what they notice with a partner, modeling how to notice specific details in the scenes. Refer to the provided or created vocabulary list as needed during the discussion and encourage students to use the words in their noticings.

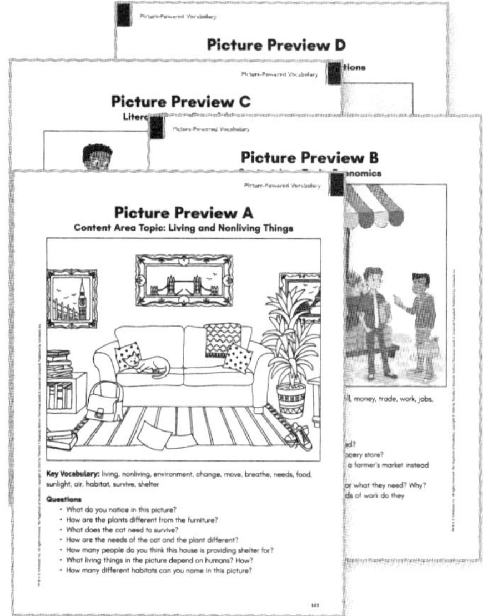

Materials	• Picture Preview A, page 103 • Picture Preview B, page 104 • Picture Preview C, page 105 • Picture Preview D, page 106 • images related to a new unit or topic • vocabulary to support images and unit or topic
Grade Band	K–8
Length of Activity	10–20 minutes
Differentiation Ideas	**English Learners:** Provide students with a vocabulary notebook where they can record words in their native language, as well as the English translation. Invite students to use the vocabulary notebook to add words they notice from their Picture Previews.
Extension Ideas	• Print the images and label with any vocabulary discussed. Hang the images with the labeled terms on the wall. • Find additional images to discuss. See if students can remember any of the vocabulary discussed in the first Picture Preview.

Picture Preview A

Content Area Topic: Living and Nonliving Things

Key Vocabulary: living, nonliving, environment, change, move, breathe, needs, food, sunlight, air, habitat, survive, shelter

Questions

- What do you notice in this picture?
- How are the plants different from the furniture?
- What does the cat need to survive?
- How are the needs of the cat and the plant different?
- How many people do you think this house is providing shelter for?
- What living things in the picture depend on humans? How?
- How many different habitats can you name in this picture?

Picture Preview B

Content Area Topic: Economics

Key Vocabulary: needs, wants, goods, services, buy, sell, money, trade, work, jobs, pay, shop, customer, local, helper, choice, commerce

Questions:

- What do you notice in this picture?
- How are people getting what they want and need?
- How is this farmer's market different from the grocery store?
- How might it help your community if you went to a farmer's market instead of a grocery store?
- Do you think people are buying what they want or what they need? Why?
- Who do you think works at this market? What kinds of work do they do each day?
- How do people pay for their purchases?

Picture Preview C

Literary Topic: Friendship

Key Vocabulary: friend, kindness, share, help, play, listen, care, teamwork, include, respect, fair, together, conflict, problem, forgive, understanding, support, loyal

Questions:

- What do you notice in these pictures?
- How can you tell the three people sitting in the second image are friends?
- (For the second image) How can you tell that this person is feeling left out? Can friends sometimes hurt our feelings?
- What makes someone a good friend?
- How could the friends include the person who is left out of the activity?
- What does it mean to be loyal to a friend? Can you be loyal and still speak up if you think something is unfair?
- What are ways we can show kindness to others, even if they aren't our friends?

Picture Preview D

Literary Topic: Change and Transitions

Key Vocabulary: change, grow, move, new, different, temporary, permanent, feelings, brave, learn, try, adapt, choice, finish, adjust, step, journey, improve, experience

Questions:

- What do you notice in this picture?
- Why might the boy be sad that he is moving?
- What parts of moving are temporary, and what parts are permanent?
- What choices does it appear the boy has made to help him handle this big change?
- How could this move be the beginning of a journey for him?
- Can you think of a time when a change helped you grow or improve?
- Is change always hard, or are there times when it is easy?
- What might the boy do to become comfortable with moving to a new place?

2.L Examples and Nonexamples Sort

Providing students with examples and nonexamples of key vocabulary helps them deepen their understanding of a word's meaning. Copy and cut apart the words and phrases on the Examples and Nonexamples Sorts on pages 108–111, enough sets for student pairs. Have students work in pairs to read and discuss the definition of the vocabulary word and read each card in the set, then determine if each example should be sorted under the *example* or *nonexample* card. After sorting all cards, students can check their answers against a full-page copy of the sort.

Materials	• Examples and Nonexamples Sort A, page 108 • Examples and Nonexamples Sort B, page 109 • Examples and Nonexamples Sort C, page 110 • Examples and Nonexamples Sort D, page 111
Grade Band	2–5
Length of Activity	5 minutes per word
Differentiation Ideas	• **Striving Learners and English Learners:** Initially limit the number of examples and nonexamples to two of each. • **Thriving Learners:** Provide small cards for students to create additional examples and nonexamples to be added to the sort.
Extension Ideas	Have students take nonexample sentences and rewrite the context to make them examples. For example: *Mark was baffled when he easily solved every question on the test.* (nonexample of *baffled*) Revised to: *Mark was baffled when he could not easily solve every question on the test he had studied hard for.*
Answers	Answers integrated into Examples and Nonexamples Sorts, pages 108–111

Strategies for Learning Words We Provide

LANGUAGE DOMAINS

Reading

Writing

Speaking

Listening

Examples and Nonexamples Sort A

Vocabulary Word: **baffled**

Definition: totally confused or puzzled

examples	nonexamples
Emma stared at the math problem completely **baffled** because she had never seen anything like it before.	Mark was **baffled** when he easily solved every question on the test.
Liam was **baffled** when his dog barked at an empty chair as if someone were sitting there.	Ella was **baffled** when she won the race after weeks of hard training every morning.
Olivia felt **baffled** when she walked into the classroom and saw balloons everywhere but had no idea why.	Noah was **baffled** when he followed a recipe and made the perfect cake.
Jason was **baffled** when his little brother started crying out of nowhere, and he didn't know what was wrong.	Ben was **baffled** when he walked into his house, knowing exactly what was for dinner: Friday night hamburgers!

Examples and Nonexamples Sort B

Vocabulary Word: **reluctant**

Definition: not wanting to do something right away

examples	nonexamples
Sonja felt **reluctant** to present her project in front of the class because she was nervous about speaking.	Ava was **reluctant** to eat her favorite chocolate cake, which she requested for her birthday.
Lucas was **reluctant** to try the strange-looking food on his plate, even though his mom said it was delicious.	Ethan was **reluctant** to go to the amusement park because he had been waiting for this trip all year.
Noah was **reluctant** to clean his messy room, dragging his feet as he picked up his toys.	Maya was **reluctant** to meet her new puppy and immediately ran to hug it.
Emerson was **reluctant** to let go of her dad's hand on the first day of school because she was feeling shy.	Carlos was **reluctant** to eat ice cream, so he grabbed a spoon and dug in immediately, finishing the whole bowl in minutes.

Examples and Nonexamples Sort C

Vocabulary Word: **hasty**

Definition: done too quickly without thinking

examples	nonexamples
Ben gave a **hasty** apology just to end the argument, but his friend knew he didn't really mean it.	Eduardo made a **hasty** decision to study all week before the test, so he felt fully prepared.
Jeremiah made a **hasty** move in the board game and immediately regretted it when he lost his turn.	Martin took a **hasty** sip of his hot chocolate after waiting for it to cool down.
Evie wrote a **hasty** answer on her test without reading the question carefully, and she got it wrong.	Lily gave a **hasty** speech after practicing it 20 times in front of the mirror.
Scarlett packed her bag in a **hasty** way and later realized she forgot her lunch at home.	Ava took an hour to finish her art project in a **hasty** fashion, making sure every detail was perfect.

Examples and Nonexamples Sort D

Vocabulary Word: **grim**

Definition: gloomy, serious, or scary

examples	nonexamples
The doctor had a **grim** expression as he delivered the bad news to the patient's family.	Sophia's face was **grim** as she laughed and danced at her birthday party.
The sky turned dark and stormy, creating a **grim** atmosphere before the thunderstorm began.	Ethan's **grim** laughter filled the air as he played tag with his best friends, dodging and weaving with a huge grin on his face.
After losing the championship game, the players sat on the bench with **grim** faces, staring at the ground.	The puppy wagged its tail with a **grim** expression as it ran toward its owner and jumped in her lap.
The soldiers marched through the battlefield with **grim** determination, knowing the fight ahead would be tough.	The classroom had a **grim** atmosphere as students cheered, high-fived, and celebrated their teacher canceling homework.

CHAPTER 2
Individual-Word Learning

Strategies for Learning Words We Provide

LANGUAGE DOMAINS

Reading

Writing

Speaking

Listening

2.M Emotion Pictures

This strategy helps students communicate with precise language for emotions, moving beyond words they might typically use such as *happy*, *sad*, and *angry*. Provide the Emotion Picture A or B on pages 113–114 for students. Pronounce each word in the list at the bottom of the page and have students chorally repeat. After students review the feelings and definitions, invite them to choose one feeling word and draw a scene of someone showing that emotion in the box on the top of the page. Students then write a description of how their drawing reflects that feeling. Model an example to show students that the sentence should be descriptive, such as: "The boy trudged back home, *shaky* (Grades 2–3) / *bedraggled* (Grades 4–8) and exhausted after the dog park, his clothes splattered with mud after his mischievous dog had dragged him through puddles, chased every squirrel in sight, and refused to come back when called." Once students finish their drawings, have them share in small groups to provide more exposure to the words.

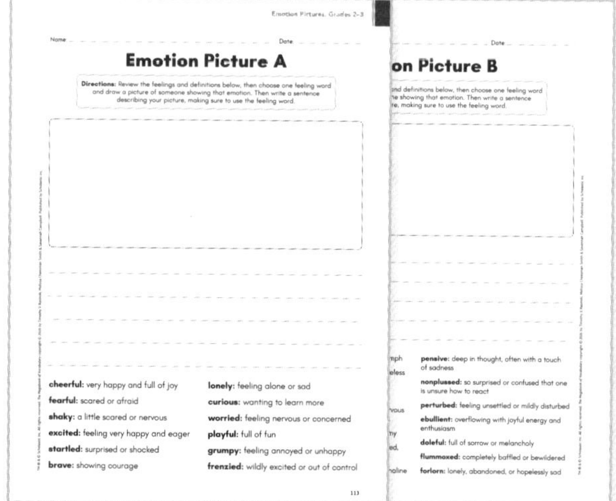

Emotion Pictures, Grades 2–3

Name ________ Date ________

Emotion Picture A

Directions: Review the feelings and definitions below, then choose one feeling word and draw a picture of someone showing that emotion. Then write a sentence describing your picture, making sure to use the feeling word.

cheerful: very happy and full of joy
fearful: scared or afraid
shaky: a little scared or nervous
excited: feeling very happy and eager
startled: surprised or shocked
brave: showing courage
lonely: feeling alone or sad
curious: wanting to learn more
worried: feeling nervous or concerned
playful: full of fun
grumpy: feeling annoyed or unhappy
frenzied: wildly excited or out of control

113

Date ________

on Picture B

nd definitions below, then choose one feeling word
e showing that emotion. Then write a sentence
e, making sure to use the feeling word.

pensive: deep in thought, often with a touch of sadness
nonplussed: so surprised or confused that one is unsure how to react
perturbed: feeling unsettled or mildly disturbed
ebullient: overflowing with joyful energy and enthusiasm
doleful: full of sorrow or melancholy
flummoxed: completely baffled or bewildered
forlorn: lonely, abandoned, or hopelessly sad

Materials	• Emotion Picture A, Grades 2–3, page 113 • Emotion Picture B, Grades 4–8, page 114
Grade Band	2–8
Length of Activity	15 minutes
Differentiation Ideas	**English Learners:** Provide examples of what they could draw a person doing for the word they picked so they have more context around the word than just the definition provided.
Extension Ideas	• Have students choose a vocabulary word not used and draw a person or write a description to capture the emotion, and then share their work in small groups. • Allow students to use the sentence they created as a hook to start writing a story.

Name: ______________________ Date: ______________

Emotion Picture A

Directions: Review the feelings and definitions below, then choose one feeling word and draw a picture of someone showing that emotion. Then write a sentence describing your picture, making sure to use the feeling word.

____

____

____

____

____

cheerful: very happy and full of joy

fearful: scared or afraid

shaky: a little scared or nervous

excited: feeling very happy and eager

startled: surprised or shocked

brave: showing courage

lonely: feeling alone or sad

curious: wanting to learn more

worried: feeling nervous or concerned

playful: full of fun

grumpy: feeling annoyed or unhappy

frenzied: wildly excited or out of control

Name: ______________________ Date: __________

Emotion Picture B

Directions: Review the feelings and definitions below, then choose one feeling word and draw a picture of someone showing that emotion. Then write a sentence describing your picture, making sure to use the feeling word.

jubilant: expressing extreme joy and triumph

despondent: deeply discouraged or hopeless

effervescent: bubbling with excitement and energy

trepidatious: hesitant and filled with nervous uncertainty

lugubrious: excessively mournful or gloomy

bedraggled: looking exhausted, disheveled, and overwhelmed

exhilarated: thrilled and filled with adrenaline

pensive: deep in thought, often with a touch of sadness

nonplussed: so surprised or confused that one is unsure how to react

perturbed: feeling unsettled or mildly disturbed

ebullient: overflowing with joyful energy and enthusiasm

doleful: full of sorrow or melancholy

flummoxed: completely baffled or bewildered

forlorn: lonely, abandoned, or hopelessly sad

2.N **Would You Rather: Vocabulary Edition**

Project a set of "Would You Rather...?" questions from pages 116–119. Then read each question while students read the definitions of those words to themselves to determine which question they would choose. Have students hold up one or two fingers, or stand in two areas of the room marked *1* and *2*, to indicate whether they prefer the first or second option. Once all students have made their choices, ask several students to share with the class or a partner why they made their selection. Continue with the next question and repeat until complete.

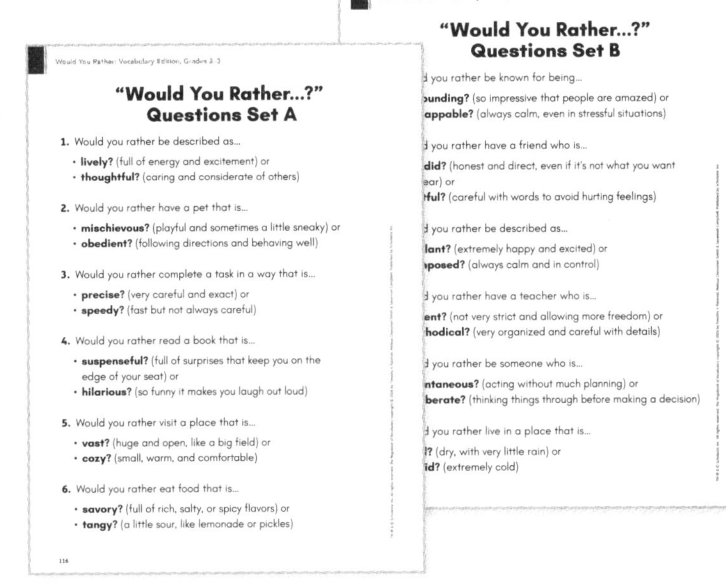

Would You Rather: Vocabulary Edition, Grades 2–3

"Would You Rather...?" Questions Set A

1. Would you rather be described as...
   - **lively?** (full of energy and excitement) or
   - **thoughtful?** (caring and considerate of others)
2. Would you rather have a pet that is...
   - **mischievous?** (playful and sometimes a little sneaky) or
   - **obedient?** (following directions and behaving well)
3. Would you rather complete a task in a way that is...
   - **precise?** (very careful and exact) or
   - **speedy?** (fast but not always careful)
4. Would you rather read a book that is...
   - **suspenseful?** (full of surprises that keep you on the edge of your seat) or
   - **hilarious?** (so funny it makes you laugh out loud)
5. Would you rather visit a place that is...
   - **vast?** (huge and open, like a big field) or
   - **cozy?** (small, warm, and comfortable)
6. Would you rather eat food that is...
   - **savory?** (full of rich, salty, or spicy flavors) or
   - **tangy?** (a little sour, like lemonade or pickles)

116

Would You Rather: Vocabulary Edition, Grades 4–8

"Would You Rather...?" Questions Set B

d you rather be known for being...
ounding? (so impressive that people are amazed) or
appable? (always calm, even in stressful situations)

d you rather have a friend who is...
did? (honest and direct, even if it's not what you want
ear) or
tful? (careful with words to avoid hurting feelings)

d you rather be described as...
lant? (extremely happy and excited) or
posed? (always calm and in control)

d you rather have a teacher who is...
ent? (not very strict and allowing more freedom) or
hodical? (very organized and careful with details)

d you rather be someone who is...
ntaneous? (acting without much planning) or
berate? (thinking things through before making a decision)

d you rather live in a place that is...
l? (dry, with very little rain) or
id? (extremely cold)

Materials	• "Would You Rather…?" Questions Set A, Grades 2–3, pages 116–117 • "Would You Rather…?" Questions Set B, Grades 4–8, pages 118–119
Grade Band	2–8
Length of Activity	20 minutes
Differentiation Ideas	**Striving Learners and English Learners:** Provide further explanation of the target words or read the definitions aloud and clarify meaning.
Extension Ideas	• Use a set of words from a text or unit of study to create "Would You Rather...?" questions with the help of an AI website. (Be sure to check any AI results to make sure they are appropriate.) This will provide multiple exposures to a word that students are already learning. • Provide students with a copy of the questions to take home and play the game with their family or friends. • Have students create their own set of questions by using words the class is studying from a text or unit of study.

Strategies for Learning Words We Provide

LANGUAGE DOMAINS

Reading

Writing

Speaking

Listening

✓

"Would You Rather...?" Questions Set A

1. Would you rather be described as...

- **lively?** (full of energy and excitement) or
- **thoughtful?** (caring and considerate of others)

2. Would you rather have a pet that is...

- **mischievous?** (playful and sometimes a little sneaky) or
- **obedient?** (following directions and behaving well)

3. Would you rather complete a task in a way that is...

- **precise?** (very careful and exact) or
- **speedy?** (fast but not always careful)

4. Would you rather read a book that is...

- **suspenseful?** (full of surprises that keep you on the edge of your seat) or
- **hilarious?** (so funny it makes you laugh out loud)

5. Would you rather visit a place that is...

- **vast?** (huge and open, like a big field) or
- **cozy?** (small, warm, and comfortable)

6. Would you rather eat food that is...

- **savory?** (full of rich, salty, or spicy flavors) or
- **tangy?** (a little sour, like lemonade or pickles)

7. Would you rather be known for being...
   - **inventive?** (good at coming up with creative ideas) or
   - **determined?** (never giving up, even when things are tough)

8. Would you rather play a game that is...
   - **strategic?** (requiring thinking and planning ahead) or
   - **energetic?** (fast-paced and full of action)

9. Would you rather be a person who is...
   - **observant?** (noticing small details that others miss) or
   - **persuasive?** (good at convincing others to agree with you)

10. Would you rather be in a place that is...
   - **bustling?** (full of energy, people, and noise) or
   - **remote?** (far away and quiet)

11. Would you rather listen to music that is...
   - **upbeat?** (fast and happy) or
   - **mellow?** (soft and slow)

12. Would you rather tell a story that is...
   - **whimsical?** (full of imagination and magic) or
   - **realistic?** (about things that could really happen)

"Would You Rather...?" Questions Set B

1. Would you rather be known for being...
   - **astounding?** (so impressive that people are amazed) or
   - **unflappable?** (always calm, even in stressful situations)

2. Would you rather have a friend who is...
   - **candid?** (honest and direct, even if it's not what you want to hear) or
   - **tactful?** (careful with words to avoid hurting feelings)

3. Would you rather be described as...
   - **jubilant?** (extremely happy and excited) or
   - **composed?** (always calm and in control)

4. Would you rather have a teacher who is...
   - **lenient?** (not very strict and allowing more freedom) or
   - **methodical?** (very organized and careful with details)

5. Would you rather be someone who is...
   - **spontaneous?** (acting without much planning) or
   - **deliberate?** (thinking things through before making a decision)

6. Would you rather live in a place that is...
   - **arid?** (dry, with very little rain) or
   - **frigid?** (extremely cold)

7. Would you rather spend time with someone who is...
   - **erratic?** (unpredictable and changing moods quickly) or
   - **obstinate?** (stubborn and refusing to change opinions)

8. Would you rather own a pet that is...
   - **docile?** (gentle, obedient, and easy to control) or
   - **vigorous?** (full of energy and always moving)

9. Would you rather visit a place that is...
   - **opulent?** (luxurious, fancy, and expensive-looking) or
   - **rustic?** (simple, natural, and rural)

10. Would you rather do a job that is...
    - **tedious?** (repetitive and boring) or
    - **grueling?** (extremely tiring and difficult)

11. Would you rather solve a problem by being...
    - **impetuous?** (acting quickly without thinking) or
    - **prudent?** (careful and thinking ahead before acting)

12. Would you rather go on an adventure that is...
    - **treacherous?** (dangerous and full of risks) or
    - **exhilarating?** (exciting and full of thrills)

LANGUAGE DOMAINS

Reading

Writing

Speaking

Listening

2.0 Choose Your Own Words

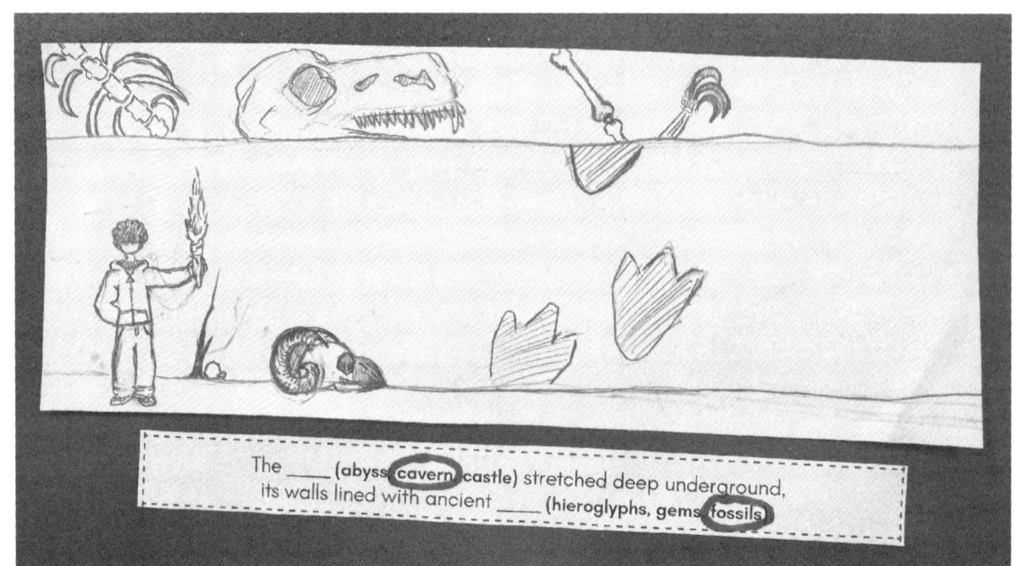

Copy and cut apart the Choose Your Own Words Sentences on pages 121–122. Have each student select a sentence strip, pick two challenging words from it, and use a print or online dictionary to determine any unknown meanings. Once meanings are clear, have students illustrate the sentence. Invite students who feel comfortable to share their picture and sentence strip with the class. Ask classmates to guess which vocabulary words are shown in the picture. After a few guesses, the student reveals the correct words and explains their meanings.

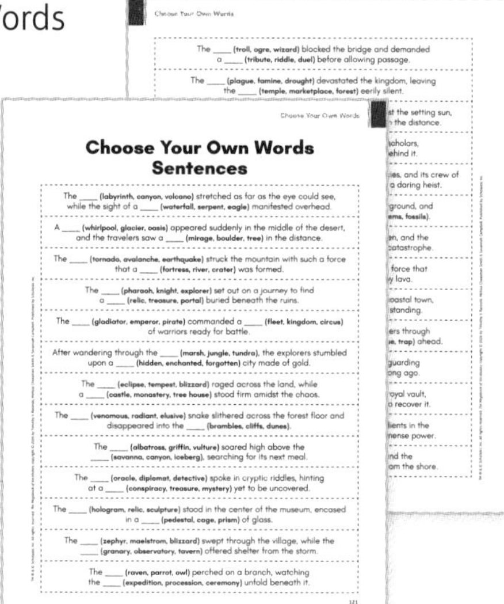
Choose Your Own Words

The ____ (troll, ogre, wizard) blocked the bridge and demanded a ____ (tribute, riddle, duel) before allowing passage.

The ____ (plague, famine, drought) devastated the kingdom, leaving the ____ (temple, marketplace, forest) eerily silent.

Choose Your Own Words

Choose Your Own Words Sentences

The ____ (**labyrinth, canyon, volcano**) stretched as far as the eye could see, while the sight of a ____ (**waterfall, serpent, eagle**) manifested overhead.

A ____ (**whirlpool, glacier, oasis**) appeared suddenly in the middle of the desert, and the travelers saw a ____ (**mirage, boulder, tree**) in the distance.

The ____ (**tornado, avalanche, earthquake**) struck the mountain with such a force that a ____ (**fortress, river, crater**) was formed.

The ____ (**pharaoh, knight, explorer**) set out on a journey to find a ____ (**relic, treasure, portal**) buried beneath the ruins.

The ____ (**gladiator, emperor, pirate**) commanded a ____ (**fleet, kingdom, circus**) of warriors ready for battle.

After wandering through the ____ (**marsh, jungle, tundra**), the explorers stumbled upon a ____ (**hidden, enchanted, forgotten**) city made of gold.

The ____ (**eclipse, tempest, blizzard**) raged across the land, while a ____ (**castle, monastery, tree house**) stood firm amidst the chaos.

The ____ (**venomous, radiant, elusive**) snake slithered across the forest floor and disappeared into the ____ (**brambles, cliffs, dunes**).

The ____ (**albatross, griffin, vulture**) soared high above the ____ (**savanna, canyon, iceberg**), searching for its next meal.

The ____ (**oracle, diplomat, detective**) spoke in cryptic riddles, hinting at a ____ (**conspiracy, treasure, mystery**) yet to be uncovered.

The ____ (**hologram, relic, sculpture**) stood in the center of the museum, encased in a ____ (**pedestal, cage, prism**) of glass.

The ____ (**zephyr, maelstrom, blizzard**) swept through the village, while the ____ (**granary, observatory, tavern**) offered shelter from the storm.

The ____ (**raven, parrot, owl**) perched on a branch, watching the ____ (**expedition, procession, ceremony**) unfold beneath it.

121

Materials	• Choose Your Own Words Sentences, pages 121–122 • Blank white paper
Grade Band	4–8
Length of Activity	30 minutes
Differentiation Ideas	**Striving Learners and English Learners:** Ensure students know the meanings of the words before they begin their drawings.
Extension Ideas	After sharing, have students write their sentences on their drawings, and then display the drawings and sentences in the classroom on a bulletin board.

Choose Your Own Words Sentences

The _____ **(labyrinth, canyon, volcano)** stretched as far as the eye could see, while the sight of a _____ **(waterfall, serpent, eagle)** manifested overhead.

A _____ **(whirlpool, glacier, oasis)** appeared suddenly in the middle of the desert, and the travelers saw a _____ **(mirage, boulder, tree)** in the distance.

The _____ **(tornado, avalanche, earthquake)** struck the mountain with such a force that a _____ **(fortress, river, crater)** was formed.

The _____ **(pharaoh, knight, explorer)** set out on a journey to find a _____ **(relic, treasure, portal)** buried beneath the ruins.

The _____ **(gladiator, emperor, pirate)** commanded a _____ **(fleet, kingdom, circus)** of warriors ready for battle.

After wandering through the _____ **(marsh, jungle, tundra)**, the explorers stumbled upon a _____ **(hidden, enchanted, forgotten)** city made of gold.

The _____ **(eclipse, tempest, blizzard)** raged across the land, while a _____ **(castle, monastery, tree house)** stood firm amidst the chaos.

The _____ **(venomous, radiant, elusive)** snake slithered across the forest floor and disappeared into the _____ **(brambles, cliffs, dunes)**.

The _____ **(albatross, griffin, vulture)** soared high above the _____ **(savanna, canyon, iceberg)**, searching for its next meal.

The _____ **(oracle, diplomat, detective)** spoke in cryptic riddles, hinting at a _____ **(conspiracy, treasure, mystery)** yet to be uncovered.

The _____ **(hologram, relic, sculpture)** stood in the center of the museum, encased in a _____ **(pedestal, cage, prism)** of glass.

The _____ **(zephyr, maelstrom, blizzard)** swept through the village, while the _____ **(granary, observatory, tavern)** offered shelter from the storm.

The _____ **(raven, parrot, owl)** perched on a branch, watching the _____ **(expedition, procession, ceremony)** unfold beneath it.

The _____ **(troll, ogre, wizard)** blocked the bridge and demanded a _____ **(tribute, riddle, duel)** before allowing passage.

The _____ **(plague, famine, drought)** devastated the kingdom, leaving the _____ **(temple, marketplace, forest)** eerily silent.

The _____ **(monolith, pyramid, amphitheater)** stood tall against the setting sun, while a _____ **(flood, thunderstorm, earthquake)** rumbled in the distance.

The _____ **(illusion, paradox, epiphany)** baffled the scholars, as they pondered the _____ **(truth, enigma, idea)** behind it.

The _____ **(zeppelin, pirate ship, caravan)** sailed through the skies, and its crew of _____ **(swashbucklers, engineers, merchants)** prepared for a daring heist.

The _____ **(abyss, cavern, castle)** stretched deep underground, and its walls were lined with ancient _____ **(hieroglyphs, gems, fossils).**

The _____ **(vortex, chasm, glacier)** split the ground open, and the _____ **(expedition, horde, army)** braced for the coming catastrophe.

The _____ **(volcano, comet, glacier)** erupted with such force that the _____ **(village, temple, bridge)** was engulfed by lava.

The _____ **(gale, monsoon, hurricane)** tore through the coastal town, while the _____ **(lighthouse, tower, statue)** remained standing.

The _____ **(oracle, sentinel, sage)** guided the adventurers through the dark forest, warning them of the _____ **(creature, curse, trap)** ahead.

The _____ **(sprite, fairy, elf)** stood tall in the forest, guarding an/a _____ **(ancient, enchanted, cursed)** relic from long ago.

The _____ **(scepter, crown, ring)** was stolen from the royal vault, and the _____ **(detective, thief, king)** was determined to recover it.

The _____ **(alchemist, sorcerer, magician)** mixed ingredients in the _____ **(cauldron, furnace, oven)** to create a potion of immense power.

The _____ **(eclipse, comet, aurora)** lit up the sky, and the _____ **(seafarers, astronomers, sailors)** watched in awe from the shore.

2.P Keyword Method

The Keyword Method (Baumann & Kame'enui, 1991) is a strategy in which students create a mental image to help remember the meaning of a word. Give students a target word from the Keyword Method Words on page 124, or your own pre-selected target words, and share the meaning with them. Then have students identify a keyword that sounds similar, at least in part, to the target word, and find a way to connect the target and keyword. For example, if the target word is *carlin*, give the definition of *old woman*. Have students identify a familiar word that sounds similar, at least in part, to the target word, such as *car*. Then have students think of how those two words could be connected by forming a visual image, in this case, perhaps *an old woman driving a car*. Have students practice the steps of Target Word → Keyword → Image → Definition to retrieve the definition. Students can share their connections with each other.

Keyword Method

Keyword Method Words

1. **Audible**
   - Keyword: Audio (relating to sound)
   - Association: Imagine listening to an audiobook on tape. "Audible" means something you can hear.
2. **Benevolent**
   - Keyword: Beneficial (doing good)
   - Association: Picture someone giving a beneficial gift, showing kindness and helping others. "Benevolent" means good-hearted or kind.
3. **Courageous**
   - Keyword: Courage (bravery)
   - Association: Imagine a superhero showing courage to save the day. "Courageous" means showing bravery in difficult situations.
4. **Eloquent**
   - Keyword: Elegance (smooth and graceful)
   - Association: Picture someone speaking in a smooth, elegant way, using beautiful words to express themselves. "Eloquent" means speaking or writing in a very clear and expressive way.
5. **Frivolous**
   - Keyword: Fun (lighthearted)
   - Association: Think of someone spending money on unnecessary, fun things like decorations. "Frivolous" means not serious or unnecessary.
6. **Meticulous**
   - Keyword: Minute (small or detailed)
   - Association: Imagine someone spending time on very minute details while organizing something. "Meticulous" means being very careful and paying attention to small details.
7. **Reluctant**
   - Keyword: Resistant (unwilling)
   - Association: Picture someone resistant to going to a party because they don't feel like it. "Reluctant" means unwilling or hesitant to do something.
8. **Vivid**
   - Keyword: Vision (clear image)
   - Association: Picture a vision of a bright, colorful rainbow. "Vivid" means very clear, bright, and detailed, like a picture in your mind.
9. **Spontaneous**
   - Keyword: Sport (unstructured play)
   - Association: Imagine someone deciding to play an unplanned game of soccer. "Spontaneous" means acting without planning or thinking ahead.
10. **Versatile**
    - Keyword: Variable (able to change)
    - Association: Think of a variable tool, like a Swiss Army knife, which can be used for many different tasks. "Versatile" means having many uses or being able to adapt easily.
11. **Consequence**
    - Keyword: Cause (what sparks a reaction)
    - Association: Think of an action (cause) and its outcome (consequence). "Consequence" means the result of an action.
12. **Absurd**
    - Keyword: Lack (lack of sense)
    - Association: Imagine something that doesn't make sense at all, like a fish flying in the sky. "Absurd" means ridiculous or illogical.
13. **Perplexed**
    - Keyword: Puzzled (confused)
    - Association: Picture a person looking at a difficult puzzle, scratching their head. "Perplexed" means confused or unsure.
14. **Friction**
    - Keyword: Chafing (rubbing)
    - Association: Imagine rubbing two sticks together, creating heat and friction. "Friction" means the resistance that one surface or object encounters when moving over another.
15. **Tangible**
    - Keyword: Touch (real or physical)
    - Association: Think of something you can touch, like a ball or a book. "Tangible" means something that can be touched or felt.
16. **Nurture**
    - Keyword: Nurse (caring for)
    - Association: Imagine caring for a plant by giving it water and sunlight. "Nurture" means to care for or encourage growth.

124

Materials	Keyword Method Words, page 124 (or words you choose)
Grade Band	4–8
Length of Activity	3 minutes per word
Differentiation Ideas	**Striving Learners and English Learners:** Have students create a quick sketch or drawing from what they were visualizing.

Extension Ideas	• Choose words from a unit of study, following these guidelines:
	  • Words have parts that can be linked to meaning (e.g., "benevolent" and "beneficial" mean good).
	  • Words have concrete, easily imagined associations that students can visualize.
	  • Words lend themselves to simple, familiar keywords that are easy to understand or relate to.

LANGUAGE DOMAINS

Reading

Writing

Speaking

Listening

Keyword Method Words

1. Audible

- Keyword: Audio (relating to sound)
- Association: Imagine listening to an audiobook on tape. "Audible" means something you can hear.

2. Benevolent

- Keyword: Beneficial (doing good)
- Association: Picture someone giving a beneficial gift, showing kindness and helping others. "Benevolent" means good-hearted or kind.

3. Courageous

- Keyword: Courage (bravery)
- Association: Imagine a superhero showing courage to save the day. "Courageous" means showing bravery in difficult situations.

4. Eloquent

- Keyword: Elegance (smooth and graceful)
- Association: Picture someone speaking in a smooth, elegant way, using beautiful words to express themselves. "Eloquent" means speaking or writing in a very clear and expressive way.

5. Frivolous

- Keyword: Fun (lighthearted)
- Association: Think of someone spending money on unnecessary, fun things like decorations. "Frivolous" means not serious or unnecessary.

6. Meticulous

- Keyword: Minute (small or detailed)
- Association: Imagine someone spending time on very minute details while organizing something. "Meticulous" means being very careful and paying attention to small details.

7. Reluctant

- Keyword: Resistant (unwilling)
- Association: Picture someone resistant to going to a party because they don't feel like it. "Reluctant" means unwilling or hesitant to do something.

8. Vivid

- Keyword: Vision (clear image)
- Association: Picture a vision of a bright, colorful rainbow. "Vivid" means very clear, bright, and detailed, like a picture in your mind.

9. Spontaneous

- Keyword: Sport (unstructured play)
- Association: Imagine someone deciding to play an unplanned game of soccer. "Spontaneous" means acting without planning or thinking ahead.

10. Versatile

- Keyword: Variable (able to change)
- Association: Think of a variable tool, like a Swiss Army knife, which can be used for many different tasks. "Versatile" means having many uses or being able to adapt easily.

11. Consequence

- Keyword: Cause (what sparks a reaction)
- Association: Think of an action (cause) and its outcome (consequence). "Consequence" means the result of an action.

12. Absurd

- Keyword: Lack (lack of sense)
- Association: Imagine something that doesn't make sense at all, like a fish flying in the sky. "Absurd" means ridiculous or illogical.

13. Perplexed

- Keyword: Puzzled (confused)
- Association: Picture a person looking at a difficult puzzle, scratching their head. "Perplexed" means confused or unsure.

14. Friction

- Keyword: Chafing (rubbing)
- Association: Imagine rubbing two sticks together, creating heat and friction. "Friction" means the resistance that one surface or object encounters when moving over another.

15. Tangible

- Keyword: Touch (real or physical)
- Association: Think of something you can touch, like a ball or a book. "Tangible" means something that can be touched or felt.

16. Nurture

- Keyword: Nurse (caring for)
- Association: Imagine caring for a plant by giving it water and sunlight. "Nurture" means to care for or encourage growth.

2.Q Character Traits Rating Chart

Select six words from a Character Traits Set on pages 126–127 or choose your own words that may apply to the characters in a shared text. Distribute the Character Traits Rating Chart on page 128 and have students fill it in with the selected words and three to four main characters from the shared text. Selected words and definitions should also be written on the back of the page for reference. As students read their book, ask them to rate characters on various traits, using a scale from 1 to 10 to indicate the extent each character embodies that trait. Allow students to adjust their scores several times as they read and characters evolve. Provide time for students to discuss in small groups to allow multiple uses of the new vocabulary and develop critical thinking about the words and characters. This strategy encourages deeper thinking about characterization and engagement with new vocabulary.

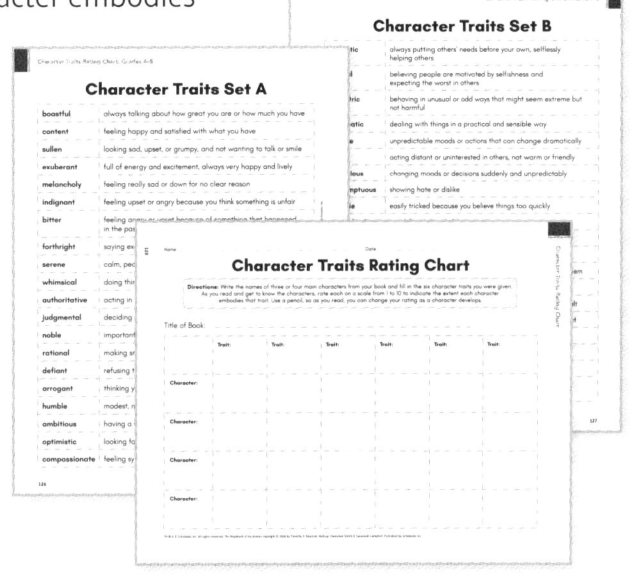

Character Traits Set B

always putting others' needs before your own, selflessly helping others
believing people are motivated by selfishness and expecting the worst in others
behaving in unusual or odd ways that might seem extreme but not harmful
dealing with things in a practical and sensible way
unpredictable moods or actions that can change dramatically
acting distant or uninterested in others, not warm or friendly
changing moods or decisions suddenly and unpredictably
showing hate or dislike
easily tricked because you believe things too quickly

Character Traits Set A

boastful	always talking about how great you are or how much you have
content	feeling happy and satisfied with what you have
sullen	looking sad, upset, or grumpy, and not wanting to talk or smile
exuberant	full of energy and excitement, always very happy and lively
melancholy	feeling really sad or down for no clear reason
indignant	feeling upset or angry because you think something is unfair
bitter	
forthright	
serene	
whimsical	
authoritative	
judgmental	
noble	
rational	
defiant	
arrogant	
humble	
ambitious	
optimistic	
compassionate	

Character Traits Rating Chart

Title of Book:

	Trait:	Trait:	Trait:	Trait:	Trait:	Trait:
Character:						
Character:						
Character:						
Character:						

Materials	• Character Traits Set A, Grades 4–5, page 126 • Character Traits Set B, Grades 6–8, page 127 • Character Traits Rating Chart, page 128
Grade Band	4–8
Length of Activity	Varies depending on the length of the book and time it takes to read it
Differentiation Ideas	**Striving Learners and English Learners:** Pronounce the word and discuss its meaning with examples to promote understanding.
Extension Ideas	• Assess students on the words through a teacher-created quiz. • Have students line up on a continuum according to how much they each exemplify the character trait being learned. • Have students choose one character trait and put all the characters by name on a continuum to increase exposure.

Strategies for Learning Words We Provide

LANGUAGE DOMAINS

Reading

Writing

Speaking

Listening

Character Traits Set A

boastful	always talking about how great you are or how much you have
content	feeling happy and satisfied with what you have
sullen	looking sad, upset, or grumpy, and not wanting to talk or smile
exuberant	full of energy and excitement, always very happy and lively
melancholy	feeling really sad or down for no clear reason
indignant	feeling upset or angry because you think something is unfair
bitter	feeling angry or upset because of something that happened in the past
forthright	saying exactly what you think in a clear and honest way
serene	calm, peaceful, and not easily upset
whimsical	doing things in a fun, silly, or unpredictable way
authoritative	acting in a way that shows you are in charge
judgmental	deciding if someone is good or bad, often in a mean way
noble	important and distinguished
rational	making smart, reasonable decisions
defiant	refusing to obey someone or something
arrogant	thinking you're better than others
humble	modest, not acting better than others or bragging
ambitious	having a strong desire to achieve goals
optimistic	looking for/expecting a positive outcome
compassionate	feeling sympathy for others and wanting to help

Character Traits Set B

altruistic	always putting others' needs before your own, selflessly helping others
cynical	believing people are motivated by selfishness and expecting the worst in others
eccentric	behaving in unusual or odd ways that might seem extreme but not harmful
pragmatic	dealing with things in a practical and sensible way
volatile	unpredictable moods or actions that can change dramatically
aloof	acting distant or uninterested in others, not warm or friendly
capricious	changing moods or decisions suddenly and unpredictably
contemptuous	showing hate or dislike
gullible	easily tricked because you believe things too quickly
methodical	careful and thoughtful in your actions
placid	calm and peaceful
caustic	really sarcastic and/or critical
haughty	acting like you're better than others and looking down on them
belligerent	hostile, aggressive, ready to fight
querulous	complaining a lot about small things or always being difficult
sanguine	always hopeful and positive, even when things aren't perfect
callous	showing a lack of compassion toward others
languid	moving in a slow or lazy manner, due to lack of energy
perceptive	able to understand details easily that others may miss
melodramatic	overacting or exaggerating emotions in a way that seems unnecessary

Name: ______________________ Date: ______________

Character Traits Rating Chart

Directions: Write the names of three or four main characters from your book and fill in the six character traits you were given. As you read and get to know the characters, rate each on a scale from 1 to 10 to indicate the extent each character embodies that trait. Use a pencil, so as you read, you can change your rating as a character develops.

Title of Book: ______________________

	Trait:	**Trait:**	**Trait:**	**Trait:**	**Trait:**	**Trait:**
Character:						
Character:						
Character:						
Character:						

2.R **Choose Your Own Adventure: Vocabulary Edition**

Pick a Choose Your Own Adventure on pages 130–133. Select a spokesperson for students and begin reading the adventure aloud, following the prompts to the end. The goal for the class is to get to the third step by choosing the correct vocabulary word that will take them further in the adventure. As the adventure unfolds and a question with three boldfaced word options appear, the spokesperson selects one of those options with input from classmates. Success depends on whether the class chooses the word that best fits the situation. If students choose the correct word, continue the game by reading the next section. If students choose an incorrect word, it's "GAME OVER!" Choose a new spokesperson and start from the beginning. Repeat until the class gets to the end of the adventure, reinforcing vocabulary through multiple exposures and with a "CONGRATULATIONS!"

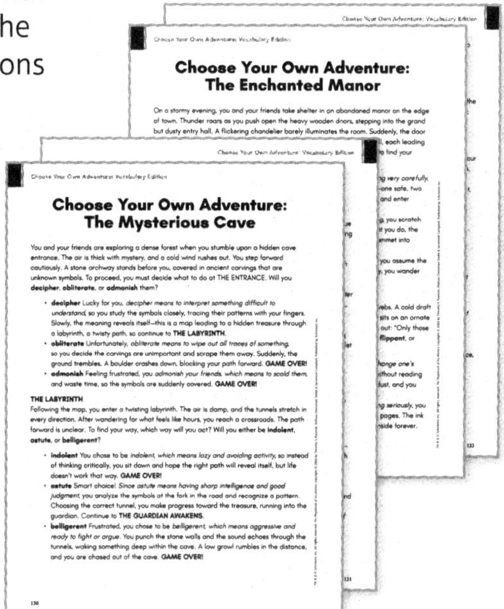

Choose Your Own Adventure: The Enchanted Manor

Choose Your Own Adventure: Vocabulary Edition

Choose Your Own Adventure: The Mysterious Cave

You and your friends are exploring a dense forest when you stumble upon a hidden cave entrance. The air is thick with mystery, and a cold wind rushes out. You step forward cautiously. A stone archway stands before you, covered in ancient carvings that are unknown symbols. To proceed, you must decide what to do at THE ENTRANCE. Will you **decipher**, **obliterate**, or **admonish** them?

- **decipher** Lucky for you, *decipher means to interpret something difficult to understand*, so you study the symbols closely, tracing their patterns with your fingers. Slowly, the meaning reveals itself—this is a map leading to a hidden treasure through a labyrinth, a twisty path, so continue to **THE LABYRINTH**.
- **obliterate** Unfortunately, *obliterate means to wipe out all traces of something*, so you decide the carvings are unimportant and scrape them away. Suddenly, the ground trembles. A boulder crashes down, blocking your path forward. **GAME OVER!**
- **admonish** Feeling frustrated, you *admonish your friends, which means to scold them*, and waste time, so the symbols are suddenly covered. **GAME OVER!**

THE LABYRINTH

Following the map, you enter a twisting labyrinth. The air is damp, and the tunnels stretch in every direction. After wandering for what feels like hours, you reach a crossroads. The path forward is unclear. To find your way, which way will you act? Will you either be **indolent**, **astute**, or **belligerent**?

- **indolent** You chose to be *indolent, which means lazy and avoiding activity*, so instead of thinking critically, you sit down and hope the right path will reveal itself, but life doesn't work that way. **GAME OVER!**
- **astute** Smart choice! *Since astute means having sharp intelligence and good judgment*, you analyze the symbols at the fork in the road and recognize a pattern. Choosing the correct tunnel, you make progress toward the treasure, running into the guardian. Continue to **THE GUARDIAN AWAKENS**.
- **belligerent** Frustrated, you chose to be *belligerent, which means aggressive and ready to fight or argue*. You punch the stone walls and the sound echoes through the tunnels, waking something deep within the cave. A low growl rumbles in the distance, and you are chased out of the cave. **GAME OVER!**

130

Materials	• Choose Your Own Adventure: The Mysterious Cave, pages 130–131 • Choose Your Own Adventure: The Enchanted Manor, pages 132–133
Grade Band	4–8
Length of Activity	Varies: 10–30 minutes
Differentiation Ideas	**Striving Learners and English Learners:** Write the sets of words from the story on the screen or board ahead of time, covering them as needed. Reveal the word choices for each scenario so students have a visual as well as an oral exposure to the words.
Extension Ideas	• Make a copy of the adventure for kids to do with a friend or family member at home, creating opportunities for expressive use of the words. • Have students illustrate a drawing of their adventure, incorporating the vocabulary words used into the picture.

Strategies for Learning Words We Provide

LANGUAGE DOMAINS

Reading

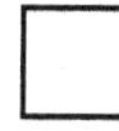

Writing

Speaking

Listening

Choose Your Own Adventure: The Mysterious Cave

You and your friends are exploring a dense forest when you stumble upon a hidden cave entrance. The air is thick with mystery, and a cold wind rushes out. You step forward cautiously. A stone archway stands before you, covered in ancient carvings that are unknown symbols. To proceed, you must decide what to do at THE ENTRANCE. Will you **decipher**, **obliterate**, or **admonish** them?

- **decipher** Lucky for you, *decipher means to interpret something difficult to understand,* so you study the symbols closely, tracing their patterns with your fingers. Slowly, the meaning reveals itself—this is a map leading to a hidden treasure through a labyrinth, a twisty path, so continue to **THE LABYRINTH**.
- **obliterate** Unfortunately, *obliterate means to wipe out all traces of something,* so you decide the carvings are unimportant and scrape them away. Suddenly, the ground trembles. A boulder crashes down, blocking your path forward. **GAME OVER!**
- **admonish** Feeling frustrated, you *admonish your friends, which means to scold them,* and waste time, so the symbols are suddenly covered. **GAME OVER!**

THE LABYRINTH

Following the map, you enter a twisting labyrinth. The air is damp, and the tunnels stretch in every direction. After wandering for what feels like hours, you reach a crossroads. The path forward is unclear. To find your way, which way will you act? Will you either be **indolent**, **astute**, or **belligerent**?

- **indolent** You chose to be *indolent, which means lazy and avoiding activity,* so instead of thinking critically, you sit down and hope the right path will reveal itself, but life doesn't work that way. **GAME OVER!**
- **astute** Smart choice! *Since astute means having sharp intelligence and good judgment,* you analyze the symbols at the fork in the road and recognize a pattern. Choosing the correct tunnel, you make progress toward the treasure, running into the guardian. Continue to **THE GUARDIAN AWAKENS**.
- **belligerent** Frustrated, you chose to be *belligerent, which means aggressive and ready to fight or argue.* You punch the stone walls and the sound echoes through the tunnels, waking something deep within the cave. A low growl rumbles in the distance, and you are chased out of the cave. **GAME OVER!**

THE GUARDIAN AWAKENS

A massive stone figure steps forward from the darkness. Its glowing eyes fix on you. *"Who dares disturb the sacred vault?"* it booms. You must respond carefully. Do you speak **ambiguously**, **brusquely**, or **eloquently**?

- **ambiguously** Since *ambiguous means speaking in a way that is unclear,* your vague response confuses the guardian. He watches you for a long moment before gesturing to a new, unfamiliar path. You must follow it, and are led to solitary confinement. **GAME OVER!**
- **brusquely** You chose to speak *brusquely, which means speaking in a blunt or harsh way* and you snap at the guardian, demanding he move aside. His eyes narrow. Instead of attacking, he challenges you to a riddle to prove your worth: *"I am not alive, but I grow. I do not have lungs, but I need air. I do not have a mouth, but water kills me. What am I?"* (*fire—if answered correctly, you may go to* **THE FINAL TRIAL, but if answered incorrectly, GAME OVER!**)
- **eloquently** Great choice! Since you chose to speak *eloquently, which means you expressed your ideas smoothly and persuasively,* you speak with wisdom, explaining your purpose. The guardian nods, impressed by your composure. He steps aside to let you pass to **THE FINAL TRIAL.**

THE FINAL TRIAL

Beyond the guardian, you enter a grand chamber. A golden goblet rests on a pedestal, glowing faintly. But beside it, a second goblet sits, identical in every way. A parchment reads: "Only those who show the right attitude will choose correctly." Will your attitude be one of **discernment**, **credulity**, or **indifference**?

- **discernment** Great attitude! Since *discernment means the ability to judge well and make wise decisions,* you examine the goblets carefully and notice that one reflects light slightly differently. You pick it up and sip and have found the treasure—immediately, knowledge floods your mind! You have chosen wisely and you WIN with powers of "all knowing." **CONGRATULATIONS!**
- **credulity** Your attitude was one of *credulity, which means a tendency to believe things too easily without questioning them,* so you trusted your friend's guess and drank the first goblet without thinking. Instantly, your vision blurs. The world spins and you do not awake. **GAME OVER!**
- **indifference** You came all this way just to feel *indifference, which means a lack of interest or caring,* so you shrug, unwilling to take a risk and choose a goblet. As you hesitate, the treasure chamber begins to crumble! You don't escape before it's too late. **GAME OVER!**

Choose Your Own Adventure: The Enchanted Manor

On a stormy evening, you and your friends take shelter in an abandoned manor on the edge of town. Thunder roars as you push open the heavy wooden doors, stepping into the grand but dusty entry hall. A flickering chandelier barely illuminates the room. Suddenly, the door slams shut behind you! You turn to find three strange inscriptions on the wall, each leading to a different path. You must decide how to proceed using the inscriptions to find your safety. Will you **scrutinize**, **deface**, or **disregard** the inscriptions?

- **scrutinize** Smart move! Since *scrutinize means to examine something very carefully*, you study the inscriptions closely. They describe three rooms ahead—one safe, two perilous. Using this knowledge, you choose the correct path forward and enter **THE HAUNTED LIBRARY.**
- **deface** Oh no! Since *deface means to spoil the surface of something*, you scratch away at the inscriptions, thinking they're just decoration. The moment you do, the walls shake, and a hidden trapdoor opens beneath your feet. You plummet into darkness. **GAME OVER!**
- **disregard** Bad choice! Since *disregard means to ignore something*, you assume the inscriptions are meaningless and randomly pick a path. Unfortunately, you wander into a collapsing hallway with no way out. **GAME OVER!**

THE HAUNTED LIBRARY

You step into a vast library filled with towering bookshelves covered in cobwebs. A cold draft rustles the pages of open books. In the center of the room, a massive tome sits on an ornate pedestal. Suddenly, the book's pages flip wildly, and a ghostly whisper calls out: "Only those who act wisely may proceed." How will you behave? Will you be **obstinate**, **flippant**, or **meticulous**?

- **obstinate** Not wise! Since *obstinate means stubbornly refusing to change one's mind*, you refuse to acknowledge the warning and charge forward without reading the book. The moment you touch the wrong shelf, the books turn to dust, and you vanish with them. **GAME OVER!**
- **flippant** Eek—bad choice!! Since *flippant means not taking something seriously*, you joke about the ghostly whisper and carelessly flip through the book's pages. The ink on the pages dissolves, and the bookshelves collapse, trapping you inside forever. **GAME OVER!**

- **meticulous** Excellent decision! Since *meticulous means showing great attention to detail*, you carefully examine the book, noticing an enchanted riddle written in its pages. You solve it, revealing a secret passage. You step through and arrive at **THE VANISHING PORTRAITS.**

THE VANISHING PORTRAITS

You enter a dimly lit hallway lined with eerie portraits. As you step forward, the figures in the paintings shift their gazes toward you. One portrait, larger than the rest, suddenly speaks: "Only those who present themselves properly may pass." You must choose how to present yourself. Will you act **unassuming**, **pompous**, or **tactful**?

- **unassuming** Not quite! Since *unassuming means being modest and not drawing attention to yourself*, you lower your head and try to blend in. The portraits sense your lack of confidence and fade into shadows, leaving you trapped in endless darkness. **GAME OVER!**
- **tactful** Brilliant choice! Since *tactful means showing sensitivity and good judgment*, you respectfully acknowledge the portraits, speaking with grace. They nod in approval and reveal a hidden staircase, leading you to **THE FINAL ENIGMA.**
- **pompous** Oh dear! Since *pompous means acting overly self-important*, you boast about your intelligence and demand passage. The portraits sneer, unimpressed. The floor beneath you crumbles, and you fall into oblivion. **GAME OVER!**

THE FINAL ENIGMA

At the top of the staircase, you find yourself in a candlelit chamber. A jeweled key rests on a pedestal, but beside it, another identical key glows faintly. A plaque reads: "The right key belongs to those who show true wisdom." How will you approach this choice? With **perceptiveness**, **naivety**, or **apathy**?

- **perceptiveness** Congratulations! Since *perceptiveness means having keen insight and understanding*, you carefully analyze both keys, realizing that only one casts a true shadow. You take the correct key, unlocking a hidden vault of ancient secrets and escaping the manor victorious. **YOU WIN!**
- **naivety** Wrong choice! Since *naivety means being too trusting or lacking experience*, you pick a key at random, believing luck is on your side. The moment you touch it, the room vanishes, and you are banished here forever. **GAME OVER!**
- **apathy** Good grief! You came all this way but now you feel only *apathy, which means a lack of interest or concern*. Instead of choosing, you hesitate too long, and the manor shifts around you. Trapped in an endless loop of corridors, you never escape. **GAME OVER!**

LANGUAGE DOMAINS

Reading

Writing

Speaking

Listening

2.S **My Character Traits**

Distribute the Character Traits List on page 135 and read aloud or have students chorally read each trait and its definition. Then have students rate themselves on a scale from 1 to 10 to show to what extent they feel they embody the trait: *1 = not at all, 10 = perfectly*. Provide explanations and examples as needed to ensure students understand the meaning of the words. Say and have students say the words as many times as possible to provide multiple exposures. Then have students review their lists and select five of their top-ranked traits and write why these words best describe them. Students can share, if they choose, to read their writing aloud in small groups or to the class.

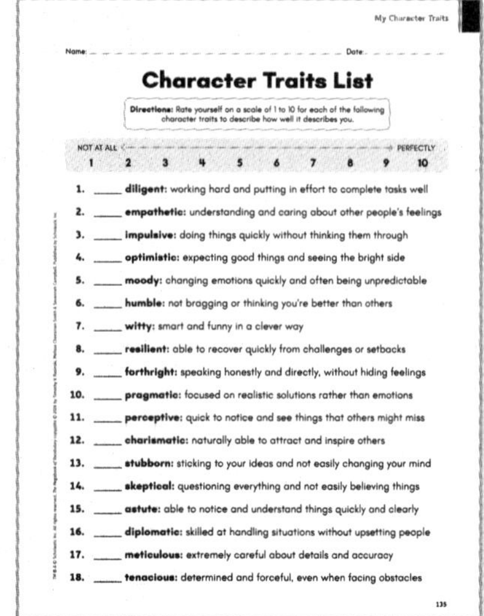

My Character Traits

Name: ________ Date: ________

Character Traits List

Directions: Rate yourself on a scale of 1 to 10 for each of the following character traits to describe how well it describes you.

NOT AT ALL ← → PERFECTLY
1 2 3 4 5 6 7 8 9 10

1. ____ **diligent:** working hard and putting in effort to complete tasks well
2. ____ **empathetic:** understanding and caring about other people's feelings
3. ____ **impulsive:** doing things quickly without thinking them through
4. ____ **optimistic:** expecting good things and seeing the bright side
5. ____ **moody:** changing emotions quickly and often being unpredictable
6. ____ **humble:** not bragging or thinking you're better than others
7. ____ **witty:** smart and funny in a clever way
8. ____ **resilient:** able to recover quickly from challenges or setbacks
9. ____ **forthright:** speaking honestly and directly, without hiding feelings
10. ____ **pragmatic:** focused on realistic solutions rather than emotions
11. ____ **perceptive:** quick to notice and see things that others might miss
12. ____ **charismatic:** naturally able to attract and inspire others
13. ____ **stubborn:** sticking to your ideas and not easily changing your mind
14. ____ **skeptical:** questioning everything and not easily believing things
15. ____ **astute:** able to notice and understand things quickly and clearly
16. ____ **diplomatic:** skilled at handling situations without upsetting people
17. ____ **meticulous:** extremely careful about details and accuracy
18. ____ **tenacious:** determined and forceful, even when facing obstacles

135

Materials	Character Traits List, page 135
Grade Band	4–8
Length of Activity	15 minutes
Differentiation Ideas	**Striving Learners and English Learners:** Check on learners before writing the paragraph to ensure they understand the meaning of the words they have chosen to best describe themselves.
Extension Ideas	• Have students rate other people they know on these traits. This should be fun and lighthearted and give students the opportunity to engage in the meaning of the word with multiple exposures, as they are now reading each word another time, each time they rate someone new. • Have students rate a well-known character from a literature study on a scale from 1 to 10 and describe why. This could be just an oral activity when they've finished a book, or while they're still reading it to study how an author develops characters.

Name: ______________________ Date: ______________

Character Traits List

Directions: Rate yourself on a scale of 1 to 10 for each of the following character traits to describe how well it describes you.

NOT AT ALL ⟵⟶ PERFECTLY

1	2	3	4	5	6	7	8	9	10

1. _____ **diligent:** working hard and putting in effort to complete tasks well
2. _____ **empathetic:** understanding and caring about other people's feelings
3. _____ **impulsive:** doing things quickly without thinking them through
4. _____ **optimistic:** expecting good things and seeing the bright side
5. _____ **moody:** changing emotions quickly and often being unpredictable
6. _____ **humble:** not bragging or thinking you're better than others
7. _____ **witty:** smart and funny in a clever way
8. _____ **resilient:** able to recover quickly from challenges or setbacks
9. _____ **forthright:** speaking honestly and directly, without hiding feelings
10. _____ **pragmatic:** focused on realistic solutions rather than emotions
11. _____ **perceptive:** quick to notice and see things that others might miss
12. _____ **charismatic:** naturally able to attract and inspire others
13. _____ **stubborn:** sticking to your ideas and not easily changing your mind
14. _____ **skeptical:** questioning everything and not easily believing things
15. _____ **astute:** able to notice and understand things quickly and clearly
16. _____ **diplomatic:** skilled at handling situations without upsetting people
17. _____ **meticulous:** extremely careful about details and accuracy
18. _____ **tenacious:** determined and forceful, even when facing obstacles

Strategies for Learning Words We Provide

LANGUAGE DOMAINS

Reading

Writing

Speaking

Listening

2.T Feelings Vocabulary

This strategy, inspired by Lily Howard Scott's concept of "Feeling Visitor" from her book, *The Words That Shape Us*, recognizes that individuals with a large emotional vocabulary tend to be emotionally, socially, and academically successful. To build a feelings word bank for students, show Owl Feelings on page 137 and have them identify which owl they feel like by studying the facial expressions and definitions for each owl. A student might say, "I'm feeling melancholy because when I saw my friend's dog, it reminded me of my dog that passed away a few weeks ago, and I still feel sad about it." Remind students that feelings are not permanent; they come and go as situations change, but it's important to name them to better understand and express themselves.

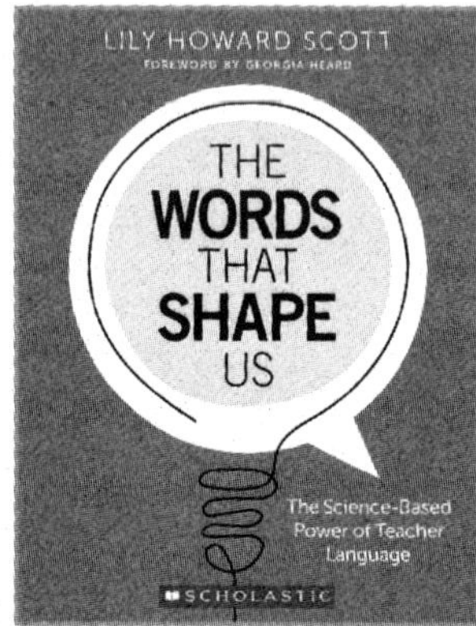

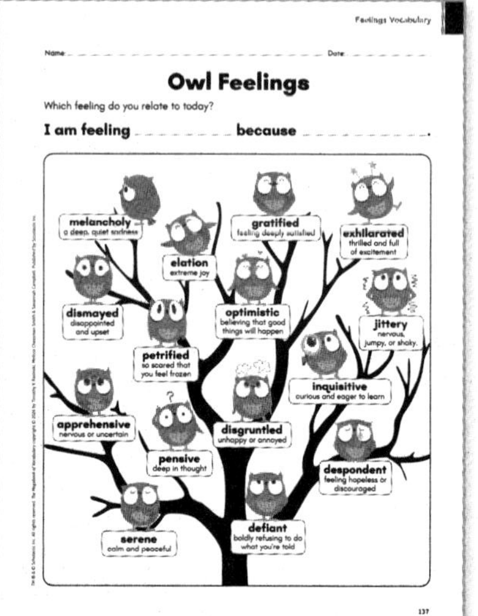
Feelings Vocabulary

Name ________ Date ________

Owl Feelings

Which feeling do you relate to today?

I am feeling ________ **because** ________.

melancholy a deep, quiet sadness
gratified feeling deeply satisfied
exhilarated thrilled and full of excitement
elation extreme joy
dismayed disappointed and upset
optimistic believing that good things will happen
jittery nervous, jumpy, or shaky
petrified so scared that you feel frozen
inquisitive curious and eager to learn
apprehensive nervous or uncertain
disgruntled unhappy or annoyed
pensive deep in thought
despondent feeling hopeless or discouraged
serene calm and peaceful
defiant boldly refusing to do what you're told

137

Materials	Owl Feelings, page 137
Grade Band	4–8
Length of Activity	5 minutes per word
Differentiation Ideas	• **Striving Learners and English Learners:** Pronounce each word with students chorally repeating to create a familiarity with those words. • **Thriving Learners:** Challenge them to choose an owl and come up with a different emotion than the one listed to be more precise in naming their feelings.
Extension Ideas	• Provide a copy of the Owl Feelings for students to take home and share with their friends and families. • Start each day with this strategy in a morning meeting to connect with students and provide a feeling of emotional safety in your classroom.

Name: ____________________ Date: ____________

Owl Feelings

Which feeling do you relate to today?

I am feeling ____________ **because** ____________ **.**

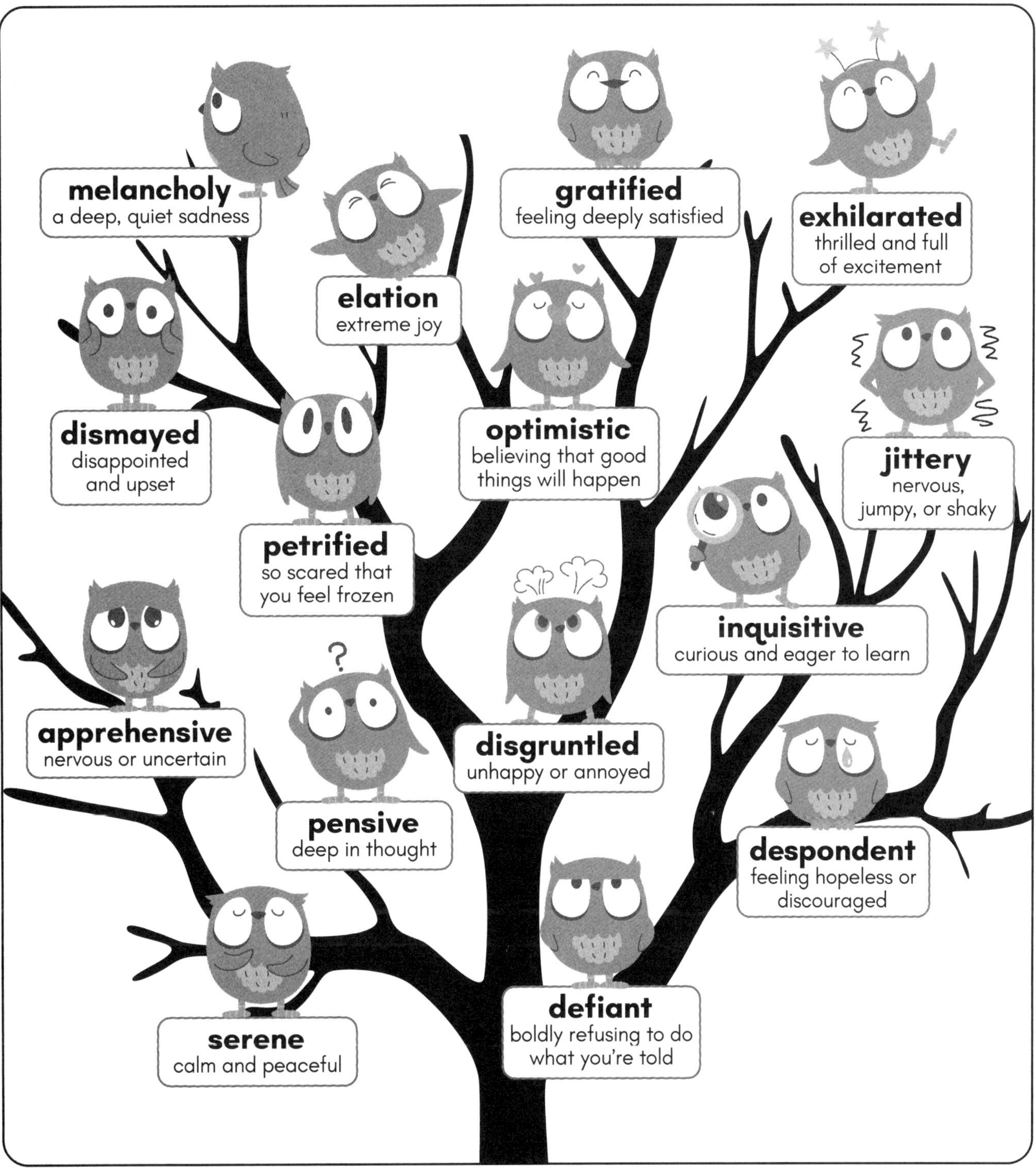

CHAPTER 2
Individual-Word Learning

Strategies for Learning Words We Provide

LANGUAGE DOMAINS

Reading

Writing

Speaking

Listening

2.U **Create a Short Story**

Choose a Create a Short Story on page 139 and distribute copies to students. Review and pronounce the vocabulary words while students chorally repeat them. Have students write a one-paragraph short story on lined paper, taking into consideration the required components in each column on the Create a Short Story page. As a means of checking their work, have the students underline each vocabulary word, sentence starter, and type of figurative language. Then invite students to read their short stories aloud to the class or in small groups.

Create a Short Story

Create a Short Story A

Directions: Write a one-paragraph short story with all these components:

Vocabulary Words (choose five)	**Sentence Starters**	**Figurative Language**
exasperated: Frustrated or very annoyed. **formidable:** Impressive and a little scary because of strength or skill. **impulsive:** Acting suddenly without thinking **perplexed:** Completely confused. **reluctant:** Unwilling or hesitant to do something. **reverberate:** To echo or repeat loudly. **wary:** Cautious or careful about something. **zealous:** Showing great energy or enthusiasm for something.	If only they had known... Nobody would have expected that...	personification simile

Create a Short Story B

Directions: Write a one-paragraph short story with all these components:

Vocabulary Words (choose five)	**Sentence Starters**	**Figurative Language**
bewildered: Extremely confused or puzzled. **catastrophe:** A terrible disaster or event. **deceptive:** Misleading or making something seem different from the truth. **intricate:** Very detailed and complicated. **menacing:** Threatening or showing danger. **sinister:** Giving the feeling that something bad will happen. **skeptical:** Doubting or not easily convinced. **treacherous:** Dangerous or not trustworthy.	Without warning... Everything seemed normal until...	onomatopoeia metaphor

139

Materials	• Create a Short Story A and B, page 139 • lined paper
Grade Band	4–8
Length of Activity	45 minutes
Differentiation Ideas	**Striving Learners and English Learners:** Begin the story with students, modeling how to incorporate the vocabulary words, sentence starters, and types of figurative language to make sure they are understanding the task.
Extension Ideas	• Direct students to extend their stories by developing characters and by developing the plotline. Have a writing contest for the most creative story. • Give bonus points for using more than five of the vocabulary words. • Encourage students to use other forms of the vocabulary words (for example, as nouns, verbs, or adverbs) in their stories.

Create a Short Story A

Directions: Write a one-paragraph short story with all these components:

Vocabulary Words (choose five)	**Sentence Starters**	**Figurative Language**
exasperated: frustrated or very annoyed **formidable:** impressive and a little scary because of strength or skill **impulsive:** acting suddenly without thinking **perplexed:** completely confused **reluctant:** unwilling or hesitant to do something **vivid:** very bright and detailed **wary:** cautious or careful about something **zealous:** showing great energy or enthusiasm for something	If only they had known... Nobody would have expected that...	personification simile

Create a Short Story B

Directions: Write a one-paragraph short story with all these components:

Vocabulary Words (choose five)	**Sentence Starters**	**Figurative Language**
bewildered: extremely confused or puzzled **catastrophe:** a terrible disaster or event **deceptive:** misleading or making something seem different from the truth **intricate:** very detailed and complicated **menacing:** threatening or showing danger **sinister:** giving the feeling that something bad will happen **skeptical:** doubting or not easily convinced **treacherous:** dangerous or not trustworthy	Without warning... Everything seemed normal until...	onomatopoeia metaphor

Strategies for Learning Words We Provide

LANGUAGE DOMAINS

Reading

Writing

Speaking

Listening

2.V Describe the Scene

Select a Describe the Scene on pages 141–144 and make copies for students, or copy a few Describe the Scenes and let each student choose one. To begin, read each word aloud and have students chorally repeat them. Then have students study the details in the picture and identify the ones that stand out by discussing them in small groups. Have students write a paragraph describing the scene, aiming to incorporate at least six of the listed words. Once they've finished, invite students to share their descriptions in small groups. This strategy will provide multiple exposures to the vocabulary words as students read, discuss, and write with the words.

Describe the Scene: Serene Beach at Sunset

Directions: Describe the scene in a paragraph, using at least six words from the list.

ethereal: extremely delicate and light in a way that seems too perfect for this world
luminous: emitting or reflecting light, often in a soft glow
solitary: done or existing alone; single
resplendent: attractive and impressive by being richly colorful or sumptuous
tranquil: free from disturbance; calm
horizon: the line where the earth or sea seems to meet the sky
opalescent: showing varying colors as an opal does
serenity: the state of being calm, peaceful, and untroubled
rippling: forming or displaying small waves on a surface
tidal: relating to the ebb and flow of tides

Describe the Scene: Snowy Mountain Landscape

Describe the Scene: Medieval Castle on a Hill

Materials	• Describe the Scene: Serene Beach at Sunset, page 141 • Describe the Scene: Snowy Mountain Landscape, page 142 • Describe the Scene: Tranquil Japanese Garden, page 143 • Describe the Scene: Medieval Castle on a Hill, page 144
Grade Band	4–8
Length of Activity	30 minutes
Differentiation Ideas	**English Learners:** Point out which part of the picture each word relates to, providing a visual context.
Extension Ideas	Have students use these paragraphs as a basis for a setting in an upcoming story they write, which will now include a ready-to-go, well-written setting.

Describe the Scene: Serene Beach at Sunset

Directions: Describe the scene in a paragraph, using at least six words from the list.

ethereal: extremely delicate and light in a way that seems too perfect for this world

luminous: emitting or reflecting light, often in a soft glow

solitary: done or existing alone; single

resplendent: attractive and impressive by being richly colorful or sumptuous

tranquil: free from disturbance; calm

horizon: the line where the earth or sea seems to meet the sky

opalescent: showing varying colors as an opal does

serenity: the state of being calm, peaceful, and untroubled

rippling: forming or displaying small waves on a surface

tidal: relating to the ebb and flow of tides

Describe the Scene: Snowy Mountain Landscape

Directions: Describe the scene in a paragraph, using at least six words from the list.

majestic: having grandeur, beauty, or dignity

frosted: covered with a thin layer of frost, ice, or snow

avalanche: a mass of snow, ice, and rocks falling rapidly down a mountainside

cavernous: like a cavern in size, shape, or atmosphere

pinnacle: the highest or most important point or peak

barren: lacking vegetation, life, or growth

blustery: characterized by strong, gusty winds

icy: covered with ice or appearing cold

imposing: grand and impressive in appearance

sequestered: isolated or hidden from view, often in a remote area

Describe the Scene: Tranquil Japanese Garden

Directions: Describe the scene in a paragraph, using at least six words from the list.

zen: a state of calm attentiveness, often associated with meditation

serenity: the state of being calm and peaceful

symmetry: the quality of being made up of exactly similar parts facing each other or around an axis

aquatic: having to do with water

deciduous: a tree that sheds its leaves seasonally

tranquil: free from disturbance

harmonious: forming a pleasing or consistent whole

truss: a framework of beams that provides support and distributes weight

transcendent: going beyond ordinary limits; surpassing

Describe the Scene: Medieval Castle on a Hill

Directions: Describe the scene in a paragraph, using at least six words from the list.

gothic: a style of architecture that is characterized by pointed arches, ribbed vaults, and flying buttresses

fortified: strengthened with defensive walls or structures

turret: a small tower, often part of a larger structure, that projects from the building

rampart: a defensive wall or embankment

bastion: a stronghold or fortified area

precarious: not securely held or in position; dangerously likely to fall or collapse

majestic: having grandeur, beauty, or dignity

fortress: a stronghold or heavily fortified building designed for defense

imposing: grand and impressive in appearance

2.W Scene Analysis

Distribute one of the Scene Analysis insert sheets on pages 146–149 to each student. Read each vocabulary word aloud, and have students chorally repeat them. Then have students work in pairs to read each word and definition, placing a check mark next to words that accurately describe the scene and an "X" next to words that don't. When they've finished, direct students to write a paragraph about the scene, following the prompt at the bottom of the page and using the words with check marks.

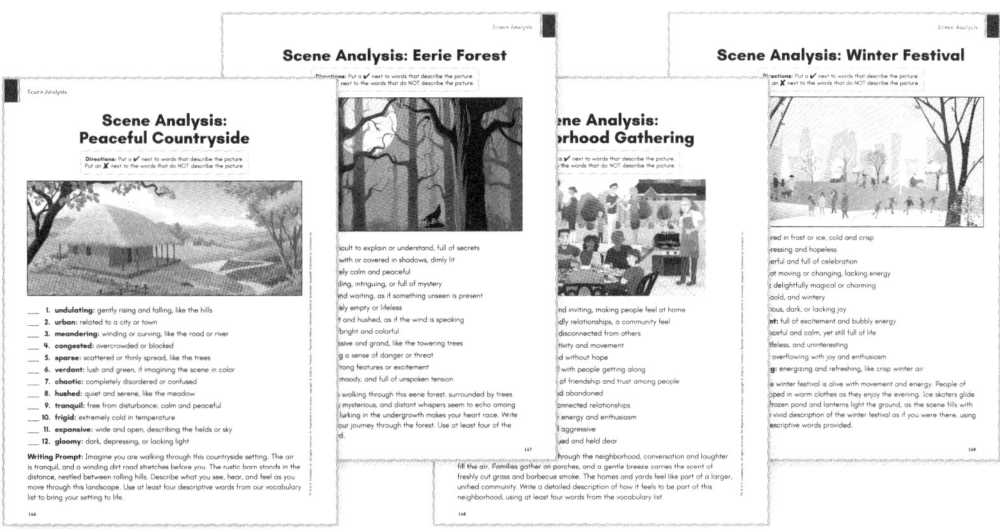

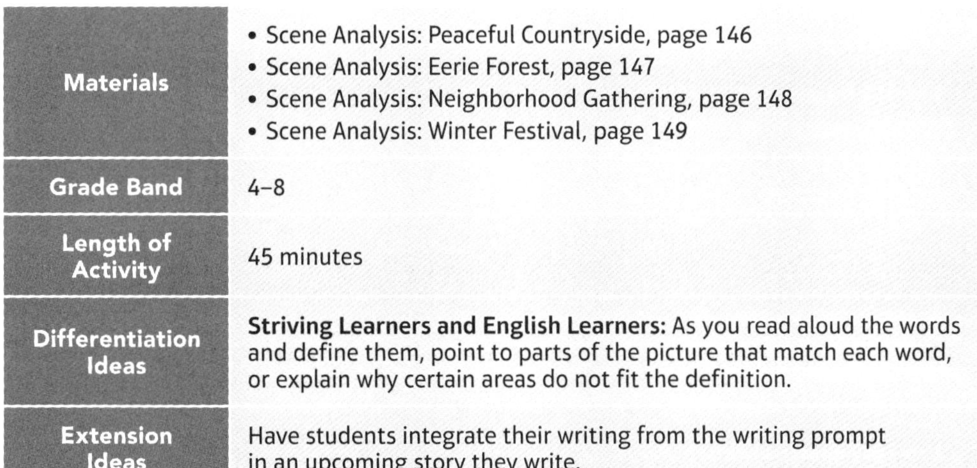

Materials	• Scene Analysis: Peaceful Countryside, page 146 • Scene Analysis: Eerie Forest, page 147 • Scene Analysis: Neighborhood Gathering, page 148 • Scene Analysis: Winter Festival, page 149
Grade Band	4–8
Length of Activity	45 minutes
Differentiation Ideas	**Striving Learners and English Learners:** As you read aloud the words and define them, point to parts of the picture that match each word, or explain why certain areas do not fit the definition.
Extension Ideas	Have students integrate their writing from the writing prompt in an upcoming story they write.

Strategies for Learning Words We Provide

LANGUAGE DOMAINS

Reading

Writing

Speaking

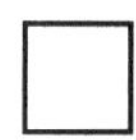

Listening

Scene Analysis: Peaceful Countryside

Directions: Put a ✔ next to words that describe the picture. Put an ✘ next to the words that do NOT describe the picture.

___ 1. **undulating:** gently rising and falling, like the hills

___ 2. **urban:** related to a city or town

___ 3. **meandering:** winding or curving, like the road or river

___ 4. **congested:** overcrowded or blocked

___ 5. **sparse:** scattered or thinly spread, like the trees

___ 6. **verdant:** lush and green, if imagining the scene in color

___ 7. **chaotic:** completely disordered or confused

___ 8. **hushed:** quiet and serene, like the meadow

___ 9. **tranquil:** free from disturbance; calm and peaceful

___ 10. **frigid:** extremely cold in temperature

___ 11. **expansive:** wide and open, describing the fields or sky

___ 12. **gloomy:** dark, depressing, or lacking light

Writing Prompt: Imagine you are walking through this countryside setting. The air is tranquil, and a winding dirt road stretches before you. The rustic barn stands in the distance, nestled between rolling hills. Describe what you see, hear, and feel as you move through this landscape. Use at least four descriptive words from our vocabulary list to bring your setting to life.

Scene Analysis: Eerie Forest

Directions: Put a ✔ next to words that describe the picture. Put an ✘ next to the words that do NOT describe the picture.

___ **1. mysterious:** difficult to explain or understand, full of secrets

___ **2. shadowy:** filled with or covered in shadows, dimly lit

___ **3. serene:** completely calm and peaceful

___ **4. enigmatic:** puzzling, intriguing, or full of mystery

___ **5. lurking:** hiding and waiting, as if something unseen is present

___ **6. barren:** completely empty or lifeless

___ **7. whispering:** soft and hushed, as if the wind is speaking

___ **8. vivid:** extremely bright and colorful

___ **9. majestic:** impressive and grand, like the towering trees

___ **10. menacing:** giving a sense of danger or threat

___ **11. bland:** lacking strong features or excitement

___ **12. brooding:** dark, moody, and full of unspoken tension

Writing Prompt: You are walking through this eerie forest, surrounded by trees and drifting fog. The air is mysterious, and distant whispers seem to echo among the branches. Something lurking in the undergrowth makes your heart race. Write a paragraph describing your journey through the forest. Use at least four of the descriptive words provided.

Scene Analysis: Neighborhood Gathering

Directions: Put a ✔ next to words that describe the picture. Put an ✘ next to the words that do NOT describe the picture.

___ **1. welcoming:** friendly and inviting, making people feel at home

___ **2. close-knit:** close, friendly relationships, a community feel

___ **3. estranged:** distant or disconnected from others

___ **4. bustling:** busy with activity and movement

___ **5. bleak:** empty, grim, and without hope

___ **6. harmonious:** peaceful with people getting along

___ **7. camaraderie:** a spirit of friendship and trust among people

___ **8. forlorn:** sad, lonely, and abandoned

___ **9. interwoven:** closely connected relationships

___ **10. animated:** full of lively energy and enthusiasm

___ **11. hostile:** unfriendly and aggressive

___ **12. cherished:** deeply valued and held dear

Writing Prompt: As you walk through the neighborhood, conversation and laughter fill the air. Families gather on porches, and a gentle breeze carries the scent of freshly cut grass and barbecue smoke. The homes and yards feel like part of a larger, unified community. Write a detailed description of how it feels to be part of this neighborhood, using at least four words from the vocabulary list.

Scene Analysis: Winter Festival

Directions: Put a ✔ next to words that describe the picture.
Put an ✘ next to the words that do NOT describe the picture.

___ 1. **frosty:** covered in frost or ice, cold and crisp

___ 2. **dismal:** depressing and hopeless

___ 3. **festive:** cheerful and full of celebration

___ 4. **stagnant:** not moving or changing, lacking energy

___ 5. **enchanting:** delightfully magical or charming

___ 6. **glacial:** icy, cold, and wintery

___ 7. **somber:** serious, dark, or lacking joy

___ 8. **effervescent:** full of excitement and bubbly energy

___ 9. **serene:** peaceful and calm, yet still full of life

___ 10. **drab:** dull, lifeless, and uninteresting

___ 11. **exuberant:** overflowing with joy and enthusiasm

___ 12. **invigorating:** energizing and refreshing, like crisp winter air

Writing Prompt: The winter festival is alive with movement and energy. People of all ages gather, wrapped in warm clothes as they enjoy the evening. Ice skaters glide smoothly across the frozen pond and lanterns light the ground, as the scene fills with joyful sounds. Write a vivid description of the winter festival as if you were there, using at least four of the descriptive words provided.

LANGUAGE DOMAINS

Reading

Writing

Speaking

Listening

2.X **Describe a Character**

Select a Describe a Character on pages 151–154 and provide each student with a copy. Have students examine the picture of the character while you pronounce each vocabulary word and students chorally repeat it. In pairs or small groups, have students read the definitions and place a star next to words they think might describe the character. Students' responses will probably vary because there is no right way to describe the characters. Then have students write an interesting description that includes several of the provided vocabulary words. Model an example to ensure students write more than just a simple description. For instance, instead of writing *She is gregarious*, students should add details to show they know the meaning of the word and give insight into the character: *Despite her competitive spirit on the court, Maya's gregarious nature shined through as she cheered for her teammates, high-fived opponents, and effortlessly made friends at every volleyball tournament she attended*. Invite students to share their descriptions with the class or in small groups.

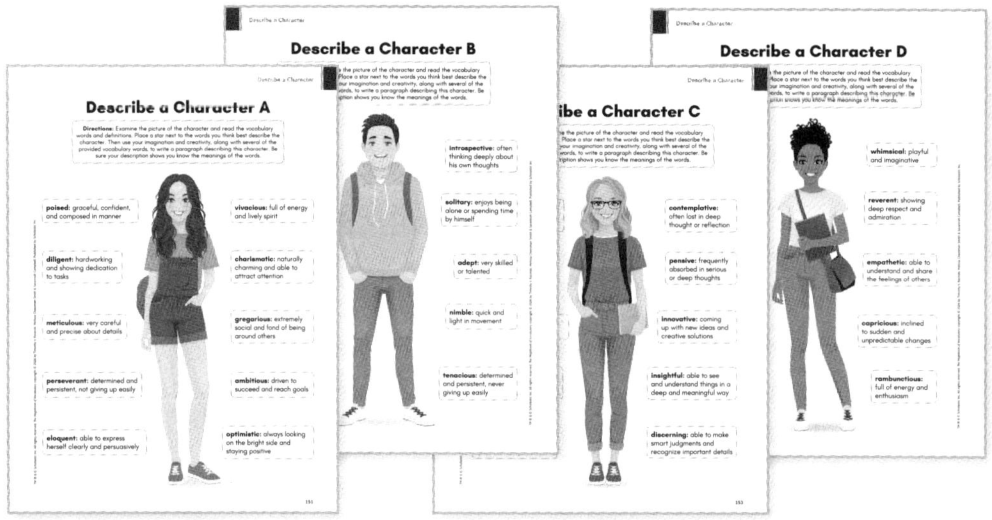
Describe a Character B

introspective: often thinking deeply about his own thoughts

solitary: enjoys being alone or spending time by himself

adept: very skilled or talented

nimble: quick and light in movement

tenacious: determined and persistent, never giving up easily

Describe a Character D

whimsical: playful and imaginative

reverent: showing deep respect and admiration

empathetic: able to understand and share the feelings of others

capricious: inclined to sudden and unpredictable changes

rambunctious: full of energy and enthusiasm

Describe a Character A

poised: graceful, confident, and composed in manner

diligent: hardworking and showing dedication to tasks

meticulous: very careful and precise about details

perseverant: determined and persistent, not giving up easily

eloquent: able to express herself clearly and persuasively

vivacious: full of energy and lively spirit

charismatic: naturally charming and able to attract attention

gregarious: extremely social and fond of being around others

ambitious: driven to succeed and reach goals

optimistic: always looking on the bright side and staying positive

Describe a Character C

contemplative: often lost in deep thought or reflection

pensive: frequently absorbed in serious or deep thoughts

innovative: coming up with new ideas and creative solutions

insightful: able to see and understand things in a deep and meaningful way

discerning: able to make smart judgments and recognize important details

Materials	• Describe a Character A, page 151 • Describe a Character B, page 152 • Describe a Character C, page 153 • Describe a Character D, page 154
Grade Band	4–8
Length of Activity	45 minutes
Differentiation Ideas	**Striving Learners and English Learners:** Read all the words aloud and have students chorally repeat them several times to ensure correct pronunciation; then use simple language to explain and describe each word.
Extension Ideas	• Have students come up with their own words to describe the character. They can use a thesaurus to come up with more words or use words they already know. • Have students use their written character description as a main character in an upcoming story they are writing.

Describe a Character A

Directions: Examine the picture of the character and read the vocabulary words and definitions. Place a star next to the words you think best describe the character. Then use your imagination and creativity, along with several of the provided vocabulary words, to write a paragraph describing this character. Be sure your description shows you know the meanings of the words.

poised: graceful, confident, and composed in manner

vivacious: full of energy and lively spirit

diligent: hardworking and showing dedication to tasks

charismatic: naturally charming and able to attract attention

meticulous: very careful and precise about details

gregarious: extremely social and fond of being around others

perseverant: determined and persistent, not giving up easily

ambitious: driven to succeed and reach goals

eloquent: able to express herself clearly and persuasively

optimistic: always looking on the bright side and staying positive

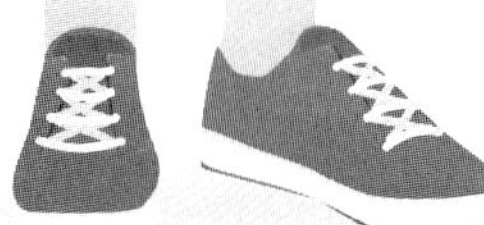

Describe a Character B

Directions: Examine the picture of the character and read the vocabulary words and definitions. Place a star next to the words you think best describe the character. Then use your imagination and creativity, along with several of the provided vocabulary words, to write a paragraph describing this character. Be sure your description shows you know the meanings of the words.

exuberant: full of energy, excitement, and cheerfulness

resilient: able to recover quickly from setbacks or challenges

zealous: passionately devoted to his interests

pensive: sometimes lost in thought, reflecting on things deeply

innovative: creative and quick to come up with new ideas

introspective: often thinking deeply about his own thoughts

solitary: enjoys being alone or spending time by himself

adept: very skilled or talented

nimble: quick and light in movement

tenacious: determined and persistent, never giving up easily

Describe a Character C

Directions: Examine the picture of the character and read the vocabulary words and definitions. Place a star next to the words you think best describe the character. Then use your imagination and creativity, along with several of the provided vocabulary words, to write a paragraph describing this character. Be sure your description shows you know the meanings of the words.

analytical: skilled at breaking down complex ideas and solving problems

intuitive: able to understand things just by feeling out a situation

curious: eager to explore and learn about new things

speculative: enjoys questioning, theorizing, and considering possibilities

methodical: working in a careful, organized, and systematic way

contemplative: often lost in deep thought or reflection

pensive: frequently absorbed in serious or deep thoughts

innovative: coming up with new ideas and creative solutions

insightful: able to see and understand things in a deep and meaningful way

discerning: able to make smart judgments and recognize important details

Describe a Character D

Directions: Examine the picture of the character and read the vocabulary words and definitions. Place a star next to the words you think best describe the character. Then use your imagination and creativity, along with several of the provided vocabulary words, to write a paragraph describing this character. Be sure your description shows you know the meanings of the words.

introspective: thoughtful and reflective about life

pensive: engaged in deep thought, often while observing nature

earthy: simple, natural, and grounded in her approach to life

unassuming: humble and modest, not seeking attention

unfettered: free-spirited and unrestrained

whimsical: playful and imaginative

reverent: showing deep respect and admiration

empathetic: able to understand and share the feelings of others

capricious: inclined to sudden and unpredictable changes

rambunctious: full of energy and enthusiasm

2.Y Word Vitamins

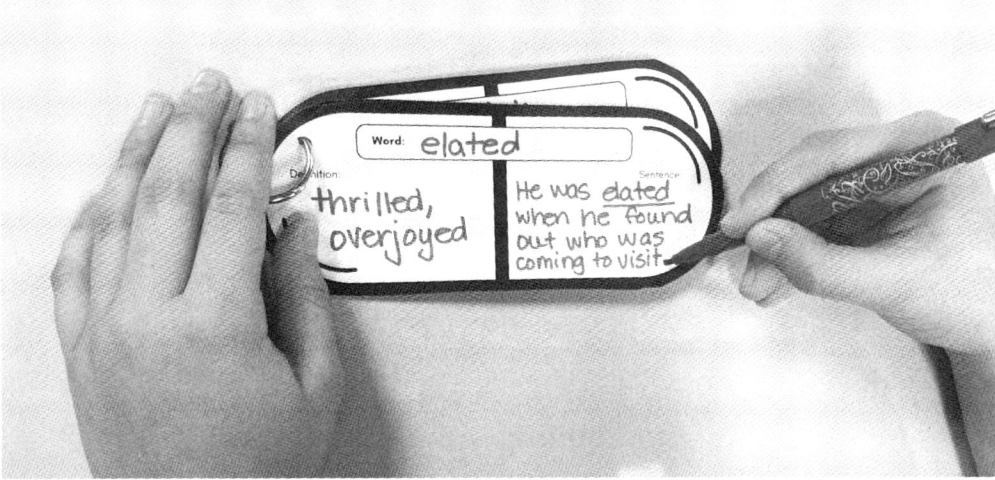

Choose words that your students would likely encounter for the first time from the Word Vitamin Vocabulary List on pages 156–157 (or choose your own). Choose one word a day to teach to students as part of a daily routine. Copy and cut apart the Word Vitamin Template on page 158 and have students write your chosen word, its definition, and a sentence containing it. Encourage students to use the word once at home and once at school that day. Have students keep all completed templates in an envelope or on a metal ring, adding new ones regularly throughout the year.

Materials	• Word Vitamin Vocabulary List, pages 156–157 • Word Vitamin Template, page 158
Grade Band	4–8
Length of Activity	10 minutes daily
Differentiation Ideas	• **Striving Learners:** Come up with a sentence together or provide the words already written on the vitamins for students. Providing the sentence ahead of time—either written on the vitamin template or created together—can help save time and support students who may be absent, ensuring they have what they need to participate when they return. • **English Learners:** Choose words for students that would better extend their vocabulary base.
Extension Ideas	Include your own set of words, or have students research and come up with new words for the class each day.

CHAPTER 2
Individual-Word Learning

Strategies for Learning Words We Provide

LANGUAGE DOMAINS

Reading

Writing
✓

Speaking

Listening
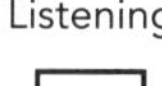

Word Vitamin Vocabulary List

WORD	DEFINITION	EXAMPLE SENTENCE
accusatory	containing or expressing accusation, accusing	She gave him an **accusatory** look when he told her a vase broke.
apathetic	having or showing little or no feeling or emotion, not caring	Even though the teacher gave her a task, she still didn't do her work and acted **apathetic**.
authoritative	showing evident authority, taking charge	The teacher had an **authoritative** quality that made the students listen.
belligerent	showing bold aggression, arguing/fighting behavior	Showing his **belligerent** attitude, the dog refused to come to the owner when called and began fighting the cat.
boastful	participating in the act of bragging	He was **boastful** about his victories.
candid	honest, sincere expression or words, blunt, to the point	The **candid** statement—spoken honestly and boldly—wasn't taken very well by the new leader.
caustic	marked by sharp sarcasm	Her **caustic** response hurt the other girl's feelings.
comical	causing laughter especially because of a startlingly or unexpectedly humorous impact	The phrase he used was so **comical** that we couldn't stop laughing.
condescending	treating someone as if they are less intelligent or knowledgeable than yourself	Her **condescending** tone made me feel worse about my mistake.
contemptuous	spiteful or hateful	Her **contemptuous** behavior toward her enemy made her feelings clear.
ecstatic	overwhelming emotion, especially happiness	My mom won the lottery and was **ecstatic**!
elated	thrilled, overjoyed	He was **elated** when he found out his grandparents were coming to visit.
erudite	having extensive knowledge acquired mainly from books	The college professor was very **erudite**.
exuberant	joyfully enthusiastic	The mood in the hallway was **exuberant** as everyone celebrated the end of the school year.
detached	not paying attention to or caring about something, free from prejudice or self-interest	I felt **detached** from the situation, like I was not involved at all.
facetious	joking, often inappropriately	The teacher did not find the student's **facetious** attitude funny at all.
flippant	lacking proper respect or seriousness	The disrespectful student got in trouble for giving a **flippant** response.

WORD	DEFINITION	EXAMPLE SENTENCE
foreboding	a feeling that something bad or scary might happen soon	The dark clouds outside looked very **foreboding**.
forthright	going straight to the point, direct, straightforward	The **forthright** boy came right out and asked the obvious question.
haughty	prideful, thinking you're better than everyone else	The **haughty** attitude she had was clear in the superior way she treated everyone else.
incredulous	unwilling to admit or accept what is offered as true, unbelieving	When he told the crazy story, I could only feel **incredulous**.
indignant	filled with anger caused by something unjust, unworthy, or mean	When I saw the lonely kid being bullied, I became **indignant**.
judgmental	judging someone or something harshly	Her **judgmental** comments about his hair caused him to get a haircut that night.
melancholy	feeling of depression	After her pet dog died, she was in a state of **melancholy**.
nostalgic	longing for return to, or of, some past period or condition	After the memorable summer camp closed, I was filled with **nostalgic** feelings.
pessimistic	making everything seem negative, anticipating the worst possible outcome	No one likes to hang out with her because she's so **pessimistic** that nothing is fun.
pompous	arrogant, acting as if you're the most important person	His **pompous** attitude didn't help him make friends.
querulous	complaining or arguing constantly	She was so **querulous** that nothing we said would make her happy.
ridiculing	making fun of a person or thing in a hateful way	When the bully pushed her, the **ridiculing** laughter rang in her ears.
sanguine	cheerfully optimistic, hopeful, confident	I got a 100 on my test and couldn't have been more **sanguine**.
somber	giving gloomy suggestions or ideas	The **somber** expression on her face let us know it would not be a good day.
sullen	gloomily or resentfully silent or moody	Her **sullen** attitude made us all feel depressed.
supercilious	coolly and snootily arrogant, proud	Her **supercilious** attitude made it seem she was better than everyone else, so she didn't make many friends.
whimsical	imaginary and fun, based on fantasy	The **whimsical** costumes at the Halloween party were super cool—totally unexpected!
wrathful	filled with strong anger or resentment	They trembled before the **wrathful** queen.

Word Vitamin Template

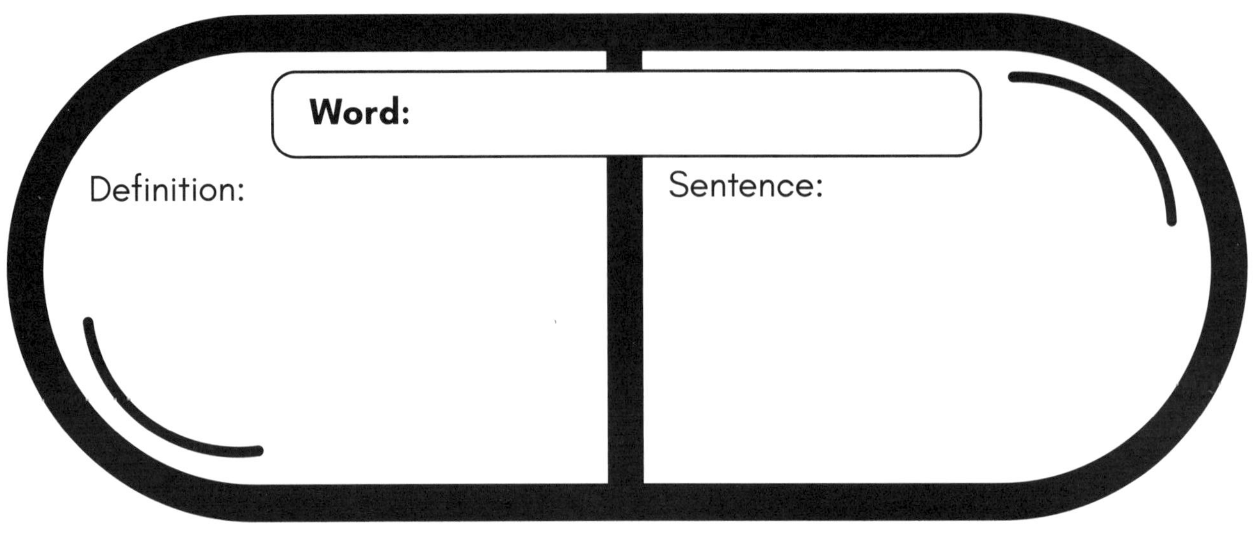

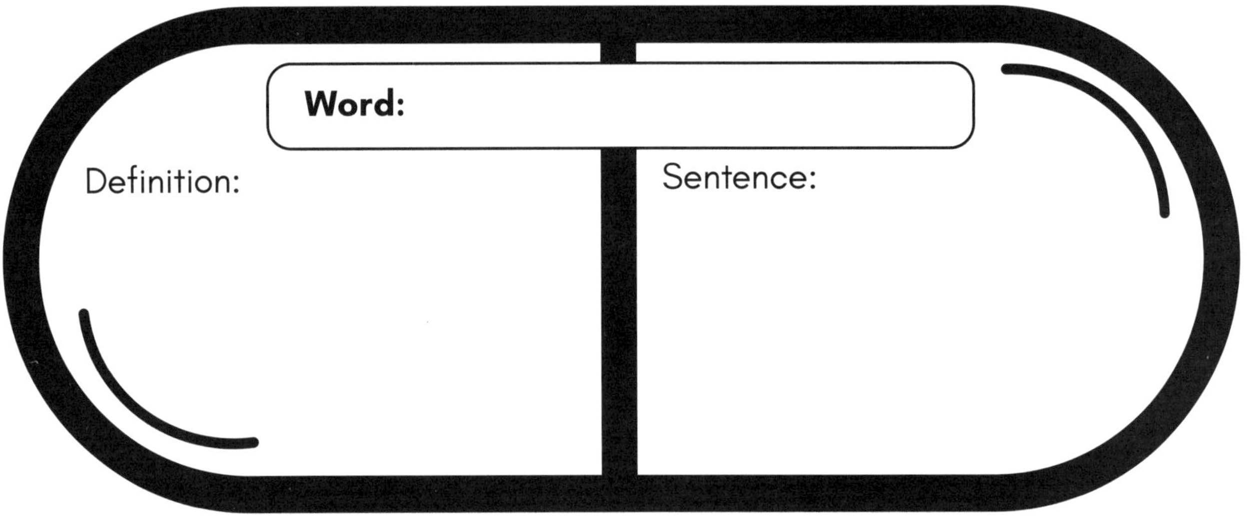

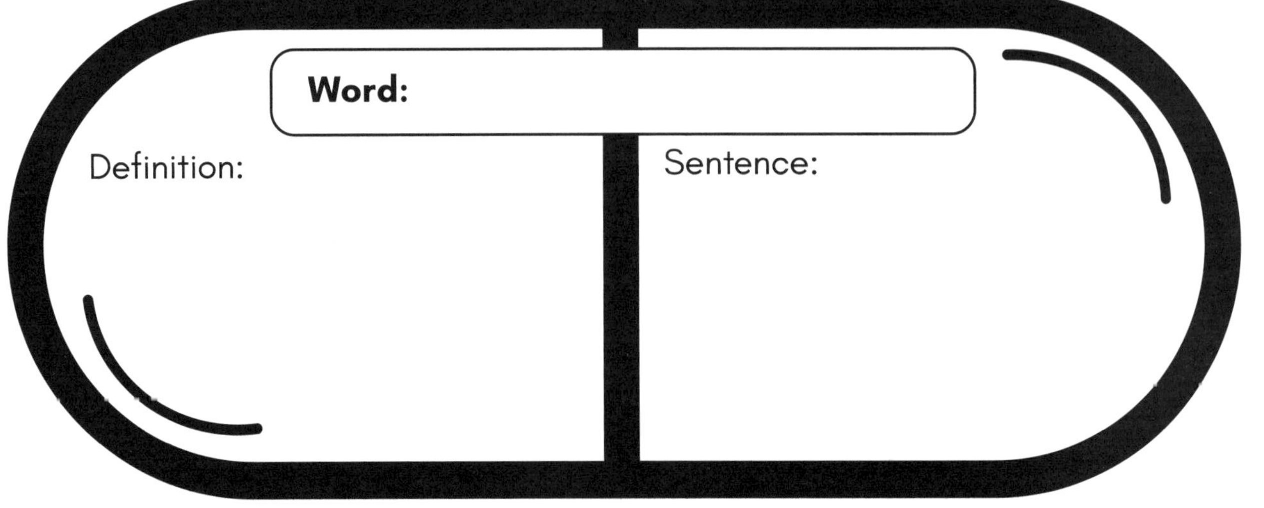

2.Z Theme, Context, Roots, Reference, and Review (TC3R)

Select words from the TC3R Method Examples on pages 160–161, or choose your own and follow the same steps. Then read students the Theme, Context, Roots, Reference, and Review for each word. Here are some general guidelines for each of those elements.

1. **Theme:** Recognize how the word might be used and under what circumstances.
2. **Context:** Pay attention to the text surrounding the word to help infer its meaning.
3. **Roots:** Analyze the root of the word to break it down and connect it to similar words students already know.
4. **Reference:** Use a print or online dictionary to give an accurate definition when needed.
5. **Review:** Reinforce the word by offering examples and practice to solidify its meaning and improve retention.

Materials	TC3R Method Examples, pages 160–161 (or a TC3R Method example you create)
Grade Band	4–8
Length of Activity	5 minutes per word
Differentiation Ideas	• **Striving Learners:** Provide the words before the class activity written on a paper with the word parts underlined. • **English Learners:** Use words that have a common base, such as *x* and *y*, so students learn meanings that will translate to many other words.
Extension Ideas	Use an AI platform and create more TC3R sets with pre-selected words. (Be sure to check any AI results to make sure they are appropriate.) This works best around a theme, helping students to group connected words together to enhance meaning.

Strategies for Learning Words We Provide

LANGUAGE DOMAINS

Reading

Writing

Speaking

Listening

TC3R Method Examples

Word: eloquent

1. **Theme:** This could refer to a speech given by a politician, so we can infer that the word might relate to how the politician speaks.
2. **Context:** "Her speech was so *eloquent* that everyone in the audience was moved to tears." The context suggests that *eloquent* has something to do with speaking or expressing oneself.
3. **Roots:** The root of *eloquent* comes from the Latin word "eloqui," meaning "to speak out." Knowing this, we can guess that the word relates to speech or communication.
4. **Reference:** Look up *eloquent* in the dictionary and find that it means "fluent or persuasive in speaking or writing."
5. **Review:** To reinforce the word, you might use it in sentences such as:
   - "The *eloquent* speaker captivated the crowd with his words."
   - "Her *eloquent* description of the scenery made me feel like I was there."

Word: benign

1. **Theme:** This could refer to a medical condition and a doctor's diagnosis. The theme suggests that the word might relate to health.
2. **Context:** "The tumor was found to be *benign*, meaning it wasn't cancerous and posed no immediate threat to her health." The context suggests that *benign* has something to do with the severity of the condition.
3. **Roots:** The root of *benign* comes from the Latin "benignus," meaning "kind" or "favorable." This hints that the word relates to something mild or non-harmful.
4. **Reference:** Looking up *benign* in a dictionary reveals that it means "harmless" or "not dangerous, especially in medical terms."
5. **Review:** After learning the word, you might practice using it in different contexts:
   - "The doctor reassured her that the cyst was *benign*."
   - "His *benign* expression made everyone feel at ease."

Word: ephemeral

1. **Theme:** This could refer to the fleeting nature of life and how moments pass quickly, suggesting that the word may relate to time.
2. **Context:** "The beauty of the sunset was *ephemeral*, lasting only a few minutes before fading into dusk." The context suggests that *ephemeral* means "something short-lived or temporary."
3. **Roots:** The root of *ephemeral* comes from the Greek "ephemeros," meaning "lasting only one day." This gives a clue that the word relates to something very brief.
4. **Reference:** A dictionary definition of *ephemeral* reveals that it means "lasting for a very short time."
5. **Review:** To reinforce the word, you can use it in other sentences:
   - "Her joy was *ephemeral*, as the excitement quickly faded."
   - "The *ephemeral* nature of the rainbow made it even more beautiful."

Word: incredulous

1. **Theme:** This could refer to a character hearing unbelievable news, so the word likely has to do with disbelief or surprise.
2. **Context:** "When she heard the news, she gave him an *incredulous* look, as if she couldn't believe what he was saying." The context suggests that *incredulous* is related to doubt or disbelief.
3. **Roots:** The root of *incredulous* comes from the Latin "incredulus," meaning "not believing" (from *in-* meaning "not" and *credere* meaning "to believe").
4. **Reference:** A dictionary definition of *incredulous* confirms that it means "unwilling or unable to believe something."
5. **Review:** Practice the word with different examples:

- "His *incredulous* expression made it clear he doubted her story."
- "I was *incredulous* when they told me I won the lottery!"

Word: conspicuous

1. **Theme:** The word relates to something or someone that can be easily noticed in a crowd.
2. **Context:** "Her bright red dress made her *conspicuous* in the sea of black outfits." The context suggests that *conspicuous* means "something that stands out and is easy to notice."
3. **Roots:** The root of *conspicuous* comes from the Latin "conspicere," meaning "to look at" or "to observe." This hints that the word involves being easily seen or noticed.
4. **Reference:** Looking up *conspicuous* in a dictionary confirms that it means "easily seen or noticed."
5. **Review:** To reinforce the word, use it in different sentences:

- "The large sign was *conspicuous* from across the street."
- "Her *conspicuous* talent made her the star of the show."

Word: plausible

1. **Theme:** This word may relate to the believability of an idea or explanation.
2. **Context:** "The detective's explanation of the crime scene seemed *plausible*, but they still had more investigating to do." The context suggests that *plausible* means "something that is reasonable or believable."
3. **Roots:** The root of *plausible* comes from the Latin "plausibilis," meaning "worthy of applause" or "acceptable." This suggests that the word relates to something that seems reasonable or likely to be true.
4. **Reference:** A dictionary definition of *plausible* shows that it means "seeming reasonable or probable."
5. **Review:** Practice with different examples:

- "His *plausible* argument convinced the jury."
- "The *plausible* explanation was supported by evidence, but it still required further investigation.

CHAPTER 2

Individual-Word Learning

Strategies for Learning Words We Provide

LANGUAGE DOMAINS

Reading

Writing

Speaking

Listening

2.AA Parts-of-Speech Word Expansion

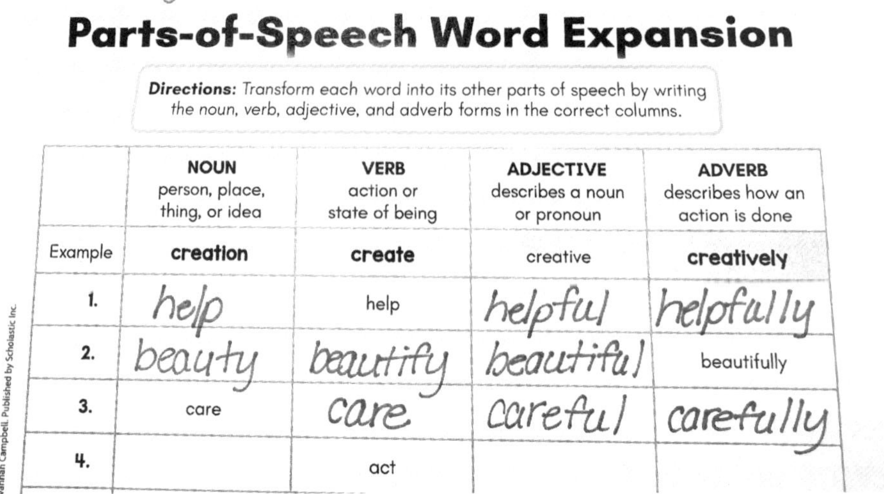

Name: Londyn Date:

Parts-of-Speech Word Expansion

Directions: *Transform each word into its other parts of speech by writing the noun, verb, adjective, and adverb forms in the correct columns.*

	NOUN person, place, thing, or idea	VERB action or state of being	ADJECTIVE describes a noun or pronoun	ADVERB describes how an action is done
Example	**creation**	**create**	creative	**creatively**
1.	help	help	helpful	helpfully
2.	beauty	beautify	beautiful	beautifully
3.	care	care	careful	carefully
4.		act		

Review the definitions of a noun, verb, adjective, and adverb. Then distribute copies of the Parts-of-Speech Word Expansion on page 163. In pairs, have students read the word in each row, determine its part of speech, and then fill in other forms of the word in the appropriate columns. For example, if the given word is *creative*, it can become *creation* as a noun, *create* as a verb, and *creatively* as an adverb. Students should rely on each other, rather than digital sources, to figure out the missing words. When they're finished, review the answers as a class to address any misconceptions or misspellings.

Materials	Parts-of-Speech Word Expansion, page 163
Grade Band	2–8
Length of Activity	10 minutes
Differentiation Ideas	**Striving Learners and English Learners:** Have students find words for just two of the three parts-of-speech categories so they can better focus on the rich conversation and not simple completion of the task.
Extension Ideas	Have students think of other base words that they can transform into all other parts of speech.
Answers	**1.** help, helpful, helpfully **2.** beauty, beautify, beautiful **3.** care, careful, carefully **4.** act, active, actively **5.** power, powerful, powerfully **6.** danger, endanger, dangerously **7.** succeed, successful, successfully **8.** freedom, free, free **9.** cleanliness, clean, cleanly **10.** hope, hopeful, hopefully **11.** education, educate, educational **12.** comfort, comfortable, comfortably **13.** attraction, attract, attractively **14.** analyze, analytical, analytically **15.** protection, protect, protectively

Name: ______________________ Date: ____________

Parts-of-Speech Word Expansion

Directions: Transform each word into its other parts of speech by writing the noun, verb, adjective, and adverb forms in the correct columns.

	NOUN person, place, thing, or idea	**VERB** action or state of being	**ADJECTIVE** describes a noun or pronoun	**ADVERB** describes how an action is done
Example	**creation**	**create**	**creative**	**creatively**
1.		help		
2.				beautifully
3.	care			
4.		act		
5.		empower		
6.			dangerous	
7.	success			
8.				freely
9.		clean		
10.	hope			
11.				educationally
12.		comfort		
13.			attractive	
14.	analysis			
15.			protective	

Strategies for Using Context Clues, pages 166–177

Strategies for Using Morphology, pages 178–225

Chapter 3 downloadables are available here.

CHAPTER 3

Student Tools for Determining Meaning

"Loving your language means a command of its vocabulary beyond the level of the everyday."

—John McWhorter

Students need tools for determining the meaning of unknown words they encounter in conversation and text to comprehend the overall message. What do we mean by "tools"? Using morphological awareness, context clues, and reference materials.

Using Morphology

A *morpheme* is the smallest unit of meaning in a word. It may be a single letter, a syllable, or an entire word. The word *uncharted* has three morphemes: *un-chart-ed*. Each morpheme affects the meaning of the word. *Morphological awareness* refers to using knowledge of word parts to determine meaning of unfamiliar words so a reader can comprehend what they read. It is a powerful and reliable skill (Spencer et al., 2017) and is essential for navigating the complexities of English. Instruction in morphology significantly improves reading, spelling, and, indeed, vocabulary, from preschool through grade eight (Bowers et al., 2010; Carlisle, 2010b).

Using Context Clues

Teaching students to search for a variety of sentence- and paragraph-level context clues has been found to improve vocabulary and reading comprehension (Stahl, 1983; Tuyen & Huyen, 2019). It's important to expose students to various types of context clues and give them opportunities to practice each one to help them use the strategy when they encounter an unknown word while reading or listening independently.

Using Reference Materials

Glossaries and dictionaries are highly effective for finding an exact definition. Glossaries within a provided text for students are great sources of knowledge and provide instant feedback about the meaning of a word. However, dictionary definitions are often confusing and time-consuming for students to access. While using reference sources should be taught as a skill, the previous two tools are more common and authentic ways students determine the meaning of an unknown word.

These three tools benefit all students, including English learners, because they allow them to deduce the meanings of unfamiliar words and deepen their understanding of language structures (Kieffer & Lesaux, 2012) when reading text independently.

Tools to Determine a Word's Meaning

1. Morphology

Use with words that have familiar, meaningful word parts.

unreliable

My alarm clock is *unreliable* and often leaves me panicking when I wake up.

Student Definition: *not able to be depended on*

Why Morphology? *Unreliable* has commonly known meanings for word parts as *un* means "not," *rely* means "to depend on," and *able* means "capable of."

2. Context Clues

Use when the sentence provides enough surrounding context.

formidable

The chess champion was a *formidable* opponent, defeating everyone he played against with a series of clever and unexpected moves.

Student Definition: *an opponent who would be difficult to defeat*

Why Context Clues? There are two great sets of useful context clues: *defeating everyone he played with* and *clever and unexpected moves.*

3. Reference Materials

Use when the morphological and context clues tools are insufficient.

curt

The stressed-out secretary used a *curt* tone when answering the phone.

Student Definition: *a short and rude answer*

Why Reference Materials? There are unfamiliar word parts and little context, so a dictionary definition may be required: *rudely brief in speech or abrupt in manner.*

Strategies for Using Context Clues

LANGUAGE DOMAINS

Reading

Writing

☐

Speaking

Listening

3.A Context Clues for Early Learners: What's My Word?

This strategy allows you to introduce new words by modeling how to use strong context clues to determine meaning. Choose a sentence from the Context Clues Sentence List on page 167 and display it for students. Read the sentence aloud, showing students how you determine meaning by looking for clues in the sentence and underlining parts of the sentence that help to determine the word's meaning. For example, "In this sentence, 'The puppy was *shivering* because it was cold outside and he had no blanket,' I think that *shivering* is something you must do when you are cold, so I'm underlining *cold* and *no blanket* because those are the words that helped me figure out how the puppy was behaving." After modeling and providing guided practice with additional sentences, ask students to work independently, using clues they find in the next sentence on the page (or in a sample sentence you've provided) to determine the meaning of the target word. Make sure that they underline parts of the sentence that help to determine the word's meaning.

Materials	Context Clues Sentence List, page 167, or words you select
Grade Band	K–1
Length of Activity	5 minutes (1–3 per day)

Differentiation Ideas	• **Striving Learners:** Give students two options for the definition. (e.g., Does *parched* mean you are hungry or thirsty?)
	• **English Learners:** Use sentences that could be illustrated by a picture.
	• **Striving Learners and English Learners:** Use sentence stems to guide responses:
	  • *I think _____ means ____ because the sentence says _________.*
	  • *The word ________ makes me think the vocabulary word ______ means ________.*

Extension Ideas	• Write the sentences on an anchor chart and read to students daily. • Give students a sentence frame with the target words and ask them to come up with a sentence using those words (oral only). • Ask students to act out words (when appropriate) after figuring out the meaning.

Context Clues Sentence List

1. The puppy was **shivering** because it was very cold outside and he had no blanket.
2. The balloon **drifted** up into the sky after Sarah accidentally let go, moving slowly higher and higher.
3. The baby was **giggling** because her dad made a funny face, and she thought it was silly.
4. The pig was **filthy** after rolling in the mud. His whole body was covered in dirt!
5. I was **starving** after running at recess, so I ate my whole sandwich very quickly.
6. The little girl was **grinning** because she was so happy to see her best friend.
7. I was **drenched** after playing in the rain without an umbrella. My clothes were soaking wet!
8. Mom said to be **gentle** with the baby kitten, so I petted it very softly.
9. I was **shocked** when I saw a huge cake with candles. I had no idea there was a surprise party for me!
10. The glass is **fragile**, so we have to be careful not to drop it, or it will break.
11. We saw a **gigantic** elephant at the zoo. It was so big it was taller than a car!
12. The clown was so **hilarious** that everyone was laughing and smiling at his jokes.
13. The wind was **howling** outside, making a loud *woo* sound through the trees.
14. The girl was **curious** about the bug, so she watched it closely and asked lots of questions.
15. After running around outside, I was **exhausted** and needed to rest.
16. The baby was **fussy** because she was tired, crying, and rubbing her eyes.
17. We had to **cooperate** to clean the room, so we all cleaned up the floor and desks together.
18. Dad had to **scrub** the dirty table really hard to get all the sticky mess off.
19. I was so **proud** when I finished my puzzle all by myself, I wanted to show everyone!
20. When I stepped on the crunchy leaf, it **crumbled** into tiny pieces.

CHAPTER 3

Student Tools for Determining Meaning

Strategies for Using Context Clues

LANGUAGE DOMAINS

Reading

Writing

Speaking

Listening

3.B Using Context Clues to Grow Word Banks

Copy and distribute one of the Using Context Clues Sets on pages 169–170. Have students read the paragraphs and highlight context clues they find to help understand the meaning of the boldfaced words. Then ask them to record their thinking on the Context Clues Organizer by writing each word and what they think that word means. If necessary, model how to fill out the organizer.

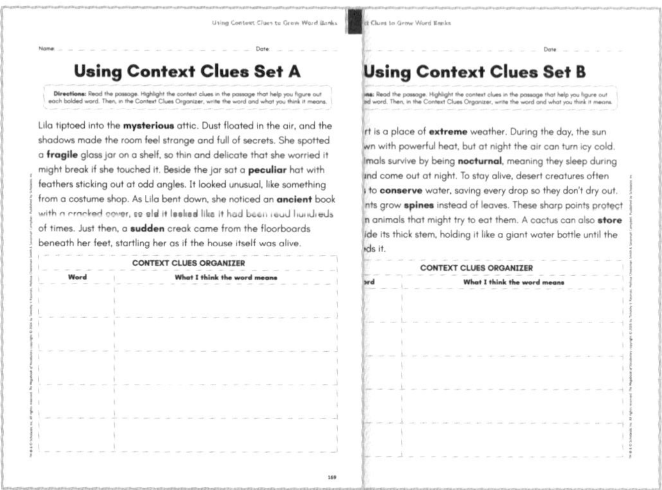

Using Context Clues to Grow Word Banks

Name: Date:

Using Context Clues Set A

Directions: Read the passage. Highlight the context clues in the passage that help you figure out each bolded word. Then, in the Context Clues Organizer, write the word and what you think it means.

Lila tiptoed into the **mysterious** attic. Dust floated in the air, and the shadows made the room feel strange and full of secrets. She spotted a **fragile** glass jar on a shelf, so thin and delicate that she worried it might break if she touched it. Beside the jar sat a **peculiar** hat with feathers sticking out at odd angles. It looked unusual, like something from a costume shop. As Lila bent down, she noticed an **ancient** book with a cracked cover, so old it looked like it had been read hundreds of times. Just then, a **sudden** creak came from the floorboards beneath her feet, startling her as if the house itself was alive.

CONTEXT CLUES ORGANIZER

Word	What I think the word means

169

Date:

Using Context Clues Set B

Read the passage. Highlight the context clues in the passage that help you figure out word. Then, in the Context Clues Organizer, write the word and what you think it means.

rt is a place of **extreme** weather. During the day, the sun wn with powerful heat, but at night the air can turn icy cold. imals survive by being **nocturnal**, meaning they sleep during nd come out at night. To stay alive, desert creatures often to **conserve** water, saving every drop so they don't dry out. nts grow **spines** instead of leaves. These sharp points protect n animals that might try to eat them. A cactus can also **store** ide its thick stem, holding it like a giant water bottle until the ds it.

CONTEXT CLUES ORGANIZER

Word	What I think the word means

Materials	• Using Context Clues Set A, page 169 • Using Context Clues Set B, page 170 • highlighters
Grade Band	2–3
Length of Activity	10 minutes per passage
Differentiation Ideas	• **Striving Learners:** Use AI to rewrite the paragraph with stronger, clearer context clues as a scaffold for students. Possible AI prompt: *Rewrite this paragraph to include stronger context clues for the word ________.* (Be sure to check any AI results to make sure they are appropriate.) Please keep all the other sentences and the content: Only add in additional context to support the meaning of the target word. • **English Learners:** Provide a bilingual glossary or word bank to refer to as needed.
Extension Ideas	• Ask students to write their own short paragraph using a new Tier 2 word with enough context for a peer to figure out the meaning. • Use the same graphic organizer across content areas like science and social studies. • Use the organizer with different texts throughout the year to help students build a growing bank of Tier 2 words they've encountered in their reading.

Name: ______________________ Date: __________

Using Context Clues Set A

Directions: Read the passage. Highlight the context clues in the passage that help you figure out each bolded word. Then, in the Context Clues Organizer, write the word and what you think it means.

Lila tiptoed into the **mysterious** attic. Dust floated in the air, and the shadows made the room feel strange and full of secrets. She spotted a **fragile** glass jar on a shelf, so thin and delicate that she worried it might break if she touched it. Beside the jar sat a **peculiar** hat with feathers sticking out at odd angles. It looked unusual, like something from a costume shop. As Lila bent down, she noticed an **ancient** book with a cracked cover, so old it looked like it had been read hundreds of times. Just then, a **sudden** creak came from the floorboards beneath her feet, startling her as if the house itself was alive.

CONTEXT CLUES ORGANIZER	
Word	**What I think the word means**

Name: ______________________________ Date: ______________

Using Context Clues Set B

Directions: Read the passage. Highlight the context clues in the passage that help you figure out each bolded word. Then, in the Context Clues Organizer, write the word and what you think it means.

The desert is a place of **extreme** weather. During the day, the sun beats down with powerful heat, but at night the air can turn icy cold. Some animals survive by being **nocturnal**, meaning they sleep during the day and come out at night. To stay alive, desert creatures often find ways to **conserve** water, saving every drop so they don't dry out. Many plants grow **spines** instead of leaves. These sharp points protect them from animals that might try to eat them. A cactus can also **store** water inside its thick stem, holding it like a giant water bottle until the plant needs it.

CONTEXT CLUES ORGANIZER	
Word	**What I think the word means**

3.C Highlight the Context Clues

Distribute one of the Highlight the Clues Sets on pages 172–173. Pronounce each boldfaced word for students and have them chorally repeat it. Ask students to add a box around each boldfaced word, then use a highlighter to mark the surrounding words that help them understand the meaning of the word. Students can then write a definition for each word based on the context clues. Clarify and refine the meaning as they share their context clues and predicted definitions. Students should write the revised definitions in the space provided.

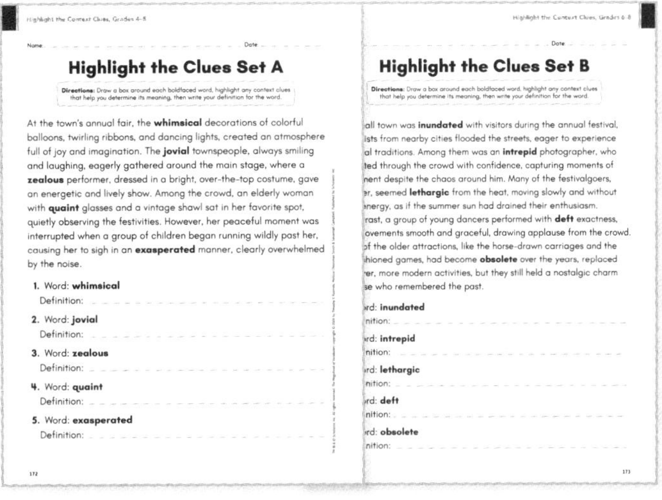

Highlight the Context Clues, Grades 4–5

Name: Date:

Highlight the Clues Set A

Directions: Draw a box around each boldfaced word, highlight any context clues that help you determine its meaning, then write your definition for the word.

At the town's annual fair, the **whimsical** decorations of colorful balloons, twirling ribbons, and dancing lights, created an atmosphere full of joy and imagination. The **jovial** townspeople, always smiling and laughing, eagerly gathered around the main stage, where a **zealous** performer, dressed in a bright, over-the-top costume, gave an energetic and lively show. Among the crowd, an elderly woman with **quaint** glasses and a vintage shawl sat in her favorite spot, quietly observing the festivities. However, her peaceful moment was interrupted when a group of children began running wildly past her, causing her to sigh in an **exasperated** manner, clearly overwhelmed by the noise.

1. Word: **whimsical**
   Definition:
2. Word: **jovial**
   Definition:
3. Word: **zealous**
   Definition:
4. Word: **quaint**
   Definition:
5. Word: **exasperated**
   Definition:

172

Highlight the Context Clues, Grades 6–8

Date:

Highlight the Clues Set B

Directions: Draw a box around each boldfaced word, highlight any context clues that help you determine its meaning, then write your definition for the word.

all town was **inundated** with visitors during the annual festival, ists from nearby cities flooded the streets, eager to experience al traditions. Among them was an **intrepid** photographer, who ted through the crowd with confidence, capturing moments of nent despite the chaos around him. Many of the festivalgoers, r, seemed **lethargic** from the heat, moving slowly and without nergy, as if the summer sun had drained their enthusiasm. rast, a group of young dancers performed with **deft** exactness, ovements smooth and graceful, drawing applause from the crowd. f the older attractions, like the horse-drawn carriages and the hioned games, had become **obsolete** over the years, replaced er, more modern activities, but they still held a nostalgic charm se who remembered the past.

rd: **inundated**
nition:
rd: **intrepid**
nition:
rd: **lethargic**
nition:
rd: **deft**
nition:
rd: **obsolete**
nition:

173

Materials	• Highlight the Clues Set A, Grades 4–5, page 172 • Highlight the Clues Set B, Grades 6–8, page 173 • highlighters
Grade Band	4–8
Length of Activity	20 minutes
Differentiation Ideas	• **Striving Learners:** Create a new passage with more obvious context clues. • **English Learners:** Read the boldfaced words and sentences aloud to clarify unknown vocabulary in the context.
Extension Ideas	• Have students use the back of the worksheet to write a sentence for each of the boldfaced words once you have reviewed the definition. • Choose five vocabulary words from an upcoming unit of study and use AI to create paragraphs with context clues for additional practice and front-loading of vocabulary. (Be sure to check any AI results to make sure they are appropriate.)
Answers	**Set A: 1.** playful, cheery, and unusual **2.** cheerful and in good humor **3.** showing great enthusiasm **4.** charmingly unusual or old-fashioned **5.** very frustrated or annoyed **Set B: 1.** to overwhelm with a large amount of something **2.** showing great courage **3.** sluggish or lacking energy **4.** skillful and quick in movement **5.** no longer in use or relevant

Strategies for Using Context Clues

LANGUAGE DOMAINS

Reading

Writing

Speaking

Listening

✓

Name: ______________________________ Date: ______________

Highlight the Clues Set A

Directions: Draw a box around each boldfaced word, highlight any context clues that help you determine its meaning, then write your definition for the word.

At the town's annual fair, the **whimsical** decorations of colorful balloons, twirling ribbons, and dancing lights, created an atmosphere full of joy and imagination. The **jovial** townspeople, always smiling and laughing, eagerly gathered around the main stage, where a **zealous** performer, dressed in a bright, over-the-top costume, gave an energetic and lively show. Among the crowd, an elderly woman with **quaint** glasses and a vintage shawl sat in her favorite spot, quietly observing the festivities. However, her peaceful moment was interrupted when a group of children began running wildly past her, causing her to sigh in an **exasperated** manner, clearly overwhelmed by the noise.

1. Word: **whimsical**
   Definition: ______________________________

2. Word: **jovial**
   Definition: ______________________________

3. Word: **zealous**
   Definition: ______________________________

4. Word: **quaint**
   Definition: ______________________________

5. Word: **exasperated**
   Definition: ______________________________

Name: ______________________ Date: __________

Highlight the Clues Set B

Directions: Draw a box around each boldfaced word, highlight any context clues that help you determine its meaning, then write your definition for the word.

The small town was **inundated** with visitors during the annual festival, as tourists from nearby cities flooded the streets, eager to experience the local traditions. Among them was an **intrepid** photographer, who navigated through the crowd with confidence, capturing moments of excitement despite the chaos around him. Many of the festivalgoers, however, seemed **lethargic** from the heat, moving slowly and without much energy, as if the summer sun had drained their enthusiasm. In contrast, a group of young dancers performed with **deft** exactness, their movements smooth and graceful, drawing applause from the crowd. Some of the older attractions, like the horse-drawn carriages and the old-fashioned games, had become **obsolete** over the years, replaced by newer, more modern activities, but they still held a nostalgic charm for those who remembered the past.

1. Word: **inundated**
   Definition: ______________________

2. Word: **intrepid**
   Definition: ______________________

3. Word: **lethargic**
   Definition: ______________________

4. Word: **deft**
   Definition: ______________________

5. Word: **obsolete**
   Definition: ______________________

CHAPTER 3

Student Tools for Determining Meaning

Strategies for Using Context Clues

LANGUAGE DOMAINS

Reading

Writing

Speaking

Listening

3.D Identifying Types of Context Clues

Review the Types of Context Clues Chart on page 175 with students, paying special attention to the examples to help them recognize context clues when they read independently. Then distribute the Types of Context Clues Set on pages 176–177 and have students read the directions and the sentence, identify the meaning of the boldfaced word, and determine which type of context clue was used.

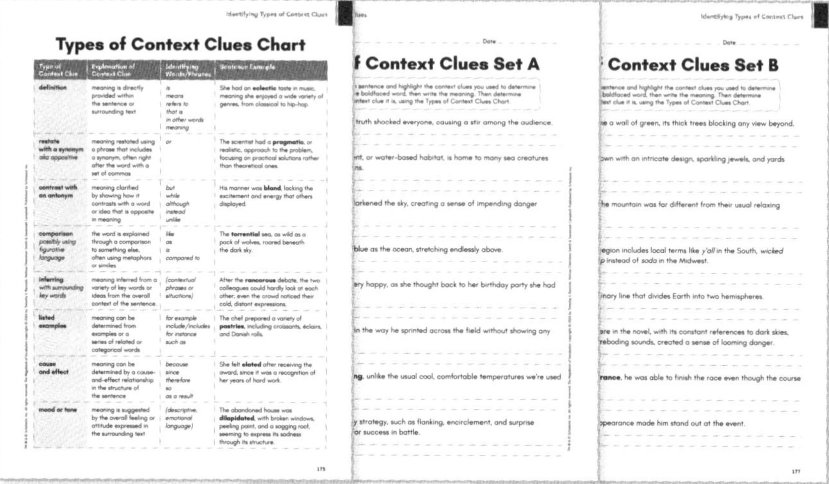

Types of Context Clues Chart

f Context Clues Set A

Context Clues Set B

Materials	• Types of Context Clues Chart, page 175 • Types of Context Clues Set A, page 176 • Types of Context Clues Set B, page 177
Grade Band	4–8
Length of Activity	20 minutes
Differentiation Ideas	**Striving Learners and English Learners:** Allow students to work with a partner so they have the opportunity to discuss answers orally first.
Extension Ideas	Have students work with a partner to identify types of context clues for new words in a shared text or book they are both reading.
Answers	**Set A: 1.** a truth that is revealed; cause and effect **2.** related to water; definition **3.** feeling that something bad might happen; mood or tone **4.** bright blue; comparison **5.** very happy; restate with a synonym **6.** a lot of energy; inferring **7.** hot and uncomfortable; contrast with an antonym **8.** organized strategies to execute a plan; listed examples **Set B: 1.** thick or crowded; comparison **2.** rich and luxurious; inferring **3.** tough or challenging to complete; contrast with an antonym **4.** everyday language spoken by people in different regions; listed examples **5.** imaginary line that divides Earth into two hemispheres; definition **6.** deep unhappiness; mood or tone **7.** continued effort despite difficulties; cause and effect **8.** messy and scruffy; restatement with a synonym

Types of Context Clues Chart

Type of Context Clue	Explanation of Context Clue	Identifying Words/Phrases	Sentence Example
definition	meaning is directly provided within the sentence or surrounding text	*is* *means* *refers to* *that is* *in other words* *meaning*	She had an **eclectic** taste in music, meaning she enjoyed a wide variety of genres, from classical to hip-hop.
restate with a synonym *aka appositive*	meaning restated using a phrase that includes a synonym, often right after the word with a set of commas	*or*	The scientist had a **pragmatic**, or realistic, approach to the problem, focusing on practical solutions rather than theoretical ones.
contrast with an antonym	meaning clarified by showing how it contrasts with a word or idea that is opposite in meaning	*but* *while* *although* *instead* *unlike*	His manner was **bland**, lacking the excitement and energy that others displayed.
comparison *possibly using figurative language*	the word is explained through a comparison to something else, often using metaphors or similes	*like* *as* *is* *compared to*	The **torrential** sea, as wild as a pack of wolves, roared beneath the dark sky.
inferring *with surrounding key words*	meaning inferred from a variety of key words or ideas from the overall context of the sentence	*(contextual phrases or situations)*	After the **rancorous** debate, the two colleagues could hardly look at each other; even the crowd noticed their cold, distant expressions.
listed examples	meaning can be determined from examples or a series of related or categorical words	*for example* *include/includes* *for instance* *such as*	The chef prepared a variety of **pastries**, including croissants, éclairs, and Danish rolls.
cause and effect	meaning can be determined by a cause-and-effect relationship in the structure of the sentence	*because* *since* *therefore* *so* *as a result*	She felt **elated** after receiving the award, since it was a recognition of her years of hard work.
mood or tone	meaning is suggested by the overall feeling or attitude expressed in the surrounding text	*(descriptive, emotional language)*	The abandoned house was **dilapidated**, with broken windows, peeling paint, and a sagging roof, seeming to express its sadness through its structure.

Name: ______________________ Date: ____________

Types of Context Clues Set A

Directions: Read each sentence and highlight the context clues you used to determine the meaning of the boldfaced word, then write the meaning. Then determine the type of context clue it is, using the Types of Context Clues Chart.

1. The **revelation** of the truth shocked everyone, causing a stir among the audience.
   Meaning: ______________________
   Type of Context Clue: ______________________
2. An **aquatic** environment, or water-based habitat, is home to many sea creatures like jellyfish and dolphins.
   Meaning: ______________________
   Type of Context Clue: ______________________
3. The **ominous** clouds darkened the sky, creating a sense of impending danger or trouble.
   Meaning: ______________________
   Type of Context Clue: ______________________
4. The sky was **azure**, as blue as the ocean, stretching endlessly above.
   Meaning: ______________________
   Type of Context Clue: ______________________
5. She felt **ecstatic**, or very happy, as she thought back to her birthday party she had last weekend.
   Meaning: ______________________
   Type of Context Clue: ______________________
6. His **vigor** was evident in the way he sprinted across the field without showing any sign of exhaustion.
   Meaning: ______________________
   Type of Context Clue: ______________________
7. The day was **sweltering**, unlike the usual cool, comfortable temperatures we're used to in the fall.
   Meaning: ______________________
   Type of Context Clue: ______________________
8. **Tactics** used in military strategy, such as flanking, encirclement, and surprise attacks, are essential for success in battle.
   Meaning: ______________________
   Type of Context Clue: ______________________

Name: ______________________ Date: ______________

Types of Context Clues Set B

Directions: Read each sentence and highlight the context clues you used to determine the meaning of the boldfaced word, then write the meaning. Then determine the type of context clue it is, using the Types of Context Clues Chart.

1. The **dense** forest was like a wall of green, its thick trees blocking any view beyond.
   Meaning: ______________________
   Type of Context Clue: ______________________
2. She wore an **opulent** gown with an intricate design, sparkling jewels, and yards of luxurious fabric.
   Meaning: ______________________
   Type of Context Clue: ______________________
3. The **grueling** climb up the mountain was far different from their usual relaxing nature walks.
   Meaning: ______________________
   Type of Context Clue: ______________________
4. The **vernacular** of the region includes local terms like *y'all* in the South, *wicked* in New England, and *pop* instead of *soda* in the Midwest.
   Meaning: ______________________
   Type of Context Clue: ______________________
5. The **equator** is an imaginary line that divides Earth into two hemispheres.
   Meaning: ______________________
   Type of Context Clue: ______________________
6. The **brooding** atmosphere in the novel, with its constant references to dark skies, shadowy figures, and foreboding sounds, created a sense of looming danger.
   Meaning: ______________________
   Type of Context Clue: ______________________
7. Because of his **perseverance**, he was able to finish the race even though the course was challenging.
   Meaning: ______________________
   Type of Context Clue: ______________________
8. His **unkempt**, scruffy, appearance made him stand out at the event.
   Meaning: ______________________
   Type of Context Clue: ______________________

Strategies for Using Morphology

Morpheme Scope and Sequence by Grade Band

There is not a single correct scope and sequence for morphology. In phonics, we would not give students complex vowel patterns if they have not yet mastered CVC words. But with morphology, students do not need to know the meaning of *rupt* before they can understand *tract*. A general guideline is to begin with Anglo-Saxon morphemes as they are clear and easy to understand. Next, delve into the Latin roots, which can be found in the vast majority of words in English. Greek roots are trickier and usually show up in content-area texts as Tier 3 words. That's why they are the last type of morpheme we teach. The scope and sequence below is a suggested order for teaching prefixes, roots, and suffixes.

Grades K–1

Morpheme	Origin	Meaning	Examples
-s, -es	Anglo-Saxon	indicates plurality/third-person singular tense	dogs, cats, lunches, boxes, swims, grabs, wishes
-ing	Anglo-Saxon	present participle	thinking, planning, charging

Grades 2–3

Morpheme	Origin	Meaning	Examples
-ed	Anglo-Saxon	marks a verb as past tense	planted, hummed, wished
-ful	Anglo-Saxon	full of	wishful, hopeful, mindful
-less	Anglo-Saxon	without	thoughtless, mindless, relentless
un-	Anglo-Saxon	not	unhappy, unwell, unkindness
re-	Latin	back, again	restart, rethink, reject
-er	Anglo-Saxon	comparative, one who	talker, thinker, farmer, singer
-est	Anglo-Saxon	most	largest, tallest, quietest
for-	Anglo-Saxon	away, against	forbid, forbade, forgiven
-or	Latin	someone who does a specific task	doctor, actor, mayor
-cian	Latin	a person with a certain skill	electrician, physician, magician
-ist	Latin	someone who...	activist, florist, humanist
fore-	Anglo-Saxon	ahead, before	forearm, forecast, forefather

Morpheme	Origin	Meaning	Examples
post-	Latin	after	postwar, posttraumatic, postlude
pre-	Latin	before	preview, prepay, precooked
-ly	Anglo-Saxon	in a _____ way	quickly, harshly, mindfully
-fully	Anglo-Saxon	in a full way, entirely, fully	hopefully, joyfully, thoughtfully
over-	Anglo-Saxon	too much/above	overeat, overcome, overlook
under-	Anglo-Saxon	below	underpaid, undersell, underhanded
out-	Anglo-Saxon	beyond	outside, output, outline
-ish	Anglo-Saxon	belonging to, somewhat, characteristic of	greenish, sickish, thinnish
-able	Latin	able to, possible	comfortable, enjoyable, reliable
-ible	Latin	able to, possible	visible, responsible, incredible
-y	Anglo-Saxon	characterized by, full of	sunny, cloudy, windy
sub-	Latin	under	subway, submerge, submarine
mid-	Anglo-Saxon	middle	midnight, midday, midpoint
mis-	Anglo-Saxon	wrong, bad	misplace, mistake, misunderstand
-en	Anglo-Saxon	made of, of that nature	lighten, darken, soften
-ness	Anglo-Saxon	condition, state of, quality of	fitness, happiness, darkness
-some	Anglo-Saxon	characterized by a particular quality or state	winsome, tiresome, adventuresome
-ward	Anglo-Saxon	shows directionality	northward, awkward, afterward
non-	Latin	not	nonsensical, nonprofit, nonfat
form	Latin	to shape	formation, reform, unformed
ject	Latin	to throw	eject, reject, project
port	Latin	to carry	reported, deport, import
rupt	Latin	to break	erupt, corrupt, disrupt
-hood	Anglo-Saxon	state or condition	childhood, adulthood, parenthood
a-	Anglo-Saxon	on/in	aloud, ashore, awake

Grades 4–5

Morpheme	Origin	Meaning	Examples
-(t)ion, -sion	Latin	the act of	repetition, action, erosion
-ive	Latin	tending to do something	active, creative, positive
-ize	Latin	to make	theorize, stabilize, maximize
aud	Latin	to hear	audio, audible, auditorium
vis, vid	Latin	to see	video, vision, revise
tract	Latin	to pull	tractor, retract, distraction
dict	Latin	to say	dictator, dictate, contradict
duct	Latin	to lead	conduct, reduction, produce
fact	Latin	to make	factory, factual, artifact
fer	Latin	to carry	transfer, prefer, referral
flex	Latin	to bend	flexible, reflex, inflection
con-	Latin	together, with	conjecture, connect, construction
in-, im-, ir-, il-	Latin	not, into	incomplete, illogical, insert, imperfect, irreplaceable
trans-	Latin	across, beyond, through	transition, transfer, transatlantic
scrib, script	Latin	to write	scribble, describe, prescription
sist	Latin	to stand	irresistible, persisted, assistance
ten	Latin	to hold	pretend, tenable, intensify
-ance	Latin	quality, state of	remembrance, resistance, extravagance
-ence	Latin	quality, state of	eloquence, existence, congruence
-ment	Latin	state or condition	enjoyment, excitement, development
-ous	Latin	full of, having the qualities of	courageous, mysterious, delicious
-ture	Latin	the act of, the result of	structure, conjecture, fixture
de-	Latin	opposite of, down	defrost, devalue, descended
dis-	Latin	not, opposite	disagree, dismiss, disconnect
en-, em-	Latin	to cause to, make able to	enable, embark, embrace

Morpheme	Origin	Meaning	Examples
ex-	Latin	out of, from	exit, export, extraction
extra-	Latin	outside, beyond	extraordinary, extradite, extravaganza
bi-	Latin	two	bicycle, biplane, binary
oct-	Latin	eight	octopus, octagon, octane
quad-	Latin	four	quadrilateral, quadrant, quadruplets
tri-	Latin	three	triangle, trilogy, triplet
uni-	Latin	one	unicorn, uniform, unity
cred	Latin	to believe	incredible, credit, discredit
gress	Latin	to step	progress, regress, congress
ped	Latin	foot	pedal, pedometer, impede
pend	Latin	to hang	depend, suspend, compendium
spect	Latin	to see	spectacles, spectator, respect
struct	Latin	to build	restructure, construction, destruction

Grades 6–8

Morpheme	Origin	Meaning	Examples
ab-	Latin	away from	absent, abrupt, absorb
ad-	Latin	toward	admit, addition, advisor
inter-	Latin	between, among	international, interaction, interrupted
geo	Greek	earth	geography, geology, geographic
graph	Greek	to write	geography, paragraph, graphics
auto	Greek	self	autobiography, automation, automatic
bio	Greek	life	biography, biology, biodegradable
a	Greek	not, without	anonymous
anti	Greek	against	antibiotics, antibacterial, antimatter

Morpheme	Origin	Meaning	Examples
log	Greek	word	logic, logistics, catalog
logy	Greek	study of	ideology, psychology, pathology
therm	Greek	heat	thermal, thermostat, thermodynamics
tele	Greek	distant	television, telegraph, telescope
pos	Latin	to put, place	position, opposition, dispose
plic	Latin	to fold	replicate, application, complicated
circum-	Latin	around, surrounding	circumlocution, circumference, circumnavigate
contra-	Latin	opposite, against	contradict, contraband, contravene
mal-	Latin	wrong, bad, ill	malnourished, malformed, malicious
ob-	Latin	to, toward, against	obstacle, obtain, objection
per-	Latin	through	perforate, perfected, perpetrate
pro-	Latin	forward, forth	procedure, profess, prohibit
super-	Latin	over/above	supervisor, supersede, superlative
polis	Greek	city	political, metropolis, police
soph	Greek	wisdom	sophisticated, philosophy, sophomore
sym, syn	Greek	together	symmetry, symbiosis, synthesis
hyper	Greek	over	hyperactive, hyperventilate, hypertension
hypo	Greek	under	hypothermia, hypothetical, hypocrisy
phone	Greek	sound	phoneme, telephone, speakerphone
photo	Greek	light	photograph, photosynthesis, photogenic
mon	Greek	one	monarch, monopoly, monologue

Morpheme	Origin	Meaning	Examples
poly	Greek	many	polychrome, polygon, polytheism
chron	Greek	time	chronicle, chronology, chrony
cracy	Greek	rule	democracy, theocracy, autocracy
arch	Greek	rule	monarch, anarchy, archbishop
aster	Greek	star	asteroid, astronaut, astrolabe
cycle	Greek	wheel, circle	bicycle, cyclical, cycle
deme	Greek	people	demographic, democracy, pandemic
epi	Greek	upon, into	epigraph, epitaph, epitome
eu	Greek	good	eulogy, eugenics, euphoria
hydro	Greek	water	hydroelectric, hydraulics, hydroplane
meter	Greek	measure	thermometer, symmetry, optometrist
micro	Greek	small	micromanage, microwave, microphone
path	Greek	feeling	sympathy, pathology, pathogen
phile	Greek	love	philosophy, philanthropy, philharmonic, bibliophile
phobia	Greek	fear, hatred	arachnophobia, agoraphobia, claustrophobia
phys	Greek	nature, natural	physical, physician, astrophysics
psych	Greek	mind	psychology, psyche, psychoanalyst
scope	Greek	to look at	microscope, telescope, horoscope
techn	Greek	skill	technical, technician, technicality

Prefixes

a- on, in

ab- away from

ad- towards

bi- two

circum- around, surrounding

con- together, with

contra- opposite, against

de- opposite of, down

dis- not, opposite

en-, em- to cause to, make able to

ex- out of, from

extra- outside, beyond

for- away, against

fore- ahead, before

in-, im-, ir-, il- not, into

inter- between, among

mal- wrong, bad, ill

mid- middle

mis- wrong, bad

non- not

ob- to, toward, against

oct- eight

out- beyond

over- too much, above

per- through

post- after

pre- before

pro- forward, forth

quad- four

re- back, again

sub- under

super- over, above

trans- across, beyond, through

tri- three

un- not

under- below

uni- one

Roots

a not, without
anti against
arch rule
aster star
aud to hear
auto self
bio life
chron time
cracy rule
cred to believe
cycle wheel, circle
deme people
dict to say
duct to lead
epi upon, into
eu good
fact to make
fer to carry
flex to bend
form to shape
geo earth

graph to write
gress to step
hydro water
hyper over
hypo under
ject to throw
log word
logy study of
meter measure
micro small
mit, mis to send
mon one
path feeling
ped foot
pend to hang
phile love
phobia fear, hatred
phon sound
photo light
phys nature, natural
plic to fold

polis city
poly many
port to carry
pos to put, place
psych mind
rupt to break
scope to look at
scrib, script to write
sist to stand
soph wisdom
spect to see
struct to build
sym, syn together
techn skill
tele distant
ten to hold
therm heat
tract to pull
vis, vid to see

Suffixes

-able able to, possible

-ance quality, state of

-cian a person with a certain skill

-ed marks a verb as past tense

-en made of, of that nature

-ence quality, state of

-er comparative, one who

-est most

-ful full of

-fully in a full way, entirely, fully

-hood state or condition

-ible able to, possible

-ing present participle

-ish belonging to, somewhat, characteristic of

-ist someone who...

-ity a state or condition

-ive tending to do something

-ize to make

-less without

-ly in a _____ way

-ment state or condition

-ness condition, state of, quality of

-or someone who does a specific task

-ous full of, having the qualities of

-s, -es indicates plurality, third-person present tense

-some characterized by a particular quality or state

-(t)ion, -sion the act of

-ture the act, result of

-ward shows directionality

-y characterized by, full of

3.E **Prefix Action**

Two of the most common prefixes, *un-* and *re-*, are great starting points for early learners to explore word parts. Create half-page word cards on cardstock with these prefixes and base words: *un, re, happy, tie, lock, fold, build, do, make, plant*, and *pack*. Choose a student to come to the front of the class and select a base word card to hold up. Have the other students act out the word on the card. Next, have the student hold up one of the prefix cards in front of the base to change the action, demonstrating how the prefixes alter the meaning of the word.

Materials	Prefix Cards: Create cards with these prefixes and base words on them: *un, re, happy, tie, lock, fold, build, do, make, plant, pack*
Grade Band	K–3
Length of Activity	20 minutes
Differentiation Ideas	**Striving Learners and English Learners:** Draw a quick sketch on the word cards as semantic clues.
Extension Ideas	• Ask students to identify real words with the activity, as well as recognize nonsense words (e.g., *unhappy* is a word but *rehappy* is not). • Have students practice writing the words in a word bank dictionary or list.
Answers	retie, relock, rebuild, redo, remake, replant, repack, unhappy, untie, unlock, unfold, undo, unpack

Strategies for Using Morphology

LANGUAGE DOMAINS

Reading

Writing

☐

Speaking

Listening

☐

LANGUAGE DOMAINS

Reading

Writing

Speaking

Listening

3.F **Suffix Spin**

Create word cards for the most frequently used suffixes (*-s*, *-es*, *-ing*, and *-ed*) and display them in a pocket chart with the base word cards from the materials list, or choose your own base words that don't require a spelling change when a suffix is added. On cardstock, copy the Suffix Spinner on page 189 and cut it out; then provide students with a paper clip and pencil to use the spinner. One student at a time spins the spinner and selects a base word from the pocket chart. Then other students write the base word with the suffix on dry-erase boards and hold up answers for you to see. Students can turn and share with a partner a sentence containing that word.

Materials	• Suffix Spinner, page 189 • base word cards; create cards with these words on them: *cat, jump, help, sing, swim, box, wish, push, talk, match* • dry-erase boards and markers • paper clips and pencils
Grade Band	K–3
Length of Activity	10 minutes
Differentiation Ideas	• **Striving Learners and English Learners:** Use the same spinners and base word cards in small groups before the whole-group activity. • **English Learners:** Provide images for each of the base word cards, or ask a student to draw a picture on each card to represent the meaning.
Extension Ideas	Instead of using the recommended base words, provide students with examples where the spelling changes (e.g., double consonant, *e*-drop, *y* change).
Answers	cats, jumps, helps, sings, swims, boxes, wishes, pushes, talks, matches, jumping, helping, singing, swimming, boxing, wishing, pushing, talking, matching, jumped, helped, boxed, wished, pushed, talked, matched

Suffix Spinner

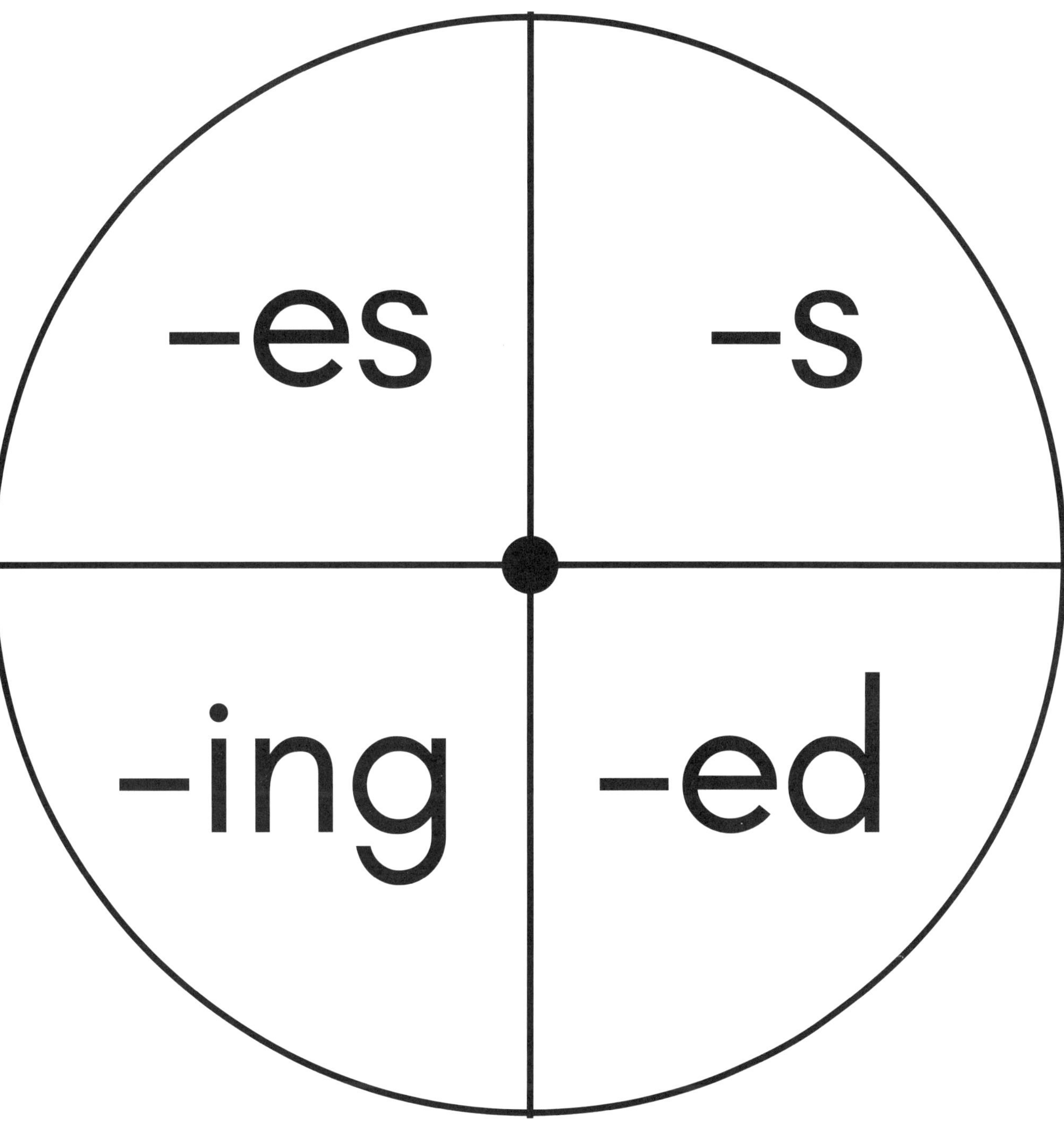

CHAPTER 3
Student Tools for Determining Meaning

Strategies for Using Morphology

LANGUAGE DOMAINS

Reading

Writing

Speaking

Listening

3.G Compound Word Match-Up

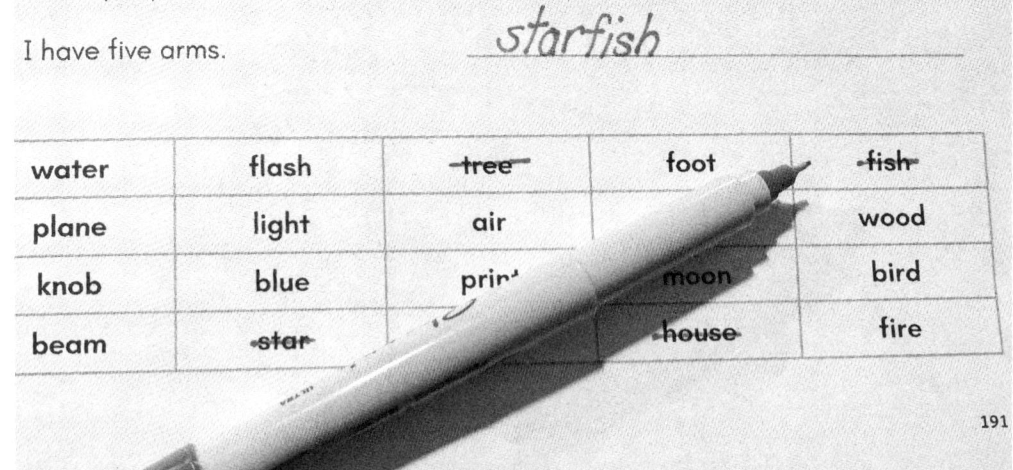

Compound words are a great introduction to multisyllabic words for our youngest learners. Discuss the concept of compound words by explaining that two words can be combined to create a new word with a related meaning. Distribute Compound Word Match-Up on page 191. Students will read the clues, then identify two words that can be combined to form a compound word, and write the new word in the correct space.

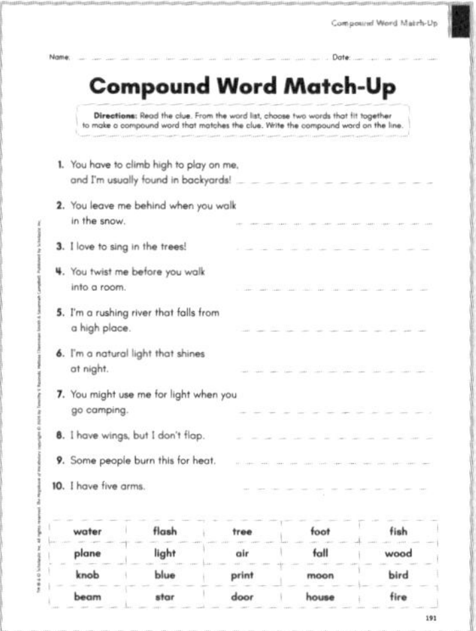

Compound Word Match-Up

Name ________ Date ________

Compound Word Match-Up

Directions: Read the clue. From the word list, choose two words that fit together to make a compound word that matches the clue. Write the compound word on the line.

1. You have to climb high to play on me, and I'm usually found in backyards! ________
2. You leave me behind when you walk in the snow. ________
3. I love to sing in the trees! ________
4. You twist me before you walk into a room. ________
5. I'm a rushing river that falls from a high place. ________
6. I'm a natural light that shines at night. ________
7. You might use me for light when you go camping. ________
8. I have wings, but I don't flap. ________
9. Some people burn this for heat. ________
10. I have five arms. ________

water	flash	tree	foot	fish
plane	light	air	fall	wood
knob	blue	print	moon	bird
beam	star	door	house	fire

191

Materials	Compound Word Match-Up, page 191
Grade Band	2–3
Length of Activity	5–10 minutes
Differentiation Ideas	**Striving Learners and English Learners:** Provide fewer words and complete as an oral-only activity in small groups.
Extension Ideas	Allow students to write their own sentences with a blank for a compound word, then share it aloud and ask the class to guess the missing compound word.
Answers	**1.** treehouse **2.** footprint **3.** bluebird **4.** doorknob **5.** waterfall **6.** moonbeam **7.** flashlight **8.** airplane **9.** firewood **10.** starfish

Name: ______________________ Date: ______________

Compound Word Match-Up

Directions: Read the clue. From the word list, choose two words that fit together to make a compound word that matches the clue. Write the compound word on the line.

1. You have to climb high to play on me, and I'm usually found in backyards! ______________
2. You leave me behind when you walk in the snow. ______________
3. I love to sing in the trees! ______________
4. You twist me before you walk into a room. ______________
5. I'm a rushing river that falls from a high place. ______________
6. I'm a natural light that shines at night. ______________
7. You might use me for light when you go camping. ______________
8. I have wings, but I don't flap. ______________
9. Some people burn this for heat. ______________
10. I have five arms. ______________

water	flash	tree	foot	fish
plane	light	air	fall	wood
knob	blue	print	moon	bird
beam	star	door	house	fire

LANGUAGE DOMAINS

Reading

Writing

Speaking

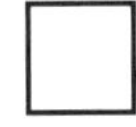

Listening

3.H Build-a-Word

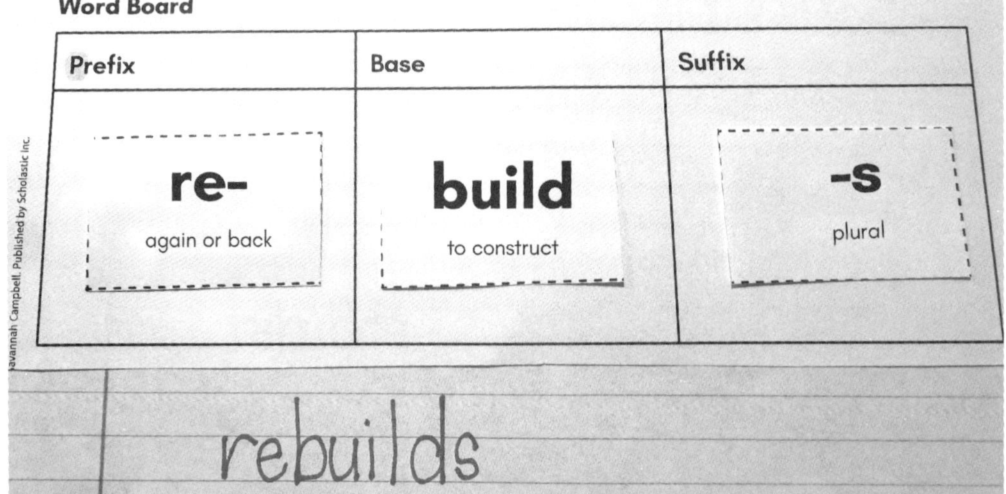

Build-a-Word is a scaffolded way to provide practice in creating and reading multisyllabic words. Have students cut out the Morpheme Cards at the bottom of Build-a-Word on page 193 and then use the cards to create words in the box at the top of the page. Ask them to list all the words they create on a separate sheet of paper. Allow them to use just a prefix, just a suffix, or a prefix and a suffix. (Idea inspired by Sarah Paul, creator of *Snippets by Sarah*.)

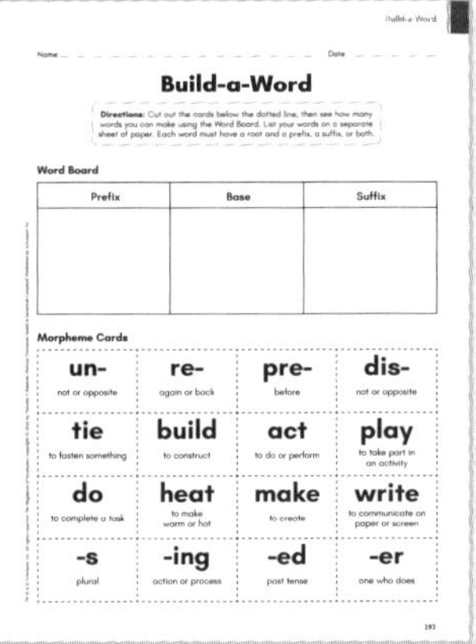

Build-a-Word

Name Date

Build-a-Word

Directions: Cut out the cards below the dotted line, then see how many words you can make using the Word Board. List your words on a separate sheet of paper. Each word must have a root and a prefix, a suffix, or both.

Word Board

Prefix	Base	Suffix

Morpheme Cards

un- not or opposite	**re-** again or back	**pre-** before	**dis-** not or opposite
tie to fasten something	**build** to construct	**act** to do or perform	**play** to take part in an activity
do to complete a task	**heat** to make warm or hot	**make** to create	**write** to communicate on paper or screen
-s plural	**-ing** action or process	**-ed** past tense	**-er** one who does

193

Materials	• Build-a-Word, page 193 • scissors
Grade Band	2–3
Length of Activity	10–15 minutes
Differentiation Ideas	**Striving Learners and English Learners:** Model an example first, and then check in later to see if more prompting is needed, or to clear up misconceptions of real words.
Extension Ideas	Turn the strategy into a game in which students score points. For example, you might pair up students and tell them, "You and your partner have five minutes to come up with as many real words as you can." Word parts are worth one point each, so words with two word parts are worth two points and words with three word parts are worth three points. Have students tabulate their scores after five minutes. Help them check that their lists include all real words, then congratulate the winner.
Answers	**Possible Answers:** unties, untied, untying, rebuilds, rebuilt, rebuilding, reacts, reacted, reacting, displays, displayed, displaying, undoes, undid, undoing, preheats, preheated, preheating, remakes, remade, remaking, rewrites, rewrote, rewriting

Name: ______________________ Date: ____________

Build-a-Word

Directions: Cut out the cards below the dotted line, then see how many words you can make using the Word Board. List your words on a separate sheet of paper. Each word must have a root and a prefix, a suffix, or both.

Word Board

Prefix	Base	Suffix

Morpheme Cards

un- not or opposite	**re-** again or back	**pre-** before	**dis-** not or opposite
tie to fasten something	**build** to construct	**act** to do or perform	**play** to take part in an activity
do to complete a task	**heat** to make warm or hot	**make** to create	**write** to communicate on paper or screen
-s plural	**-ing** action or process	**-ed** past tense	**-er** one who does

Strategies for Using Morphology

LANGUAGE DOMAINS

Reading

Writing

Speaking

Listening

3.1 Affix Addition

In this activity, students learn how adding morphemes to a base or root word changes the meaning of a word. Copy the Word Mat on page 195 and write a base or root word in the center square, prefixes in the squares to the left, and suffixes in the squares to the right. Make copies of the completed Word Mat for each small group. Then have students build as many real words as possible within a time limit by combining parts from the mat. When time is up, have groups share the words they created and tally how many real words all groups found. Repeat for extra practice.

Potential Word Mats

Prefixes	Base/Root	Suffixes
re, in, over	act	or, ion, ive
ex, im, re	port	ed, ing, er
re, de, e	ject	ed, ing, s
re, con, de	struct	ure, ion, ed
re, con, un	form	ed, ing, s

Prefixes	Base/Root	Suffixes
re, de, sub	tract	ing, ed, ion
pre, de, sub	scribe	er, ion, ing
re, un, dis	play	ed, ing, able
re, un, dis	cover	ed, ing, s
pre, mis, re	read	er, ing, s

Materials	• Word Mat, page 195 • timer
Grade Band	2–5
Length of Activity	10 minutes
Differentiation Ideas	• **Striving Learners and English Learners:** Allow students to create words with JUST a prefix or a suffix instead of both. • **English Learners:** Provide a visual for the root word to make the concept more concrete. • **Thriving Learners:** Encourage students to create a short paragraph utilizing the words they wrote from the word mat.
Extension Ideas	Ask students to use MULTIPLE prefixes or suffixes in their responses. They can create their own mats or use the one provided. For example, *struct* can become *deconstruction* or *reconstructed*. Students may use prefixes or suffixes that are not on the mat, but are known to the student.

Word Mat

CHAPTER 3
Student Tools for Determining Meaning

Strategies for Using Morphology

LANGUAGE DOMAINS

Reading

Writing

Speaking

Listening
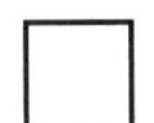

3.J Decoding Multisyllabic Words

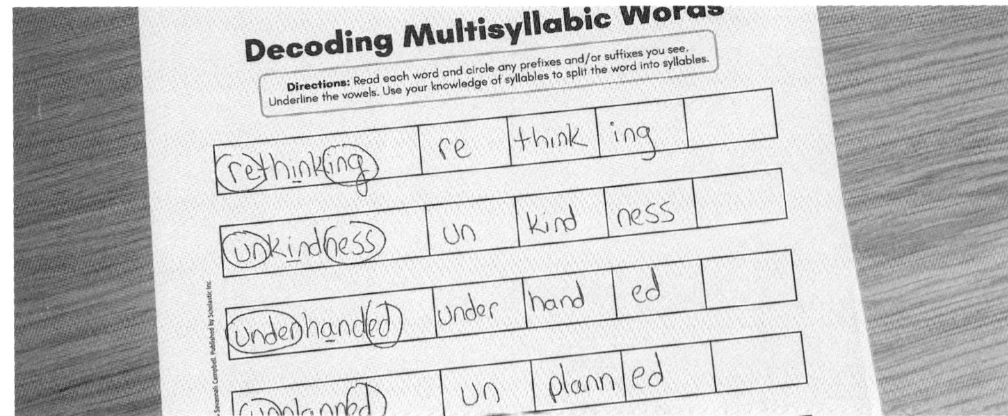

Copy the Decoding Multisyllabic Words template on page 197. In the first box of each line, write a word from the Decoding Multisyllabic Words Word Lists on page 198 or another word you have chosen, then copy for students. Use the following steps to have students accurately decode the word. First, have students circle any known prefixes and suffixes. Then, students should underline each vowel and determine whether it is part of a vowel team, a magic-*e* pattern, or an *r*-controlled vowel. Since every syllable must contain at least one vowel, this step helps them determine the number of remaining syllables. Finally, students should use their knowledge of syllables, phonics patterns, and morphemes to divide the rest of the word into the correct syllables or meaningful parts in the order they appear, writing one syllable or morpheme in each remaining box.

Materials	• Decoding Multisyllabic Words, page 197 • Decoding Multisyllabic Words Word Lists, pages 198
Grade Band	2–8
Length of Activity	10–15 minutes

Differentiation Ideas	• **Striving Learners:**
	  • Focus on a single prefix or suffix at a time, and then slowly interleave additional affixes.
	  • Repeat the strategy in small groups.
	  • Pull multisyllabic words from the selections you will read to the whole class.
	  • Provide boxes for students to split the words. Each box should represent a single morpheme.
	• **English Learners:** Ensure there are visuals to illustrate the meaning of each affix. Connect the morpheme back to the student's first language, finding cognates when possible.

Extension Ideas	• Use this strategy as a warm-up before reading a text that you've selected for students to read that day. Choose 3–5 multisyllabic words that are key to understanding the text. Ask students to split the words on dry-erase boards and then discuss the meaning of each word and its parts. • Instead of using dry-erase boards, use dry-erase notecards so students can see each syllable separately.
Answers	Answers integrated into Decoding Multisyllabic Word Word Lists, page 198

Decoding Multisyllabic Words

Directions: Read each word and circle any prefixes and/or suffixes you see. Underline the vowels. Use your knowledge of syllables to split the word into syllables.

1.				
2.				
3.				
4.				
5.				
6.				
7.				
8.				

Decoding Multisyllabic Words Word Lists

Grades 2–3:

rethinking ***re-think-ing***
unkindness ***un-kind-ness***
underhanded ***under-hand-ed***
unplanned ***un-plann-ed***
misleading ***mis-lead-ing***
redoing ***re-do-ing***
misspelling ***mis-spell-ing***
reminders ***re-mind-er-s***
unreliable ***un-re-li-able***
outlandishly ***out-land-ish-ly***
reformation ***re-form-a-tion***
deported ***de-port-ed***
darkening ***dark-en-ing***
misunderstanding ***mis-under-stand-ing***
precooked ***pre-cook-ed***
ejected ***e-ject-ed***

Grades 4–5:

transferring ***trans-ferr-ing***
construction ***con-struct-ion***
extracted ***ex-tract-ed***
incredible ***in-cred-ible***
reconstructed ***re-con-struct-ed***
disposable ***dis-pos-able***
unremarkable ***un-re-mark-able***
exceedingly ***ex-ceed-ing-ly***
excitement ***ex-cite-ment***
referral ***re-ferr-al***
contradiction ***contra-dict-ion***
incomplete ***in-com-plete***
respectable ***re-spect-able***
distracting ***dis-tract-ing***
production ***pro-duct-ion***
irresistible ***ir-re-sist-ible***

Grades 6–8:

delineate ***de-lin-e-ate***
antibiotic ***anti-bio-tic***
opposition ***op-pos-i-tion***
compendium ***com-pend-i-um***
circumnavigate ***circum-nav-i-gate***
malformation ***mal-form-a-tion***
independence ***in-de-pend-ence***
cartography ***cart-o-graph-y***
absently ***ab-sent-ly***
international ***inter-nat-ion-al***
thermodynamic ***thermo-dy-nam-ic***
symmetry ***sym-metr-y***
perfected ***per-fect-ed***
complicated ***com-pli-cat-ed***
democracy ***dem-o-cracy***

3.K Word Parts: Breaking It Up

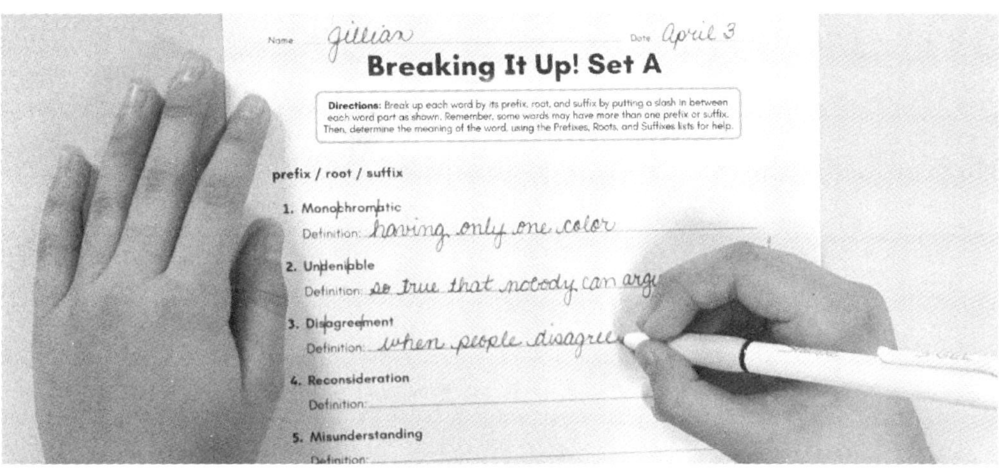

Understanding meaningful word parts, or morphemes, is essential for building vocabulary and decoding multisyllabic words. In this strategy, students practice breaking words into morphemes. Give students one of the Breaking It Up! Sets on pages 200–201 and have them separate each word by prefix, root, and suffix, recognizing that some words may have multiple prefixes or suffixes. When they're finished, ask students to define each word using their knowledge of word parts. This process helps deepen vocabulary knowledge and word analysis skills.

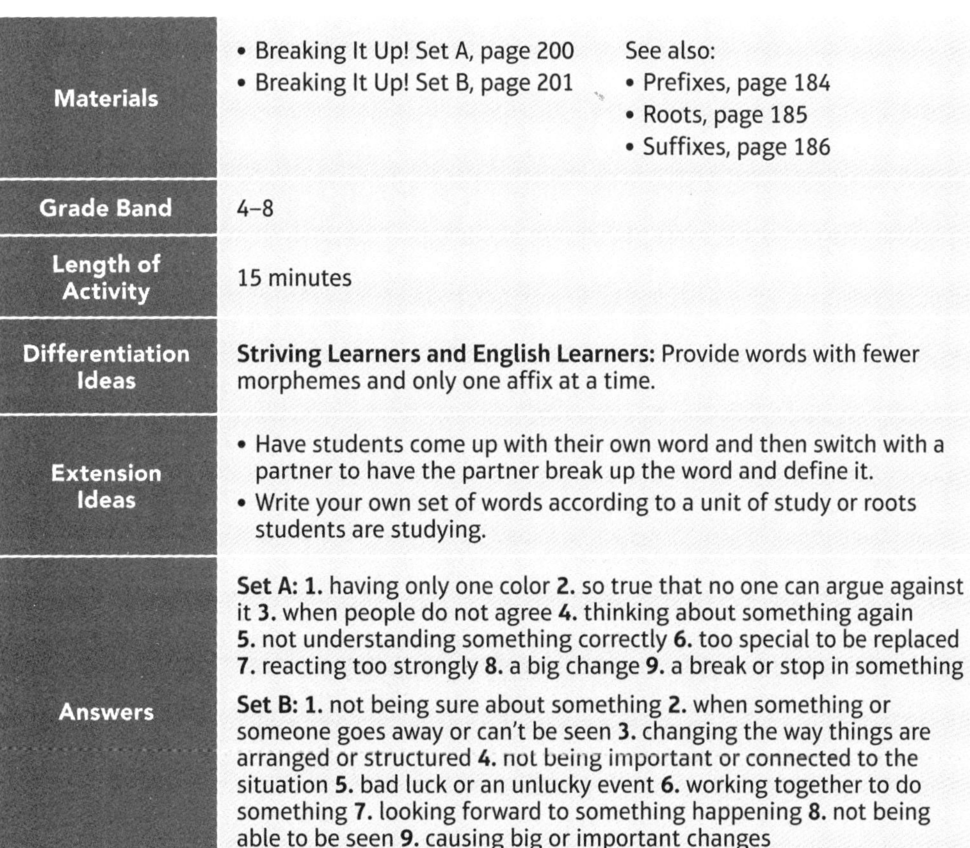

Materials	• Breaking It Up! Set A, page 200 • Breaking It Up! Set B, page 201 See also: • Prefixes, page 184 • Roots, page 185 • Suffixes, page 186
Grade Band	4–8
Length of Activity	15 minutes
Differentiation Ideas	**Striving Learners and English Learners:** Provide words with fewer morphemes and only one affix at a time.
Extension Ideas	• Have students come up with their own word and then switch with a partner to have the partner break up the word and define it. • Write your own set of words according to a unit of study or roots students are studying.
Answers	**Set A: 1.** having only one color **2.** so true that no one can argue against it **3.** when people do not agree **4.** thinking about something again **5.** not understanding something correctly **6.** too special to be replaced **7.** reacting too strongly **8.** a big change **9.** a break or stop in something **Set B: 1.** not being sure about something **2.** when something or someone goes away or can't be seen **3.** changing the way things are arranged or structured **4.** not being important or connected to the situation **5.** bad luck or an unlucky event **6.** working together to do something **7.** looking forward to something happening **8.** not being able to be seen **9.** causing big or important changes

CHAPTER 3

Student Tools for Determining Meaning

Strategies for Using Morphology

LANGUAGE DOMAINS

Reading

Writing

Speaking

Listening

Name: ______________________ Date: __________

Breaking It Up! Set A

Directions: Break up each word by its prefix, root, and suffix by putting a slash in between each word part as shown. Remember, some words may have more than one prefix or suffix. Then determine the meaning of the word, using the Prefixes, Roots, and Suffixes lists for help.

prefix / root / suffix

1. **monochromatic**

   Definition: ______________________

2. **undeniable**

   Definition: ______________________

3. **disagreement**

   Definition: ______________________

4. **reconsideration**

   Definition: ______________________

5. **misunderstanding**

   Definition: ______________________

6. **irreplaceable**

   Definition: ______________________

7. **overreaction**

   Definition: ______________________

8. **transformation**

   Definition: ______________________

9. **interruption**

   Definition: ______________________

Name: ______________________________ Date: ______________

Breaking It Up! Set B

Directions: Break up each word by its prefix, root, and suffix by putting a slash in between each word part as shown. Remember, some words may have more than one prefix or suffix. Then determine the meaning of the word, using the Prefixes, Roots, and Suffixes lists for help.

prefix / root / suffix

1. **uncertainty**

   Definition: ______________________________

2. **disappearance**

   Definition: ______________________________

3. **reorganization**

   Definition: ______________________________

4. **irrelevance**

   Definition: ______________________________

5. **misfortune**

   Definition: ______________________________

6. **cooperation**

   Definition: ______________________________

7. **anticipation**

   Definition: ______________________________

8. **invisibility**

   Definition: ______________________________

9. **revolutionary**

   Definition: ______________________________

Strategies for Using Morphology

LANGUAGE DOMAINS

Reading

Writing

Speaking

Listening

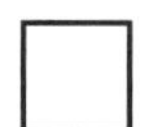

3.L Morphology Word Wall

Each week, introduce a new Greek or Latin root to the class and display it on a designated wall in your classroom titled *Morphology Word Wall.* Share the meaning of the root and provide a few examples of words that contain it. Over the course of the week, students search for words that include the featured morpheme. These words might come from independent reading, classroom texts, or conversations. When students encounter a word, have them use the Word Cards on page 203 to write the word, the sentence containing the word, and the morphemes (prefixes, root, suffixes) that make up the word. Encourage students to explain how each morpheme contributes to the word's meaning before adding it to the wall. As the week progresses, the wall becomes a growing collection of connected vocabulary.

Materials	• teacher-selected Greek or Latin morphemes • Word Cards, page 203
Grade Band	4–8
Length of Activity	Varies
Differentiation Ideas	• **Striving Learners:** Scaffold by completing the Word Cards together in small groups several times before asking students to complete the cards on their own. • **English Learners:** Provide oral rehearsal opportunities before writing on the Word Card. When possible, connect the English roots to cognates in a student's home language (e.g., *port* in English and *puerto* in Spanish). • **Thriving Learners:** Allow thriving learners to create etymology reports tracing how a word evolved.
Extension Ideas	• Let students choose a favorite word and create a poster breaking it down, including its origin, morphemes, meaning, and a drawing to illustrate it. • Play a mystery word game using the student Word Cards. Provide clues to the word, such as, "This is a word with three morphemes" or "This is a word with a prefix meaning 'not.'" Each correct guess receives a point.

Word Cards

Word					
Sentence					
Morphemes					

Word					
Sentence					
Morphemes					

Word					
Sentence					
Morphemes					

Strategies for Using Morphology

LANGUAGE DOMAINS

Reading

Writing

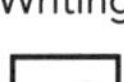

Speaking

Listening

3.M **Double the Suffix!**

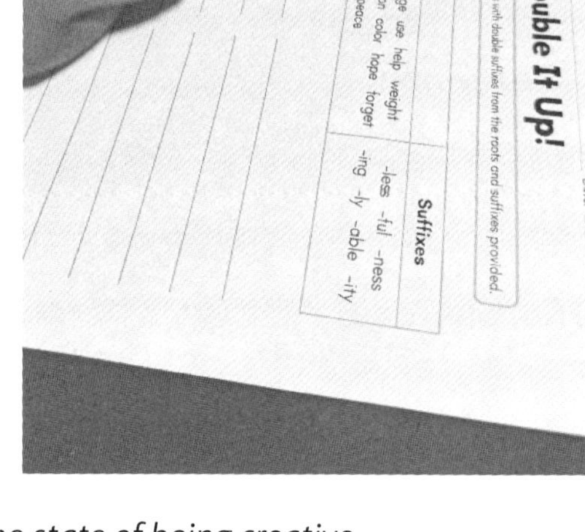

Review the definition of suffix, *a word part added to the end of a word that changes its meaning, part of speech, or tense*, and definitions of the following suffixes:

-less without / *fearless = without fear*

-ful full of / *joyful = full of joy*

-ness condition, state of, quality of / *kindness = the state of being kind*

-ing present participle / *running = the act of running*

-ly in a _____ way / *quickly = in a quick way*

-able able to/possible / *breakable = able to be broken*

-ity a state or condition / *creativity = the state of being creative*

Copy and distribute Double It Up! on page 205. Tell students they will focus on adding two suffixes to a single word. Ask students to create as many real "double suffix" words as possible from the list. Working with a partner, have them determine if their combinations formed actual words by sharing their thoughts and/or using an online resource.

Materials	Double It Up!, page 205
Grade Band	4–8
Length of Activity	15 minutes
Differentiation Ideas	**Striving Learners:** Model multiple examples out loud, such as: *If* questionable *is a word, is* questionableing*? No, that doesn't sound right, what about* questionably*? Yes, this could work.*
Extension Ideas	Have students add a new word or suffix to the Double It Up! sheet to create more words or to challenge another student with.
Answers	**Possible Answers:** thank: thankfulness, thanklessness, thankfully; faith: faithfulness, faithfully; care: carefulness, carefully; fear: fearfulness, fearfully; manage: manageability, manageably; use: usefulness, usefully; help: helpfulness, helplessness, helpfully; weight: weightlessness, weightily; power: powerfulness, powerlessness, powerfully; thought: thoughtfulness, thoughtfully, thoughtlessness; surprise: surprisingly; question: questionably; color: colorfulness, colorfully; forget: forgetfulness, forgetfully; enjoy: enjoyably; respect: respectfulness, respectfully; peace: peacefulness, peacefully

Name: ______________________ Date: ______________

Double It Up!

Directions: Create as many words as possible with double suffixes from the roots and suffixes provided.

Roots	Suffixes
thank faith care fear manage use help weight power thought surprise question color hope forget enjoy respect peace	-less -ful -ness -ing -ly -able -ity -y

CHAPTER 3
Student Tools for Determining Meaning

Strategies for Using Morphology

LANGUAGE DOMAINS

Reading

Writing

Speaking

Listening

3.N **Derivational Word Webs**

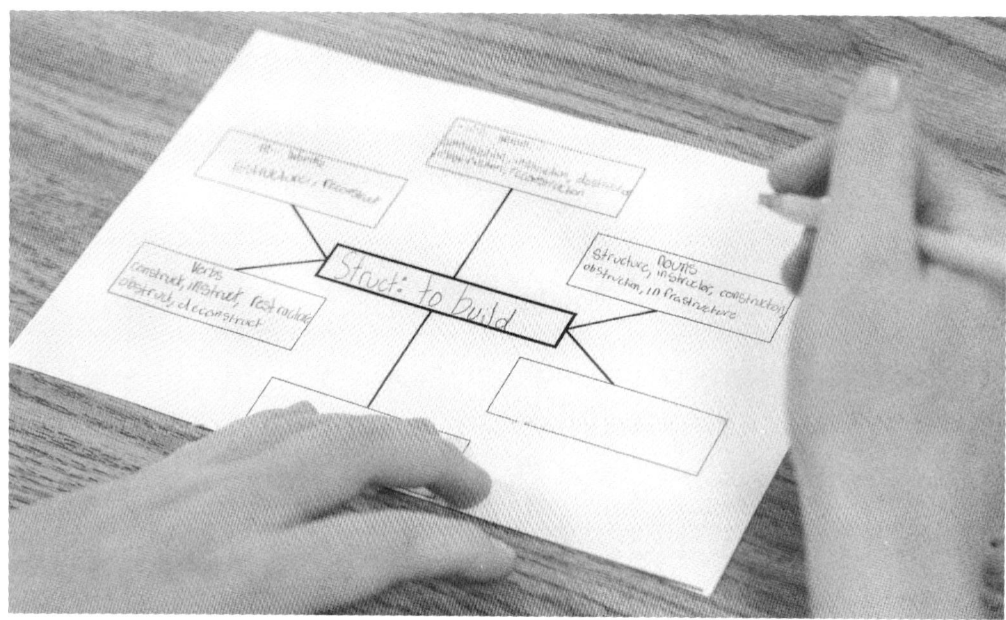

Copy and distribute the Word Web on page 207, and project a blank version for modeling. Have students write a root word in the center, such as *struct*, along with a brief definition. Label the surrounding boxes with categories such as "*-ion* words," "*re-* words," or "nouns" to guide word generation. See Word Part Suggestions on pages 208–209. As you model, provide examples and invite students to suggest words such as *construction*, *instruct*, *structure*, and *restructure*, discussing how affixes change meaning and/or parts of speech. Leave some boxes blank so students can create their own categories.

Materials	• Word Web, page 207 • Word Part Suggestions, pages 208–209
Grade Band	4–8
Length of Activity	10 minutes per activity
Differentiation Ideas	• **Striving Learners:** Provide a partially filled-in Word Web with some affixes of example words already listed. • **English Learners:** Provide a Word Bank with definitions, as well as a bilingual dictionary to support access to the words. • **Thriving Learners:** Invite students to create new categories based on affixes, parts of speech, or context.
Extension Ideas	• Discuss the meaning of each morpheme to deepen understanding. • Turn the strategy into a game where students take turns and earn points for each new word they think of within that category.
Answers	Answers integrated in Word Part Suggestions, pages 208–209

Name: ____________________ Date: __________

Word Web

Directions: Place a root word in the middle box and then fill in the surrounding boxes based on your teacher's instructions.

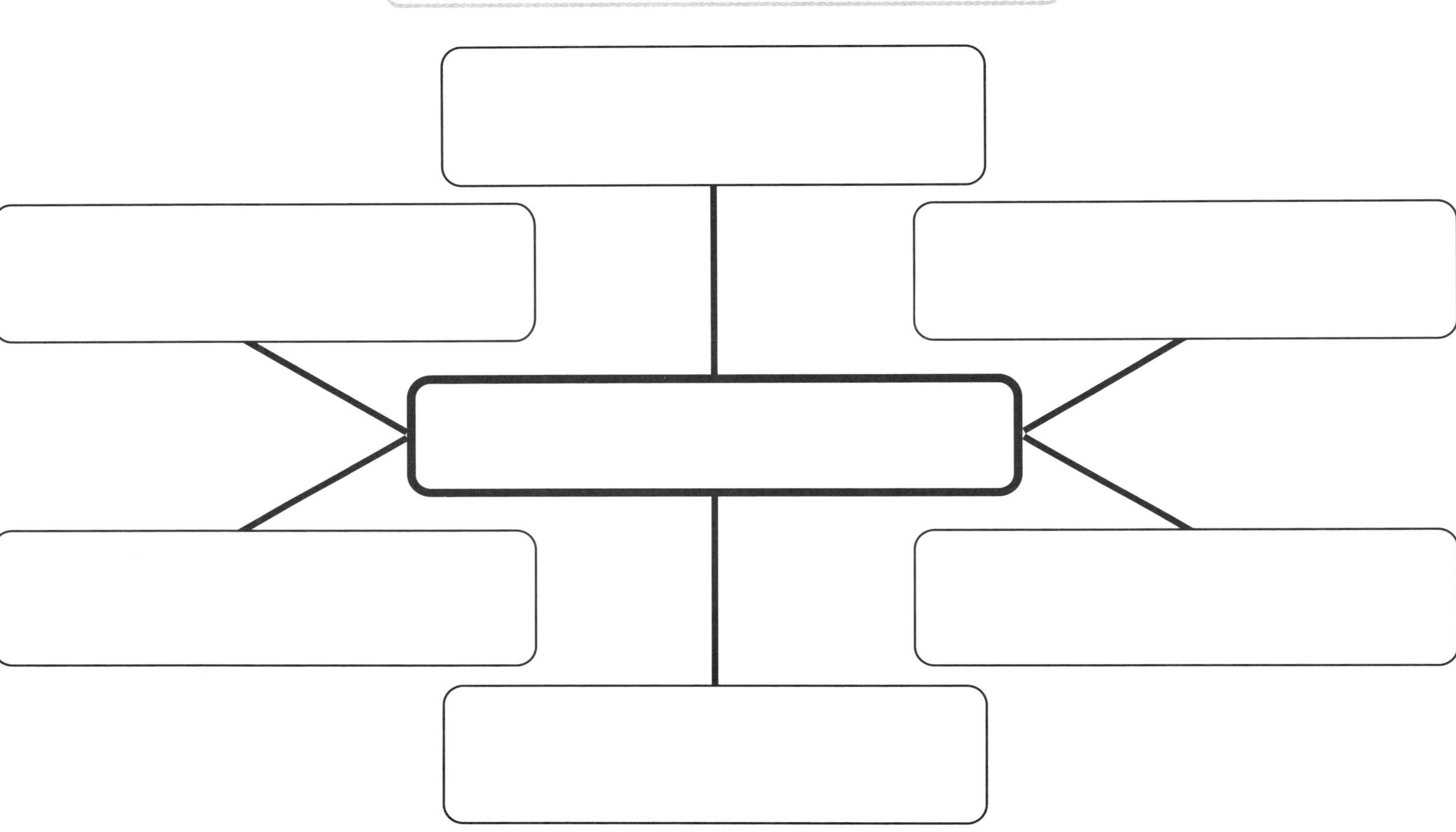

Word Part Suggestions

1. Root: **struct** *(to build)*
   - ***-ion* words:** construction, instruction, destruction, obstruction, reconstruction
   - ***re-* words:** restructure, reconstruct
   - **nouns:** structure, instructor, construction, obstruction, infrastructure
   - **verbs:** construct, instruct, restructure, obstruct, deconstruct

2. Root: **scrib/script** *(to write)*
   - ***pre-* words:** prescribe, prescription
   - ***-ion* words:** description, transcription, subscription, inscription, prescription
   - **jobs:** scribe, scriptwriter, transcriber, subscriber
   - **technology:** manuscript, typescript, transcript, postscript

3. Root: **port** *(to carry)*
   - **words with prefixes:** export, import, deport, comport, report
   - **words with suffixes:** portable, porter, portability
   - **nouns:** portfolio, porter, export, transport, import
   - **verbs:** report, support, transport, deport, import

4. Root: **vis/vid** *(to see)*
   - ***tele-* words:** television, televise, telecast, teleconference
   - **nouns:** division, visit, visitor, video
   - ***-ion* words:** vision, revision, supervision, provision, division
   - **adjectives:** visible, invisible, advisable

5. Root: **tract** *(to pull or drag)*
   - ***re-* words:** retract, retraction, retractable
   - **verbs:** attract, detract, extract, protract
   - **machines/tools:** tractor, extractor, retractor, protractor
   - ***-ion* words:** traction, distraction, retraction, contraction

6. Root: **mit/mis** *(to send)*
   - ***trans-* words:** transmit, transmission, transmittable
   - ***sub-* words:** submit, submission, submittal
   - **nouns:** mission, missile, omission, transmission
   - **verbs:** submit, emit, transmit, dismiss

7. Root: **rupt** *(to break)*
   - ***-ion* words:** eruption, corruption, interruption, disruption
   - **unexpected things:** eruption, interruption, abrupt event, disruption
   - **verbs:** erupt, disrupt, interrupt, bankrupt, rupture
   - **adjectives:** disruptive, corrupt, abrupt

8. Root: **ject** *(to throw)*
   - ***re-* words:** reject, reproject, rejection, rejected
   - ***-ion* words:** projection, rejection, ejection, objection
   - **tools/objects:** projector, injector, object
   - **adjectives:** dejected, subjective, objective

9. Root: **form** *(to shape)*
   - ***re-* words:** reform, reformat, reformulate
   - ***trans-* words:** transform, transformation, transformative, transformer
   - ***-ation* words:** formation, transformation, reformation, deformation
   - **art/design:** format, formation, uniform, conform

10. Root: **phon** *(sound)*
    - **tools/devices:** microphone, phonograph, megaphone, earphone
    - **words to describe sounds:** symphony, cacophony, euphony, polyphony
    - **nouns:** phoneme, telephone, cellphone, smartphone, saxophone
    - **adjectives:** euphonious, symphonic, phonological

11. Root: **cred** *(to believe, trust)*
    - ***-ible/-able* words:** credible, incredible, creditable
    - **nouns:** creed, creditor, incredulity, credence
    - **verbs:** accredit, discredit, credit, miscredit
    - **people:** credible witness, accredited agent, incredulous person
    - **adjectives:** credible, incredulous, creditworthy

12. Root: **spect** *(to look, see)*
    - ***re-* words:** respect, reinspection, retrospect
    - ***-ion* words:** inspection, reflection, introspection, prospection
    - **nouns:** spectator, spectacle, speculation, prospect
    - **verbs:** inspect, suspect, respect, introspect
    - **adjectives:** spectacular, prospective, introspective

CHAPTER 3

Student Tools for Determining Meaning

Strategies for Using Morphology

LANGUAGE DOMAINS

Reading

Writing

Speaking

Listening

3.0 Creating Words From Word Parts

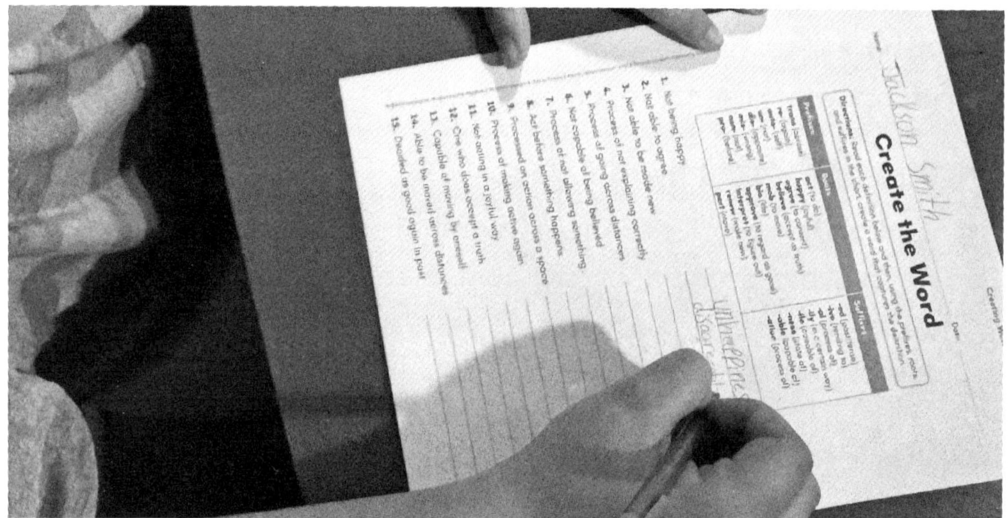

Copy and distribute Create the Word on page 211. Have students work in pairs to read each definition, then use one of each word part—prefix, root, and suffix—to create the word that matches the definition. The answers will each have one prefix, root, and suffix. Model the first one if necessary. Review answers with students to fix any errors.

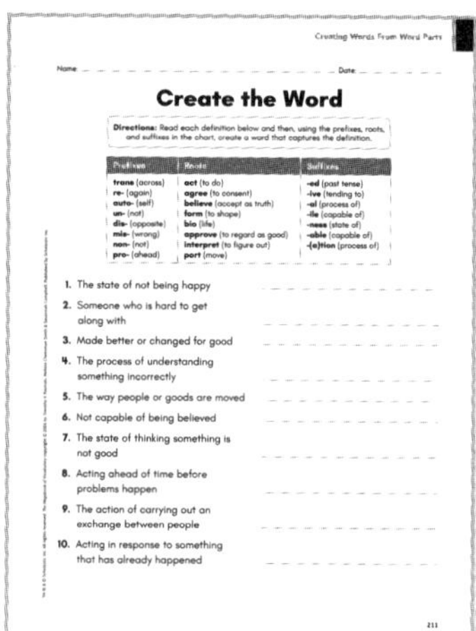

Creating Words From Word Parts

Name: __________ Date: __________

Create the Word

Directions: Read each definition below and then, using the prefixes, roots, and suffixes in the chart, create a word that captures the definition.

Prefixes	Roots	Suffixes
trans (across)	**act** (to do)	**-ed** (past tense)
re- (again)	**agree** (to consent)	**-ive** (tending to)
auto- (self)	**believe** (accept as truth)	**-al** (process of)
un- (not)	**form** (to shape)	**-ile** (capable of)
dis- (opposite)	**bio** (life)	**-ness** (state of)
mis- (wrong)	**approve** (to regard as good)	**-able** (capable of)
non- (not)	**interpret** (to figure out)	**-(a)tion** (process of)
pro- (ahead)	**port** (move)	

1. The state of not being happy __________
2. Someone who is hard to get along with __________
3. Made better or changed for good __________
4. The process of understanding something incorrectly __________
5. The way people or goods are moved __________
6. Not capable of being believed __________
7. The state of thinking something is not good __________
8. Acting ahead of time before problems happen __________
9. The action of carrying out an exchange between people __________
10. Acting in response to something that has already happened __________

211

Materials	Create the Word, page 211
Grade Band	4–8
Length of Activity	15 minutes
Differentiation Ideas	Have students come up with their own words from a set of prefixes, roots, or suffixes that you have been studying in class.
Extension Ideas	Have students think of other base words that they can transform into all other parts of speech.
Answers	**1.** unhappiness **2.** disagreeable **3.** reformed **4.** misinterpretation **5.** transportation **6.** unbelievable **7.** disapproval **8.** proactive **9.** transaction **10.** reactive

Name: ______________________ Date: ____________

Create the Word

Directions: Read each definition below and then, using the prefixes, roots, and suffixes in the chart, create a word that captures the definition.

Prefixes	Roots	Suffixes
trans (across) **re-** (again) **auto-** (self) **un-** (not) **dis-** (opposite) **mis-** (wrong) **non-** (not) **pro-** (ahead)	**act** (to do) **agree** (to consent) **believe** (accept as truth) **form** (to shape) **bio** (life) **approve** (to regard as good) **interpret** (to figure out) **port** (move)	**-ed** (past tense) **-ive** (tending to) **-al** (process of) **-ile** (capable of) **-ness** (state of) **-able** (capable of) **-(a)tion** (process of)

1. The state of not being happy ____________
2. Someone who is hard to get along with ____________
3. Made better or changed for good ____________
4. The process of understanding something incorrectly ____________
5. The way people or goods are moved ____________
6. Not capable of being believed ____________
7. The state of thinking something is not good ____________
8. Acting ahead of time before problems happen ____________
9. The action of carrying out an exchange between people ____________
10. Acting in response to something that has already happened ____________

Strategies for Using Morphology

LANGUAGE DOMAINS

Reading
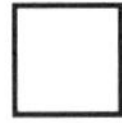

Writing

Speaking

Listening

3.P Morphology Word Chains

Provide students with dry-erase boards and markers. Have them write the first base word from the Morphology Chain Ideas on pages 213–215 at the top of their board. Then ask them to alter the word by adding or changing morphemes based on clues you give them, creating a list or chain of words. Model the first example, if needed.

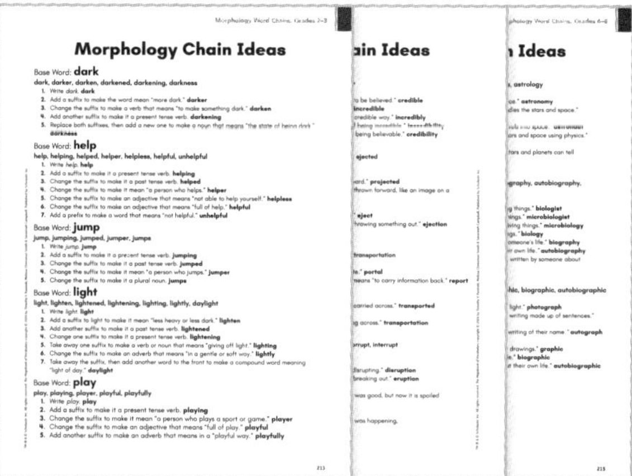

Morphology Word Chains, Grades 2–3

Morphology Chain Ideas

Base Word: **dark**
dark, darker, darken, darkened, darkening, darkness
1. Write *dark*. **dark**
2. Add a suffix to make the word mean "more dark." **darker**
3. Change the suffix to make a verb that means "to make something dark." **darken**
4. Add another suffix to make it a present tense verb. **darkening**
5. Replace both suffixes, then add a new one to make a noun that means "the state of being dark." **darkness**

Base Word: **help**
help, helping, helped, helper, helpless, helpful, unhelpful
1. Write *help*. **help**
2. Add a suffix to make it a present tense verb. **helping**
3. Change the suffix to make it a past tense verb. **helped**
4. Change the suffix to make it mean "a person who helps." **helper**
5. Change the suffix to make an adjective that means "not able to help yourself." **helpless**
6. Change the suffix to make an adjective that means "full of help." **helpful**
7. Add a prefix to make a word that means "not helpful." **unhelpful**

Base Word: **jump**
jump, jumping, jumped, jumper, jumps
1. Write *jump*. **jump**
2. Add a suffix to make it a present tense verb. **jumping**
3. Change the suffix to make it a past tense verb. **jumped**
4. Change the suffix to make it mean "a person who jumps." **jumper**
5. Change the suffix to make it a plural noun. **jumps**

Base Word: **light**
light, lighten, lightened, lightening, lighting, lightly, daylight
1. Write *light*. **light**
2. Add a suffix to light to make it mean "less heavy or less dark." **lighten**
3. Add another suffix to make it a past tense verb. **lightened**
4. Change one suffix to make it a present tense verb. **lightening**
5. Take away one suffix to make a verb or noun that means "giving off light." **lighting**
6. Change the suffix to make an adverb that means "in a gentle or soft way." **lightly**
7. Take away the suffix, then add another word to the front to make a compound word meaning "light of day." **daylight**

Base Word: **play**
play, playing, player, playful, playfully
1. Write *play*. **play**
2. Add a suffix to make it a present tense verb. **playing**
3. Change the suffix to make it mean "a person who plays a sport or game." **player**
4. Change the suffix to make an adjective that means "full of play." **playful**
5. Add another suffix to make an adverb that means in a "playful way." **playfully**

213

Materials	• Morphology Word Chain Ideas, Grades 2–3, page 213 • Morphology Word Chain Ideas, Grades 4–5, page 214 • Morphology Word Chain Ideas, Grades 6–8, page 215 • dry-erase boards and markers, enough for each student
Grade Band	2–8
Length of Activity	5–10 minutes each
Differentiation Ideas	• **Striving Learners and English Learners:** Give them a word bank to choose from. • **Striving Learners and English Learners:** Use color-coding to differentiate between prefixes, suffixes, and roots.
Extension Ideas	• Ask students to pick 2–3 words and write sentences for each one. • Give students a root, then ask them to come up with as many forms of the word as possible using that root.
Answers	Answers integrated on Morphology Chain Ideas, pages 213–215

Morphology Chain Ideas

Base Word: dark

dark, darker, darken, darkened, darkening, darkness

1. Write *dark*. **dark**
2. Add a suffix to make the word mean "more dark." **darker**
3. Change the suffix to make a verb that means "to make something dark." **darken**
4. Add another suffix to make it a present tense verb. **darkening**
5. Replace both suffixes, then add a new one to make a noun that means "the state of being dark." **darkness**

Base Word: help

help, helping, helped, helper, helpless, helpful, unhelpful

1. Write *help*. **help**
2. Add a suffix to make it a present tense verb. **helping**
3. Change the suffix to make it a past tense verb. **helped**
4. Change the suffix to make it mean "a person who helps." **helper**
5. Change the suffix to make an adjective that means "not able to help yourself." **helpless**
6. Change the suffix to make an adjective that means "full of help." **helpful**
7. Add a prefix to make a word that means "not helpful." **unhelpful**

Base Word: jump

jump, jumping, jumped, jumper, jumps

1. Write *jump*. **jump**
2. Add a suffix to make it a present tense verb. **jumping**
3. Change the suffix to make it a past tense verb. **jumped**
4. Change the suffix to make it mean "a person who jumps." **jumper**
5. Change the suffix to make it a plural noun. **jumps**

Base Word: light

light, lighten, lightened, lightening, lighting, lightly, daylight

1. Write *light*. **light**
2. Add a suffix to light to make it mean "less heavy or less dark." **lighten**
3. Add another suffix to make it a past tense verb. **lightened**
4. Change one suffix to make it a present tense verb. **lightening**
5. Take away one suffix to make a verb or noun that means "giving off light." **lighting**
6. Change the suffix to make an adverb that means "in a gentle or soft way." **lightly**
7. Take away the suffix, then add another word to the front to make a compound word meaning "light of day." **daylight**

Base Word: play

play, playing, player, playful, playfully

1. Write *play*. **play**
2. Add a suffix to make it a present tense verb. **playing**
3. Change the suffix to make it mean "a person who plays a sport or game." **player**
4. Change the suffix to make an adjective that means "full of play." **playful**
5. Add another suffix to make an adverb that means in a "playful way." **playfully**

Morphology Chain Ideas

Root: **cred**

credit, credible, incredible, incredibly, incredibility, credibility

1. Write *credit.* **credit**
2. Change the suffix to make an adjective that means "able to be believed." **credible**
3. Add a prefix to make a word that means "not believable." **incredible**
4. Add another suffix to make an adverb that means "in an incredible way." **incredibly**
5. Change the suffix to make a noun that means "the state of being incredible." **incredibility**
6. Remove the prefix to make a noun the means "the state of being believable." **credibility**

Root: **ject**

reject, rejected, projected, projection, project, eject, ejection, ejected

1. Write *reject.* **reject**
2. Add a suffix to make it past tense. **rejected**
3. Change the prefix to make a word that means "threw forward." **projected**
4. Change the suffix to make a noun that means "something thrown forward, like an image on a screen." **projection**
5. Remove the suffix. **project**
6. Change the prefix to make a word that means "throw out." **eject**
7. Change the suffix to make a noun that means "the act of throwing something out." **ejection**
8. Change the suffix to make the verb past tense. **ejected**

Root: **port**

port, portal, report, import, imported, transported, transport, transportation

1. Write *port.* **port**
2. Add a suffix to make a noun that means "a doorway or gate." **portal**
3. Remove the suffix, then add a prefix to make a word that means "to carry information back." **report**
4. Change the prefix to mean "to carry in." **import**
5. Add a suffix to make the verb past tense. **imported**
6. Change the prefix to make a past tense verb that means "carried across." **transported**
7. Remove the suffix. **transport**
8. Add a suffix to make a noun that means "the act of carrying across." **transportation**

Root: **rupt**

disrupt, disrupted, disruption, eruption, erupted, corrupted, corrupt, interrupt

1. Write *disrupt.* **disrupt**
2. Add a suffix to make the verb past tense. **disrupted**
3. Change the suffix to make a noun that means "the act of disrupting." **disruption**
4. Change the prefix to make a noun that means "the act of breaking out." **eruption**
5. Change the suffix to make a past tense verb. **erupted**
6. Change the prefix to make a word that means "something was good, but now it is spoiled or turned bad." **corrupted**
7. Remove the suffix. **corrupt**
8. Change the prefix to make a word that means "something was happening, but it got stopped in the middle." **interrupted**

Morphology Chain Ideas

Root: **astro**

astronomical, astronomy, astronomer, astronaut, astrophysics, astrology

1. Write *astronomical.* **astronomical**
2. Change the suffix to make a noun for "the study of stars and space." **astronomy**
3. Change the suffix to make a word that means "a person who studies the stars and space." **astronomer**
4. Change the suffix to make a word that means "a person who travels into space." **astronaut**
5. Change the ending to make a noun for "a science that studies stars and space using physics." **astrophysics**
6. Change the ending to make a noun that means "the belief that stars and planets can tell the future or explain people's lives." **astrology**

Root: **bio**

biological, biologist, microbiologist, microbiology, biology, biography, autobiography, autobiographical

1. Write *biological.* **biological**
2. Change one suffix to make a noun for "a person who studies living things." **biologist**
3. Add a root to make a noun for "a person who studies tiny living things." **microbiologist**
4. Change the suffix to make a noun that means "the study of tiny living things." **microbiology**
5. Remove the beginning to make a noun for "the study of living things." **biology**
6. Change the ending to make a noun for "a book that tells about someone's life." **biography**
7. Add a root to make a noun for "a book someone writes about their own life." **autobiography**
8. Change the ending to make an adjective that means "something written by someone about their own life." **autobiographical**

Root: **graph**

photography, photograph, paragraph, autograph, graph, graphic, biographic, autobiographic

1. Write *photography.* **photography**
2. Remove the suffix to make a noun meaning "a picture made with light." **photograph**
3. Change the beginning form to make a noun meaning "a piece of writing made up of sentences." **paragraph**
4. Change the beginning to make a noun meaning "a person's own writing of their name." **autograph**
5. Remove the beginning to return to the root. **graph**
6. Add a suffix to make an adjective meaning "shown by pictures or drawings." **graphic**
7. Add a root to make an adjective that means "about someone's life." **biographic**
8. Add a root to make an adjective meaning "someone writing about their own life." **autobiographic**

LANGUAGE DOMAINS

Reading

Writing

Speaking

Listening

3.Q Root Trees

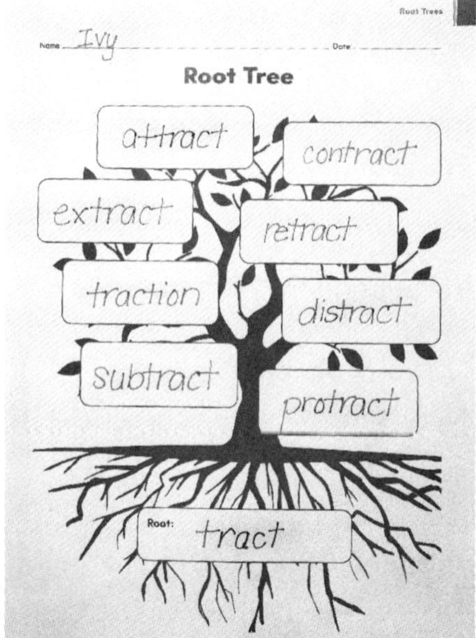

Students will explore roots and words that contain them. Choose a root from Word Lists for Root Trees on page 218, then copy and distribute the Root Tree graphic organizer on page 217. Have students write the root and its definition in the box at the bottom of the tree. Then, with students, generate words that contain the root and write those words in the boxes in branches of the tree, using the Word Lists for Root Trees as a reference. Discuss the meaning of the words as you add them to the tree.

A Spanish example for English Learners is given below.

Materials	• Root Tree graphic organizer, page 217 • Word Lists for Root Trees, page 218
Grade Band	4–8
Length of Activity	15 minutes
Differentiation Ideas	• **Striving Learners:** Have students work in pairs or small groups to brainstorm words that contain the given root and discuss how each word connects to the root, reinforcing their placement on the word tree. • **English Learners:** When appropriate, allow students to add words in their first language, for example allow them to add *describir* and *escritura* to a "scrib" root tree.
Extension Ideas	When they've completed their Root Trees, have students place them inside a vocabulary binder. If they find new words with a specific root, have them revisit their trees to add those words.
Answers	Answers integrated into Word Lists for Root Trees, page 218

Name: Date:

Root Tree

Word Lists for Root Trees

Root: **aud** (to hear)

Words for Branches: audible, audience, audition, auditorium, auditory, inaudible, audiology, audiovisual, audio

Root: **cred** (to believe)

Words for Branches: credit, credential, credible, credibility, incredible, credence, discredit, accreditation, creditor, miscredited

Root: **dict** (to say, tell)

Words for Branches: predict, dictate, dictionary, contradict, verdict, benediction, dictation, indict, prediction, dictator

Root: **fer** (to carry)

Words for Branches: transfer, refer, confer, infer, prefer, referred, defer, differ, inference, suffering

Root: **form** (to shape)

Words for Branches: transform, inform, reform, conform, deform, formation, uniform, formulate, informant, formal

Root: **ject** (to throw)

Words for Branches: eject, reject, dejected, rejection, project, inject, subjective, projection, objection, trajectory

Root: **mit, mis** (to send)

Words for Branches: submit, permission, emit, admit, dismiss, remit, transmission, mission, submission, intermission

Root: **port** (to carry)

Words for Branches: transport, import, export, support, deport, report, portable, portfolio, porter, transportation

Root: **rupt** (to break)

Words for Branches: disrupt, interrupt, erupt, rupture, corrupt, abrupt, bankruptcy, corruptible

Root: **scribe, script** (to write)

Words for Branches: inscribe, description, prescription, manuscript, subscribe, scribble, transcribe, proscribe, subscription, postscript

Root: **spect** (to look)

Words for Branches: inspector, inspect, respect, prospective, spectator, spectacle, introspection, perspective, retrospect, speculate

Root: **struct** (to build)

Words for Branches: construct, destruct, structure, instruction, reconstruction, obstruction, infrastructure, constructor, restructure, destruction

Root: **therm** (heat)

Words for Branches: thermometer, thermal, thermostat, geothermal, hypothermia, thermodynamics, endothermic, exothermic

Root: **tract** (to pull)

Words for Branches: attract, retract, extract, contract, distract, traction, subtract, protract, tractor, contraction

Root: **vis, vid** (to see)

Words for Branches: vision, visible, visual, evidence, revise, supervise, television, provision, visibility, envision

Root: **phil, phile** (love)

Words for Branches: philosophy, philosopher philanthropist, bibliophile, anglophile, philosopher, francophile

Root: **bio** (life)

Words for Branches: biography, autobiography, biology, biologist, antibiotic, biomass

3.R **Be the Bard: Morphemes Create Words!**

Students explore language creatively by inventing words, just as William Shakespeare did. Using the Prefixes, Roots, and Suffixes lists on pages 184–186, have students combine any word parts with existing words to form unique, original words. Encourage them to be silly and creative! Share some examples to get them going: **automand** *an order that one gives to himself or herself*, **terrameter** *a device for measuring land*, and **contraduct** *to lead a group against another group*. After creating their words, ask students to share them and their definitions. This strategy (Rasinski et al., 2011) encourages students to experiment with language like true wordsmiths.

Materials	• Prefixes, page 184 • Roots, page 185 • Suffixes, page 186
Grade Band	4–8
Length of Activity	15 minutes
Differentiation Ideas	**Striving Learners and English Learners:** Model a think-aloud process for creating words that will help guide them. Focus on the "creative" part and make sure it is clear these are made-up words, so there is no right and wrong.
Extension Ideas	• Allow students to create a drawing of their word and definition for classroom display. • Challenge students to use their newly created word at home with friends or family and see if anyone asks about it in conversation, then students can report back the next day.

LANGUAGE DOMAINS

Reading

Writing

Speaking

Listening

Strategies for Using Morphology

LANGUAGE DOMAINS

Reading

Writing

Speaking

Listening

3.S **Vocabulary Sussers: Guess the Definition**

When students encounter a challenging word, they can use word parts, as well as context clues, to help break down the word's meaning, and this strategy combines both those important skills. Explain that *suss* is a fun British word that means to "realize or discover something." (Ness & Miles, 2025). Tell the students they will be the "sussers" today, which means they will be attempting to unlock the meaning of some very challenging words, but no worries—they will have clues to help! Put students in small groups and provide small dry-erase boards and markers. Display Vocabulary Sussers Words on page 221 with just the first row containing the word, definitions of the two word parts, and the sentence showing. Give groups a minute or so to discuss the information and come up with a definition for the word and write it on a dry-erase board to display. Reveal the correct answer and acknowledge any group that "sussed it out" with an acceptable definition by giving them a point! Continue with the remaining seven words and determine a winner! (Strategy inspired by Molly Ness and Katie Pace Miles's *Making Words Stick*.)

Vocabulary Sussers: Guess the Definition

Vocabulary Sussers Words

Word	Word Parts	Sentence	Definition
circumspect	**circum-** (around) **spect** (to look)	Knowing how quickly things could go wrong, Jenna remained **circumspect** as she considered her options before responding.	cautious; thinking carefully about risks
intractable	**in-** (not) **tract** (to pull)	No matter how many strategies the coach tried, the team's behavior remained **intractable**, frustrating every effort to bring order.	hard to manage or control
perspicacious	**per-** (through) **spic** (to look)	Only the most **perspicacious** readers noticed the subtle hint the author dropped in the second chapter.	mentally sharp, able to notice and understand things easily
ebullient	**e-** (out) **bullire** (to boil)	Jamie's **ebullient** personality made the room feel brighter the moment she walked in, even on a gloomy Monday.	full of energy and enthusiasm
irrevocable	**re-** (again) **voc** (to call)	Once the decision was made public, it became **irrevocable**, no matter how much public opinion shifted.	cannot be changed or undone
equanimity	**equ-** (equal) **anim** (mind/spirit)	While others panicked, Trevor faced the sudden change with **equanimity**, his tone and manner unchanged.	calmness, especially under pressure
magnanimous	**magn-** (great) **anim** (soul/spirit)	Though the mistake cost her the promotion, she remained **magnanimous**, congratulating her colleague with genuine warmth.	generous or forgiving, especially toward a rival
obfuscate	**ob-** (toward) **fusc** (dark)	The technical language seemed to **obfuscate** the real issue, leaving even experienced readers unsure of what to think.	to make unclear or confusing

221

Materials	• Vocabulary Sussers Words, page 221 • dry-erase boards and markers
Grade Band	4–8
Length of Activity	15–20 minutes
Differentiation Ideas	**Striving Learners and English Learners:** Provide the word parts and sentence written so it can be referred back to when discussing. Use cognates if available.
Extension Ideas	Have students write their own sentences or give more examples of how the Vocabulary Sussers Words can be used for bonus points.
Answers	Answers integrated on Vocabulary Sussers Words, page 221

Vocabulary Sussers Words

Word	Word Parts	Sentence	Definition
circumspect	**circum-** (around) **spect** (to look)	Knowing how quickly things could go wrong, Jenna remained **circumspect** as she considered her options before responding.	cautious; thinking carefully about risks
intractable	**in-** (not) **tract** (to pull)	No matter how many strategies the coach tried, the team's behavior remained **intractable**, frustrating every effort to bring order.	hard to manage or control
perspicacious	**per-** (through) **spic** (to look)	Only the most **perspicacious** readers noticed the subtle hint the author dropped in the second chapter.	mentally sharp, able to notice and understand things easily
ebullient	**e-** (out) **bullire** (to boil)	Jamie's **ebullient** personality made the room feel brighter the moment she walked in, even on a gloomy Monday.	full of energy and enthusiasm
irrevocable	**re-** (again) **voc** (to call)	Once the decision was made public, it became **irrevocable**, no matter how much public opinion shifted.	cannot be changed or undone
equanimity	**equ-** (equal) **anim** (mind/spirit)	While others panicked, Trevor faced the sudden change with **equanimity**, his tone and manner unchanged.	calmness, especially under pressure
magnanimous	**magn-** (great) **anim** (soul/spirit)	Though the mistake cost her the promotion, she remained **magnanimous**, congratulating her colleague with genuine warmth.	generous or forgiving, especially toward a rival
obfuscate	**ob-** (toward) **fusc** (dark)	The technical language seemed to **obfuscate** the real issue, leaving even experienced readers unsure of what to think.	to make unclear or confusing

CHAPTER 3
Student Tools for Determining Meaning

Strategies for Using Morphology

LANGUAGE DOMAINS

Reading

Writing

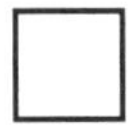

Speaking

Listening

3.T **Word Origins: A Word a Day!**

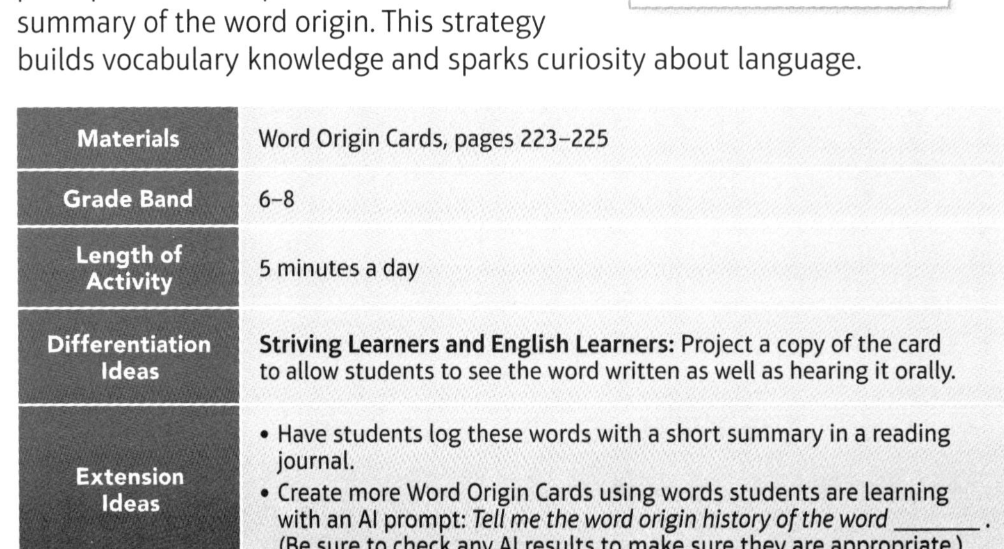

Etymology, the study of word histories, helps students understand where words come from and how they evolve across time and cultures. Copy and cut apart the Word Origin Cards on pages 223–225, and have one student select a card and read it aloud. Have students repeat the word before you read about its origin and again after you've read about it. Then have students pair up and come up with a one-sentence summary of the word origin. This strategy builds vocabulary knowledge and sparks curiosity about language.

Materials	Word Origin Cards, pages 223–225
Grade Band	6–8
Length of Activity	5 minutes a day
Differentiation Ideas	**Striving Learners and English Learners:** Project a copy of the card to allow students to see the word written as well as hearing it orally.
Extension Ideas	• Have students log these words with a short summary in a reading journal. • Create more Word Origin Cards using words students are learning with an AI prompt: *Tell me the word origin history of the word* _______ . (Be sure to check any AI results to make sure they are appropriate.)

Word Origin Cards

goodbye

The word ***goodbye*** evolved from the phrase **"God be with ye,"** which was commonly used in the 16th century as a farewell blessing. Over time, people began shortening it in speech, turning it into ***God b'w'ye*** and later into ***good-b'wy***. The influence of similar greetings like ***good day*** and ***good night*** likely caused a shift, transforming it into the modern spelling ***goodbye***. This change reflects how language evolves through frequent use, convenience, and pronunciation shifts over generations.

robot

The word ***robot*** comes from the Czech word ***robota***, meaning "forced labor" or "drudgery." It was first introduced in the 1920 play ***R.U.R. (Rossum's Universal Robots)***. The play depicted artificial humanoid workers created to serve humans, but they eventually rebelled. Although the concept of artificial beings existed before, ***robot*** became the widely accepted term for mechanical workers.

nightmare

Originally, ***nightmare*** had nothing to do with bad dreams. The word ***mare*** referred to a folklore creature believed to have sat on sleeping people's chests, causing suffocation and terror. The term ***night-mare*** came to describe the sensation of sleep paralysis or disturbing visions associated with supernatural forces. Over centuries, as scientific understanding of sleep grew, ***nightmare*** shifted from meaning an actual demonic entity to simply a frightening dream.

salary

The word ***salary*** comes from the Latin word ***salarium***, which referred to the payments made to Roman soldiers for the purchase of salt, a valuable commodity in ancient times. Over time, the term evolved to represent a regular payment or compensation for work, even though salt itself was no longer involved. The connection to salt highlights its historical importance in trade and sustenance.

quarantine

Quarantine comes from the Italian word ***quaranta***, meaning "forty." During the Black Plague in the 14th century, ships arriving in Venice were required to anchor for forty days to ensure they weren't carrying the disease. The practice was called "**quaranta giorni**" (forty days), and the term gradually came to refer to any period of isolation to prevent the spread of disease.

panic

The word ***panic*** has its roots in Greek mythology. It is named after Pan, the god of the wild, shepherds, and flocks. Pan was believed to cause sudden, irrational fear in people, especially in isolated or wild places. This fear, often characterized by confusion and hysteria, became known as ***panic***, reflecting the overwhelming, uncontrollable emotions it provoked.

ostracize

In ancient Athens, Greece, citizens could vote to banish a person from the city for 10 years. They didn't use paper; they wrote the name of the person they wanted to kick out on a broken piece of pottery, called an ***ostrakon***. If enough people voted for someone to be banished, they were ***ostracized***.

geek

The term ***geek*** originally referred to a circus performer in the early 20th century, particularly one who would perform bizarre acts such as biting the heads off chickens. This use of ***geek*** comes from the old English dialect word ***geck***, meaning a "fool" or "simpleton." Over time, the word evolved into a label for people who were highly focused on specialized knowledge or technology, shedding its negative connotations in favor of a more positive, if quirky, identity.

sinister

The word ***sinister*** comes from the Latin word ***sinister***, meaning "left" or "on the left side." In ancient times, left-handedness was considered unlucky or even evil, leading to the word ***sinister*** being associated with bad or ominous occurrences. Over time, ***sinister*** came to describe anything threatening, harmful, or evil, though its original connection to left-handedness remains in the language.

clue

Clue comes from the Old English word ***clew***, meaning "a ball of thread." This word is related to the myth of Theseus and the Minotaur. In the myth, Ariadne gives Theseus a ball of thread (a ***clew***) to help him find his way out of the labyrinth. Over time, ***clew*** evolved into ***clue*** and came to represent anything that helps solve a puzzle or mystery.

genius

Genius originates from the Latin word ***genius***, referring to a guiding spirit or guardian deity. The Romans believed every person had a ***genius*** that influenced their character and fate. Over time, the word came to refer to exceptional intellectual or creative ability, as people began associating the idea of extraordinary talents with the influence of a powerful inner spirit.

lunatic

Lunatic comes from the Latin word ***lunaticus***, meaning "moonstruck," derived from ***luna***, meaning "moon." Ancient people believed that the phases of the moon could influence mental health, particularly causing madness or erratic behavior. The word originally referred to people whose mental states seemed to fluctuate with the moon, and over time, it evolved to describe someone exhibiting extreme or irrational behavior.

muscle

Muscle comes from the Latin word ***musculus***, which means "little mouse." The term was used to describe the shape and movement of muscles, as people thought muscles resembled small mice moving under the skin. This comparison to a mouse is still reflected in the modern scientific name for muscles.

fiasco

The word ***fiasco*** comes from the Italian phrase "**far fiasco**," meaning "to make a bottle" or "to fail badly." It is believed to have originated in the glass-making trade, where a defective bottle was said to be a ***fiasco***. Over time, the term broadened to refer to any complete failure or disaster, especially one that happens in a dramatic or public manner.

sabotage

Sabotage comes from the French word ***sabot***, meaning "a wooden shoe" or "clog." In the 19th century, workers reportedly threw their wooden shoes into machines to stop them from working, or "sabotaged" them. The term evolved to mean any deliberate act of destruction or disruption, especially in a workplace or industrial context.

sympathy

Sympathy comes from the Greek word ***sympatheia***, meaning "fellow feeling" or "compassion." It is formed from ***sym-*** (together) and ***pathos*** (feeling), and originally referred to a sense of shared emotion or understanding between people. Over time, it came to specifically refer to feelings of care and compassion for another's misfortune.

Chapter 4 downloadables are available here.

CHAPTER 4

Exploration of Word Relationships

"Human vocabulary is still not capable, and probably never will be, of knowing, recognizing, and communicating everything that can be humanly experienced and felt."

—José Saramago

Building vocabulary is not only about teaching students strategies for finding the meaning of words they don't know, but also about deepening their understanding of words they do know (Schmitt, 2014). It's important for us to focus on the *depth* as well as the *breadth* of word knowledge. To do that, Beck & McKeown (2007b) recommend immersing students in "relationships among words," which includes understanding types of words, such as synonyms, antonyms, and homonyms, as well as word-related concepts such as multiple meanings, word categories, figurative language, nuances, analogies, and connotations. This kind of deeper exploration of words helps students make connections between words and concepts, fostering a richer understanding of language (Greenwood & Flanigan, 2007; Nation, 2013). For example, teaching students nuances of words such as *happy* and *joyful* or *angry* and *furious* can significantly enhance their comprehension of words when they read and listen, as well as their use of words when they write and speak.

Exploring word relationships is especially critical for English learners. As Beck & McKeown (2007b) note, word relationships such as multiple-meaning words (*bank* as a financial institution versus *bank* of a river) and idioms (*Hold your horses!*) can be confusing for English learners. These linguistic complexities can create barriers to comprehension and communication and must be explicitly taught.

When we focus on word relationships, we provide all students with essential tools for academic success. By helping students make connections between words and concepts, we allow them to gain a more nuanced understanding of the English language, enabling them to read, write, speak, and listen more confidently. Effective vocabulary instruction is not just about teaching students new words, but also equipping them with the strategies they need to navigate the complexities of language and succeed academically.

Common Word Relationships

Grades Kindergarten and 1

- simple multiple-meaning words
- sorting objects into categories
- naming attributes of a category
- synonyms and antonyms
- words and uses: *Can you name some objects that are rounded?*
- simple shades of meaning (verbs): *see* vs. *stare*
- simple shades of meaning (adjectives): *small* vs. *tiny*
- simple conjunctions to show relationships: *and, but, because*

Grades 2 and 3

- multiple-meaning words
- literal vs. nonliteral meanings: *bright idea*
- words and uses: *Who are hardworking people?*
- shades of meaning (state of mind): *surprised, shocked, stunned*
- shades of meaning (degree of certainty): *maybe, probably, definitely*
- specific adjectives and adverbs: *fuzzy, sticky, gently, bravely*
- words showing spatial relationships: *between, under*
- words showing temporal relationships: *later, soon*

Grades 4 and 5

- multiple-meaning words
- similes and metaphors
- idioms, adages, proverbs
- synonyms and antonyms
- words that signal precise actions and emotions: *stomp, relieved*
- words that signal states of being: *exist, survive*
- words that signal contrast: *although, however*
- words particular to a content-area topic: *renewable, solar*

Grades 6 and 8

- multiple-meaning words
- figures of speech (personification, allusions, irony, puns)
- analogies (part/whole, cause and effect)
- positive and negative connotations

Strategies for Understanding Relationships Among Words

LANGUAGE DOMAINS

Reading

Writing

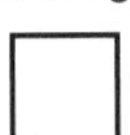

Speaking

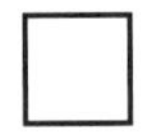

Listening

4.A **Multiple-Meaning Picture Match-Up**

When first learning a word, students often have a limited, single-meaning understanding of it. This strategy aims to expand that understanding by prompting students to identify a second meaning of a target word. Provide student pairs a set of Multiple-Meaning Picture Cards on page 229. Call out one word from the list: *bat*, *bark*, *ring*, *duck*, *jam*, *watch*, or *spring*, and have student pairs find two pictures that capture the meaning of that word.

Materials	Multiple-Meaning Picture Cards, page 229
Grade Band	K–1
Length of Activity	15–20 minutes
Differentiation Ideas	• **Striving Learners and English Learners:** Pre-teach the pictures before the activity, so that students know the names of the pictures beforehand. Encourage students to name the word in their home language, while you introduce the term in English. • **Thriving Learners:** Provide additional and more challenging multiple-meaning words and ask students to create images for another picture match-up with the class.
Extension Ideas	Play charades: Have students draw one of the Multiple-Meaning Word Cards out of a hat and act out the word for their classmates to guess.
Answers	**bat:** equipment used in baseball, a flying animal; **bark:** sound a dog makes, outer layer of a tree; **ring:** a piece of jewelry, a bell making a sound; **duck:** a water bird, the act of crouching down; **jam:** a fruit spread, a traffic backup; **watch:** a clock for your wrist, a person looking at something; **spring:** a season after winter when flowers grow, a metal coil

Multiple-Meaning Picture Cards

bat	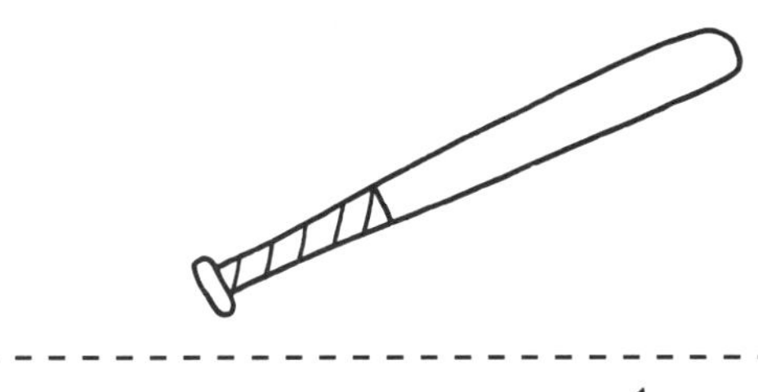	
bark		
ring	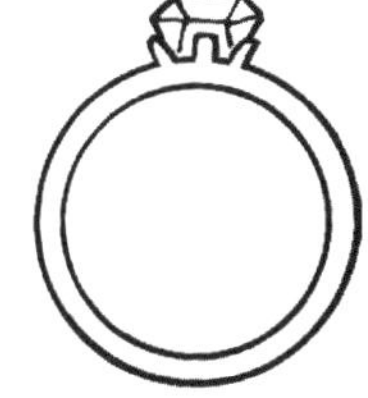	
duck		
jam		
watch		
spring		

CHAPTER 4

Exploration of Word Relationships

Strategies for Understanding Relationships Among Words

LANGUAGE DOMAINS

Reading

Writing

☐

Speaking

Listening

4.B Category Connections

This oral vocabulary strategy prompts students to make connections between categories and words within those categories. Present students with a category, such as Things That Are Cold, and have them turn to a partner or small group and take turns naming words that belong in that category.

Potential Categories: Colors, Animals, Foods, Drinks, Shapes, Numbers, Sports, Tools, Musical Instruments, Musicians, Things in the Kitchen, Things in the Bathroom, Things at the Beach, Things in the Forest, Toys, Items of Clothing, Farm Animals, Ocean Animals, Zoo Animals, Pets, Healthy Foods, Unhealthy Foods, Cold Things, Hot Things, Types of Weather, Types of Transportation, Sticky Things, Things You See on the Way to School, Things You See at School

Materials	teacher-chosen word categories
Grade Band	K–1
Length of Activity	10–15 minutes
Differentiation Ideas	• **English Learners:** Provide a set of pictures that fit the target category and allow them to tell you the name of the objects in their native language, then tell them the object's name in English. During the activity, invite students to share the name of objects in their native language with the class. • **Thriving Learners:** Add parameters: Ask students to tell you only words that fit the category that start with a particular letter (rolling a letter dice) or words that describe things that are a particular color (use a color wheel).
Extension Ideas	List three words in a category and have students figure out the name of the category, like *ball, car, doll* (toys) or *apple, banana, grapes* (fruits).

4.C Mystery Antonyms Box

This strategy introduces young learners to antonyms in a hands-on way. Place a variety of objects or pictures inside a "Mystery Antonyms Box." See Ideas for the Mystery Antonyms Box on page 232 for ideas. Then allow each student or small group of students to take turns pulling out an object or picture and describing it. Prompt them for specific attributes using guided questions or sentence starters. For example, if a student pulls out a toy car, prompt them to recognize it as something that is *fast*, so the opposite would be something that is *slow*. Once students have described an object or picture's attributes, ask them to search for classmates with an object or picture that represents the opposite of theirs. Follow up by writing all the antonyms on an anchor chart for future reference.

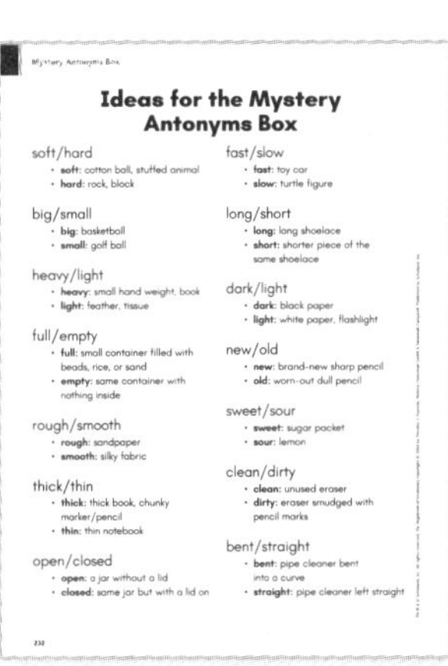

Mystery Antonyms Box

Ideas for the Mystery Antonyms Box

soft/hard
- **soft**: cotton ball, stuffed animal
- **hard**: rock, block

big/small
- **big**: basketball
- **small**: golf ball

heavy/light
- **heavy**: small hand weight, book
- **light**: feather, tissue

full/empty
- **full**: small container filled with beads, rice, or sand
- **empty**: same container with nothing inside

rough/smooth
- **rough**: sandpaper
- **smooth**: silky fabric

thick/thin
- **thick**: thick book, chunky marker/pencil
- **thin**: thin notebook

open/closed
- **open**: a jar without a lid
- **closed**: same jar but with a lid on

fast/slow
- **fast**: toy car
- **slow**: turtle figure

long/short
- **long**: long shoelace
- **short**: shorter piece of the same shoelace

dark/light
- **dark**: black paper
- **light**: white paper, flashlight

new/old
- **new**: brand-new sharp pencil
- **old**: worn-out dull pencil

sweet/sour
- **sweet**: sugar packet
- **sour**: lemon

clean/dirty
- **clean**: unused eraser
- **dirty**: eraser smudged with pencil marks

bent/straight
- **bent**: pipe cleaner bent into a curve
- **straight**: pipe cleaner left straight

232

Materials	• Ideas for the Mystery Antonyms Box, page 232 • box • chart paper • pictures or objects that represent antonyms
Grade Band	K–1
Length of Activity	25 minutes
Differentiation Ideas	**Striving Learners and English Learners:** Use sentence frames to help students find the antonym. For example, you could lead them to say: "This cotton ball is soft. This rock is _____."
Extension Ideas	• Have students create antonym riddles: "I'm thinking of an object. It is not big, it is not soft. My object is _____." • Take students outside and let them find real-world antonyms (a big leaf and a small rock, a puddle and a dry patch of grass, etc.).

Strategies for Understanding Relationships Among Words

LANGUAGE DOMAINS

Reading

Writing

Speaking

Listening

Ideas for the Mystery Antonyms Box

soft/hard

- **soft:** cotton ball, stuffed animal
- **hard:** rock, block

big/small

- **big:** basketball
- **small:** golf ball

heavy/light

- **heavy:** small hand weight, book
- **light:** feather, tissue

full/empty

- **full:** small container filled with beads, rice, or sand
- **empty:** same container with nothing inside

rough/smooth

- **rough:** sandpaper
- **smooth:** silky fabric

thick/thin

- **thick:** thick book, chunky marker/pencil
- **thin:** thin notebook

open/closed

- **open:** a jar without a lid
- **closed:** same jar but with a lid on

fast/slow

- **fast:** toy car
- **slow:** turtle figure

long/short

- **long:** long shoelace
- **short:** shorter piece of the same shoelace

dark/light

- **dark:** black paper
- **light:** white paper, flashlight

new/old

- **new:** brand-new sharp pencil
- **old:** worn-out dull pencil

sweet/sour

- **sweet:** sugar packet
- **sour:** lemon

clean/dirty

- **clean:** unused eraser
- **dirty:** eraser smudged with pencil marks

bent/straight

- **bent:** pipe cleaner bent into a curve
- **straight:** pipe cleaner left straight

4.D Time Words and Phrases

Temporal words and phrases relate to time and are used to communicate the sequence of events in a story or series of actions. Explain the importance of using temporal words and phrases to capture when things happen. Then project and review the Time Words and Phrases Reference Sheet on page 234, and pair up students to come up with a sentence orally to describe each Time Vocabulary picture on page 235. Encourage students to include at least one temporal word or phrase in their sentences.

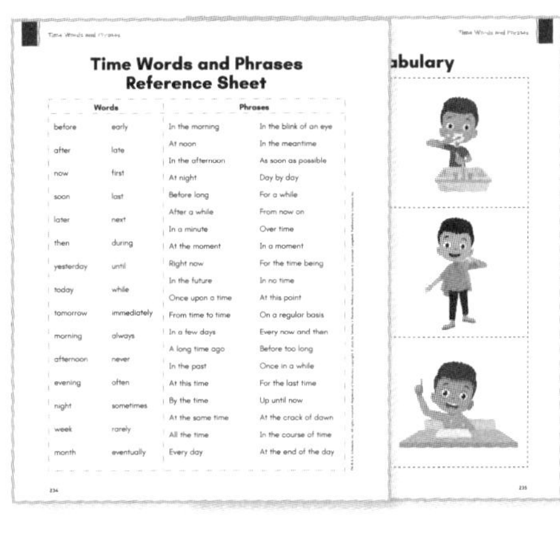

Time Words and Phrases

Time Words and Phrases Reference Sheet

Words	
before	early
after	late
now	first
soon	last
later	next
then	during
yesterday	until
today	while
tomorrow	immediately
morning	always
afternoon	never
evening	often
night	sometimes
week	rarely
month	eventually

Phrases	
In the morning	In the blink of an eye
At noon	In the meantime
In the afternoon	As soon as possible
At night	Day by day
Before long	For a while
After a while	From now on
In a minute	Over time
At the moment	In a moment
Right now	For the time being
In the future	In no time
Once upon a time	At this point
From time to time	On a regular basis
In a few days	Every now and then
A long time ago	Before too long
In the past	Once in a while
At this time	For the last time
By the time	Up until now
At the same time	At the crack of dawn
All the time	In the course of time
Every day	At the end of the day

234

Time Words and Phrases

abulary

235

Materials	• Time Words and Phrases Reference Sheet, page 234 • Time Vocabulary, page 235
Grade Band	K–3
Length of Activity	20 minutes
Differentiation Ideas	**Striving Learners and English Learners:** Provide a smaller set of time words or phrases to choose from by highlighting those most commonly used.
Extension Ideas	Have students glue the reference sheet into a writer's notebook to reference later in their writing.
Answers	**Possible Answers: 1.** First, he wakes up and stretches in bed. **2.** Next, he brushes his teeth in the bathroom. **3.** Then, he eats breakfast at the table. **4.** After breakfast, he gets dressed. **5.** Soon after, he walks to school. **6.** Now, he is at school and working in class.

LANGUAGE DOMAINS

Reading

Writing

Speaking

Listening

Time Words and Phrases Reference Sheet

Words		Phrases	
before	early	in the morning	in the blink of an eye
after	late	at noon	in the meantime
now	first	in the afternoon	as soon as possible
soon	last	at night	day by day
later	next	before long	for a while
then	during	after a while	from now on
yesterday	until	in a minute	over time
today	while	at the moment	in a moment
tomorrow	immediately	right now	for the time being
morning	always	in the future	in no time
afternoon	never	once upon a time	at this point
evening	often	from time to time	on a regular basis
night	sometimes	in a few days	every now and then
week	rarely	a long time ago	before too long
month	eventually	in the past	once in a while
		at this time	for the last time
		by the time	up until now
		at the same time	at the crack of dawn
		all the time	in the course of time
		every day	at the end of the day

Time Vocabulary

Strategies for Understanding Relationships Among Words

LANGUAGE DOMAINS

Reading

Writing

Speaking

Listening

4.E Spatial Words and Phrases

Explain to students that words that relate to how things take up space and where they are located are important because they help us understand our environment and communicate clearly. For students who are not yet reading, this activity can be done orally. For students who are reading and writing, it can be done by filling in the blanks on the worksheet. Project Spatial Relationship Words and Phrases on page 237 and review it with students. Then distribute Spatial Relationships on page 238 and have students study the picture and use the words from Spatial Relationship Words and Phrases to describe the placement of objects in relation to one another. From there, ask them to share and discuss their answers to reinforce understanding and provide multiple exposures to the spatial vocabulary words and phrases.

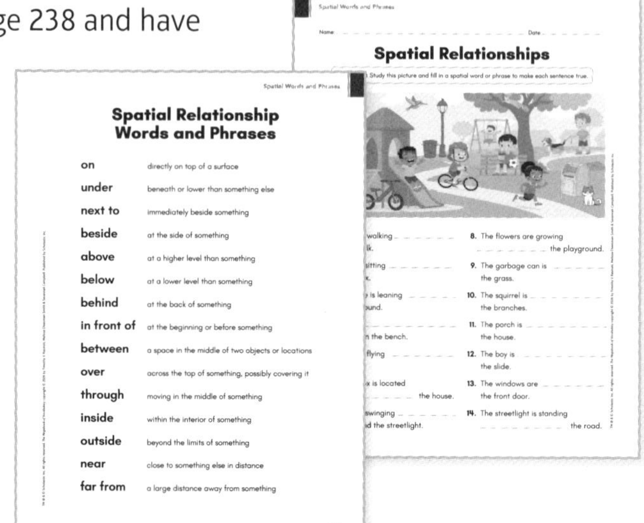

Spatial Relationship Words and Phrases

on	directly on top of a surface
under	beneath or lower than something else
next to	immediately beside something
beside	at the side of something
above	at a higher level than something
below	at a lower level than something
behind	at the back of something
in front of	at the beginning or before something
between	a space in the middle of two objects or locations
over	across the top of something, possibly covering it
through	moving in the middle of something
inside	within the interior of something
outside	beyond the limits of something
near	close to something else in distance
far from	a large distance away from something

Spatial Relationships

8. The flowers are growing ________ the playground.
9. The garbage can is ________ the grass.
10. The squirrel is ________ the branches.
11. The porch is ________ the house.
12. The boy is ________ the slide.
13. The windows are ________ the front door.
14. The streetlight is standing ________ the road.

Materials	• Spatial Relationship Words and Phrases, page 237 • Spatial Relationships, page 238
Grade Band	K–3
Length of Activity	20 minutes
Differentiation Ideas	**Striving Learners and English Learners:** Select a smaller set of spatial words for students to choose from.
Extension Ideas	• Have students create their own picture and write five sentences using spatial relationship words to share with the class. • Provide students with a copy of the reference sheet to glue into a writer's notebook to use as a reference when writing.

Spatial Relationship Words and Phrases

on	directly on top of a surface
under	beneath or lower than something else
next to	immediately beside something
beside	at the side of something
above	at a higher level than something
below	at a lower level than something
behind	at the back of something
in front of	at the beginning or before something
between	a space in the middle of two objects or locations
over	across the top of something, possibly covering it
through	moving in the middle of something
inside	within the interior of something
outside	beyond the limits of something
near	close to something else in distance
far from	a large distance away from something

Name: ______________________ Date: ____________

Spatial Relationships

Directions: Study this picture and fill in a spatial word or phrase to make each sentence true.

1. The dog is walking ______________ the sidewalk.
2. The cat is sitting ______________ the mailbox.
3. The bicycle is leaning ______________ the playground.
4. The ball is ______________ the child on the bench.
5. The bird is flying ______________ the park.
6. The mailbox is located ______________ the house.
7. The boy is swinging ______________ the tree and the streetlight.
8. The flowers are growing ______________ the playground.
9. The garbage can is ______________ the grass.
10. The squirrel is ______________ the branches.
11. The porch is ______________ the house.
12. The boy is ______________ the slide.
13. The windows are ______________ the front door.
14. The streetlight is standing ______________ the road.

4.F **Synonym and Antonym Mini-Posters**

Use a list of provided words (below), or your own words with a number of potential synonyms and antonyms, and write each word at the top of a sheet of chart paper. Then create a T-chart below the word with *Synonyms* and *Antonyms* as headers. Create enough charts for student pairs. Post the charts around the room. Review with students that synonyms are words with similar meanings and antonyms are words with opposite meanings. Have partners visit each chart and add a synonym and/or antonym to it. Then walk around and read the words students came up with and determine if they are all actual synonyms and antonyms for the vocabulary word. The goal is to engage in discussion and deepen understanding of words.

Simple Words: *happy, big, fast, hot, smart, old, strong, beautiful, clean, light, brave, kind, hard, funny,* and *loud*

Challenging Words: *fierce, tiny, curious, messy, gentle, lonely, creative, busy, comfortable, mellow, smart, delicious, friendly, excited, strange, cozy, surprising, tasty,* and *boring*

Materials	• words with synonyms and antonyms • chart paper for mini-posters
Grade Band	2–5
Length of Activity	45 minutes
Differentiation Ideas	**Striving Learners and English Learners:** Allow students to use a thesaurus to help them come up with synonyms and antonyms.
Extension Ideas	• Choose your own words from a text or unit of study. • Have student partners share their favorite word they heard today that they do not often use, then challenge them to use the word when speaking with someone the next day.

LANGUAGE DOMAINS

Reading

Writing

Speaking

Listening

☑

CHAPTER 4

Exploration of Word Relationships

Strategies for Understanding Relationships Among Words

LANGUAGE DOMAINS

Reading

Writing

Speaking

Listening

4.G **Analogies**

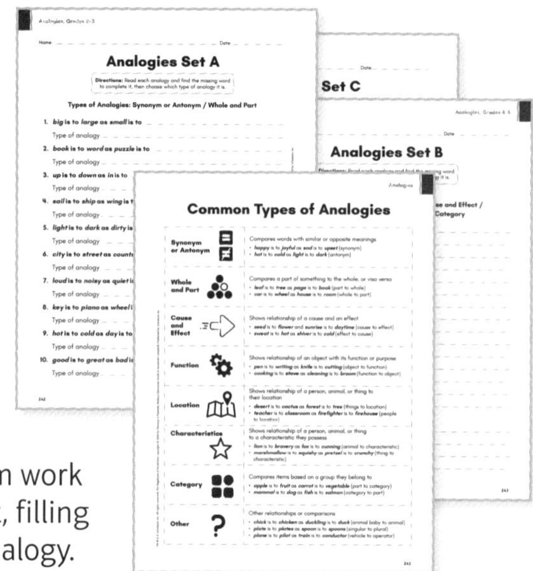

An analogy is a comparison or relationship between two words or ideas. For younger students, describe the two types of analogies they will practice, *synonym or antonym* and *whole and part*, using the examples from Common Types of Analogies on page 241. For older students, review all the types using Common Types of Analogies. Once students are familiar with types of analogies, distribute an Analogies Set on pages 242–244 and have them work individually or in pairs to complete it, filling in the missing words and types of analogy.

Materials	• Common Types of Analogies, page 241 • Analogies Set A, Grades 2–3, page 242 • Analogies Set B, Grades 4–5, page 243 • Analogies Set C, Grades 6–8, page 244
Grade Band	2–8
Length of Activity	20 minutes each
Differentiation Ideas	**Striving Learners and English Learners:** Start with simple analogies such as *"color: red* as *shape:*______. " Students can also be given an Analogies Set below their grade level to simplify language, but still be working on the skill.
Extension Ideas	Allow students to create their own analogies using words from a text or unit of study, and then share with classmates.
Answers	**Set A: 1.** tiny; synonym **2.** piece; whole and part **3.** out; antonym **4.** airplane; whole and part **5.** clean; antonym **6.** state, whole and part **7.** silent; synonym **8.** car (or anything with wheels); whole and part **9.** night; antonym **10.** terrible; synonym **Set B: 1.** fearful; antonym **2.** flower; category **3.** hardness; characteristic **4.** racetrack; location **5.** gloomy; synonym **6.** book; whole and part **7.** dim; synonym **8.** gathering; function **9.** difficult; antonym **10.** disorganized; cause/effect **Set C: 1.** direction; function **2.** serene; synonym **3.** gem or gemstone; category **4.** timid; cause/effect **5.** airplane; function **6.** game; category **7.** brushing teeth; function **8.** tiny; characteristic **9.** Antarctic; location **10.** contraction; cause/effect (Accept all reasonable alternatives.)

Common Types of Analogies

Synonym or Antonym		Compares words with similar or opposite meanings • ***happy*** is to ***joyful*** as ***sad*** is to ***upset*** (synonym) • ***hot*** is to ***cold*** as ***light*** is to ***dark*** (antonym)
Whole and Part		Compares a part of something to the whole, or visa versa • ***leaf*** is to ***tree*** as ***page*** is to ***book*** (part to whole) • ***car*** is to ***wheel*** as ***house*** is to ***room*** (whole to part)
Cause and Effect	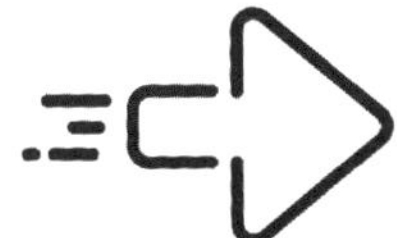	Shows relationship of a cause and an effect • ***seed*** is to ***flower*** and ***sunrise*** is to ***daytime*** (cause to effect) • ***sweat*** is to ***hot*** as ***shiver*** is to ***cold*** (effect to cause)
Function		Shows relationship of an object with its function or purpose • ***pen*** is to ***writing*** as ***knife*** is to ***cutting*** (object to function) • ***cooking*** is to ***stove*** as ***cleaning*** is to ***broom*** (function to object)
Location		Shows relationship of a person, animal, or thing to their location • ***desert*** is to ***cactus*** as ***forest*** is to ***tree*** (things to location) • ***teacher*** is to ***classroom*** as ***firefighter*** is to ***firehouse*** (people to location)
Characteristics		Shows relationship of a person, animal, or thing to a characteristic they possess • ***lion*** is to ***bravery*** as ***fox*** is to ***cunning*** (animal to characteristic) • ***marshmallow*** is to ***squishy*** as ***pretzel*** is to ***crunchy*** (thing to characteristic)
Category		Compares items based on a group they belong to • ***apple*** is to ***fruit*** as ***carrot*** is to ***vegetable*** (part to category) • ***mammal*** is to ***dog*** as ***fish*** is to ***salmon*** (category to part)
Other		Other relationships or comparisons • ***chick*** is to ***chicken*** as ***duckling*** is to ***duck*** (animal baby to animal) • ***plate*** is to ***plates*** as ***spoon*** is to ***spoons*** (singular to plural) • ***plane*** is to ***pilot*** as ***train*** is to ***conductor*** (vehicle to operator)

Name: ______________________ Date: ____________

Analogies Set A

Directions: Read each analogy and find the missing word to complete it, then choose which type of analogy it is.

Types of Analogies: Synonym or Antonym / Whole and Part

1. ***big*** **is to** ***large*** **as** ***small*** **is to** ______________________

   Type of analogy ______________________

2. ***book*** **is to** ***word*** **as** ***puzzle*** **is to** ______________________

   Type of analogy ______________________

3. ***up*** **is to** ***down*** **as** ***in*** **is to** ______________________

   Type of analogy ______________________

4. ***sail*** **is to** ***ship*** **as** ***wing*** **is to** ______________________

   Type of analogy ______________________

5. ***light*** **is to** ***dark*** **as** ***dirty*** **is to** ______________________

   Type of analogy ______________________

6. ***city*** **is to** ***street*** **as** ***country*** **is to** ______________________

   Type of analogy ______________________

7. ***loud*** **is to** ***noisy*** **as** ***quiet*** **is to** ______________________

   Type of analogy ______________________

8. ***key*** **is to** ***piano*** **as** ***wheel*** **is to** ______________________

   Type of analogy ______________________

9. ***hot*** **is to** ***cold*** **as** ***day*** **is to** ______________________

   Type of analogy ______________________

10. ***good*** **is to** ***great*** **as** ***bad*** **is to** ______________________

    Type of analogy ______________________

Name: ______________________ Date: __________

Analogies Set B

Directions: Read each analogy and find the missing word to complete it, then choose which type of analogy it is.

Types of Analogies:
Synonym or Antonym / Whole and Part / Cause and Effect / Function / Location / Characteristics / Category

1. ***strong*** **is to** ***weak*** **as** ***brave*** **is to** ______________________

   Type of analogy ______________________

2. ***tiger*** **is to** ***animal*** **as** ***tulip*** **is to** ______________________

   Type of analogy ______________________

3. ***cloud*** **is to** ***fluffiness*** **as** ***stone*** **is to** ______________________

   Type of analogy ______________________

4. ***chef*** **is to** ***kitchen*** **as** ***race car driver*** **is to** ______________________

   Type of analogy ______________________

5. ***bright*** **is to** ***radiant*** **as** ***dark*** **is to** ______________________

   Type of analogy ______________________

6. ***branch*** **is to** ***tree*** **as** ***chapter*** **is to** ______________________

   Type of analogy ______________________

7. ***sunny*** **is to** ***bright*** **as** ***dull*** **is to** ______________________

   Type of analogy ______________________

8. ***shovel*** **is to** ***digging*** **as** ***rake*** **is to** ______________________

   Type of analogy ______________________

9. ***happy*** **is to** ***miserable*** **as** ***easy*** **is to** ______________________

   Type of analogy ______________________

10. ***clean*** **is to** ***tidy*** **as** ***messy*** **is to** ______________________

    Type of analogy ______________________

Name: ________________ Date: ________

Analogies Set C

Directions: Read each analogy and find the missing word to complete it, then choose which type of analogy it is.

Types of Analogies:
Synonym or Antonym / Whole and Part / Cause and Effect / Function / Location / Characteristics / Category

1. ***clock*** **is to** ***timekeeping*** **as** ***compass*** **is to** ________

   Type of analogy ________

2. ***angry*** **is to** ***furious*** **as** ***calm*** **is to** ________

   Type of analogy ________

3. ***gold*** **is to** ***metal*** **as** ***diamond*** **is to** ________

   Type of analogy ________

4. ***faithful*** **is to** ***brave*** **as** ***fearful*** **is to** ________

   Type of analogy ________

5. ***driving*** **is to** ***car*** **as** ***flying*** **is to** ________

   Type of analogy ________

6. ***soccer*** **is to** ***sport*** **as** ***chess*** **is to** ________

   Type of analogy ________

7. ***frying pan*** **is to** ***cooking*** **as** ***toothbrush*** **is to** ________

   Type of analogy ________

8. ***whale*** **is to** ***enormous*** **as** ***hummingbird*** **is to** ________

   Type of analogy ________

9. ***North Pole*** **is to** ***Arctic*** **as** ***South Pole*** **is to** ________

   Type of analogy ________

10. ***heat*** **is to** ***expansion*** **as** ***cold*** **is to** ________

    Type of analogy ________

4.H **Multiple Meanings: Draw or Act!**

Copy and cut apart a Multiple-Meaning Cards Set on pages 246–249. Give student pairs a card, which includes one word with two meanings, and allow them a few minutes to plan a way to act out or draw one meaning of the word. Then have partners perform their word or display the drawing of their word in front of the class, without revealing it. Have the class guess which multiple-meaning word is being shared. Project the Word List at the bottom of each card set if students need support.

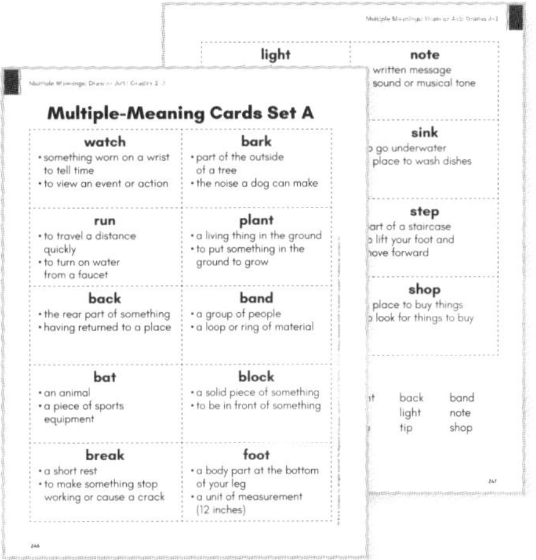

Multiple-Meaning Cards Set A

watch	**bark**
• something worn on a wrist to tell time • to view an event or action	• part of the outside of a tree • the noise a dog can make
run • to travel a distance quickly • to turn on water from a faucet	**plant** • a living thing in the ground • to put something in the ground to grow
back • the rear part of something • having returned to a place	**band** • a group of people • a loop or ring of material
bat • an animal • a piece of sports equipment	**block** • a solid piece of something • to be in front of something
break • a short rest • to make something stop working or cause a crack	**foot** • a body part at the bottom of your leg • a unit of measurement (12 inches)

246

light	**note**
	written message sound or musical tone
	sink go underwater place to wash dishes
	step art of a staircase lift your foot and ove forward
	shop place to buy things look for things to buy

back band
light note
tip shop

247

Materials	• Multiple-Meaning Cards Set A, Grades 2–3, pages 246–247 • Multiple-Meaning Cards Set B, Grades 4–5, page 248 • Multiple-Meaning Cards Set C, Grades 6–8, page 249 • paper and colored pencils or markers
Grade Band	2–8
Length of Activity	30 minutes
Differentiation Ideas	**Striving Learners and English Learners:** Give students their word earlier with some extra explaining and support so they have some practice before they participate. This could, in fact, remove barriers for all students.
Extension Ideas	Have students draw quick sketches of each word along with the definition as partners are presenting.

Strategies for Understanding Relationships Among Words

LANGUAGE DOMAINS

Reading

Writing

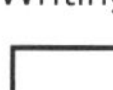

Speaking

Listening

Multiple-Meaning Cards Set A

watch • something worn on a wrist to tell time • to view an event or action	**bark** • part of the outside of a tree • the noise a dog can make
run • to travel a distance quickly • to turn on water from a faucet	**plant** • a living thing in the ground • to put something in the ground to grow
back • the rear part of something • having returned to a place	**band** • a group of people • a loop or ring of material
bat • an animal • a piece of sports equipment	**block** • a solid piece of something • to be in front of something
break • a short rest • to make something stop working or cause a crack	**foot** • a body part at the bottom of your leg • a unit of measurement (12 inches)

light	**note**
• something that helps you see • not heavy	• a written message • a sound or musical tone
root	**sink**
• a part of a plant underground • to cheer someone on	• to go underwater • a place to wash dishes
slip	**step**
• to lose your balance and fall • to slide smoothly	• part of a staircase • to lift your foot and move forward
tip	**shop**
• a helpful piece of advice • to give extra money	• a place to buy things • to look for things to buy

Word List

watch	bark	run	plant	back	band
bat	block	break	foot	light	note
root	sink	slip	step	tip	shop

Multiple-Meaning Cards Set B

prompt • a statement that shows what to write about • a message or cue to take action	**perspective** • a way of thinking about something • a physical view of something like a sunset	**voice** • the sound made when singing or talking • a way of expressing your opinion
pound • a unit of weight • to hit with force	**stands** • a place where people sit or watch something • to be upright on your feet	**cart** • a vehicle to carry something around • the act of moving something
table • a flat surface with legs • to put something aside	**like** • to enjoy or take pleasure in • similar or the same	**act** • to perform in a show • a part of a play
change • to make something different • money back after a purchase	**charge** • to give power to something • to ask for money in exchange for something	**check** • to look at something carefully • a paper to write on to pay for something
fair • to treat everyone equally • a fun event with rides and games	**play** • to have fun or do an activity • a performance or show	**quarter** • a coin worth 25 cents • one of four equal parts
spot • a small mark or stain • a place or location	**throw** • to toss in the air • to cause someone else to win on purpose	**ring** • a circular piece of jewelry worn on the finger • a sound like a bell ringing

Word List

prompt	perspective	voice	pound	stands	cart
table	like	act	change	charge	check
fair	play	quarter	spot	throw	ring

Multiple-Meaning Cards Set C

wrap	**train**	**spike**
• to cover something up • a type of sandwich with a tortilla	• a vehicle that moves on tracks • to practice something to get better	• a sharp pointed edge • a sudden increase or rise in something
scale • a tool used to measure weight • the size of something compared to a bigger or smaller version	**press** • to push with your hand • a machine used to flatten something	**form** • to shape or structure something • a document with spaces to fill out information
flat • smooth and even with no bumps • a place to live, like an apartment (British)	**file** • a tool used to smooth something • a collection of documents	**draw** • to make a picture with a pencil, pen, or markers • to pull something toward you
motion • the act of moving or changing • a proposal made during a meeting	**reflection** • an image seen in a mirror or water • thinking carefully about something	**outlook** • the way one sees or thinks about something • a place where you have a certain view to study something
produce • to make or create something • fruits and vegetables grown on a farm	**rare** • uncommon or hard to find • meat that is lightly cooked	**bank** • a place where money is kept • the land alongside a river
bill • a paper showing how much you paid for something • a type of beak on a bird	**grade** • a score or mark to show how you did in school • a level or year in school	**brush** • a tool with bristles to clean something • to sweep or clean lightly

Word List

wrap	train	spike	scale	press	form
flat	file	draw	motion	reflection	outlook
produce	rare	bank	bill	grade	brush

CHAPTER 4

Exploration of Word Relationships

Strategies for Understanding Relationships Among Words

LANGUAGE DOMAINS

Reading

Writing

Speaking

Listening

4.1 Homonyms Sort

Students will identify different types of homonyms to help them think about word relationships and the nuances of language. Copy and cut apart the Homonyms Sort on page 251, enough sets for pairs of students. Review the three types of homonyms: *homophones*: words that sound the same but have different meanings (e.g., *bear/bare*); *homographs*: words that are spelled the same but have different pronunciations (e.g., wind [breeze]/wind [to twist]); and *multiple-meaning* words one word with more than one definition. Have students pair up the matching words, then sort the word sets into multiple-meaning words, homophones, or homographs under the appropriate header cards on page 252.

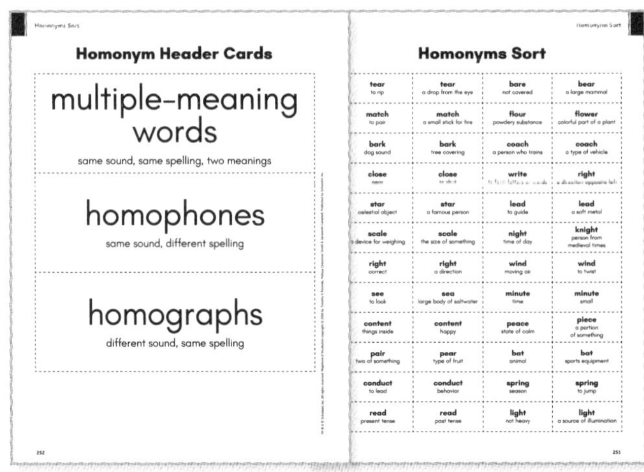

Homonym Header Cards

multiple-meaning words
same sound, same spelling, two meanings

homophones
same sound, different spelling

homographs
different sound, same spelling

252

Homonyms Sort

tear to rip	**tear** a drop from the eye	**bare** not covered	**bear** a large mammal
match to pair	**match** a small stick for fire	**flour** powdery substance	**flower** colorful part of a plant
bark dog sound	**bark** tree covering	**coach** a person who trains	**coach** a type of vehicle
close [illegible]	**close** [illegible]	**write** [illegible]	**right** [illegible]
star celestial object	**star** a famous person	**lead** to guide	**lead** a soft metal
scale a device for weighing	**scale** the size of something	**night** time of day	**knight** person from medieval times
right correct	**right** a direction	**wind** moving air	**wind** to twist
see to look	**sea** large body of saltwater	**minute** time	**minute** small
content things inside	**content** happy	**peace** state of calm	**piece** a portion of something
pair two of something	**pear** type of fruit	**bat** animal	**bat** sports equipment
conduct to lead	**conduct** behavior	**spring** season	**spring** to jump
read present tense	**read** past tense	**light** not heavy	**light** a source of illumination

251

Materials	• Homonyms Sort, page 251 • Homonym Header Cards, page 252
Grade Band	2–8
Length of Activity	30 minutes
Differentiation Ideas	**Striving Learners and English Learners:** Complete the activity in a small group so you can pronounce the words for students as they are reading them on the worksheet. This will help clarify the difference between examples of homophones and homographs.
Extension Ideas	Have students think of their own sets to try to stump a partner.
Answers	**multiple-meaning words:** match, match; bark, bark; coach, coach; star, star; scale, scale; right, right; bat, bat; spring, spring; light, light **homophones:** bare, bear; flour, flower; write, right; night, knight; see, sea; peace, piece; pair, pear **homographs:** tear, tear; close, close; lead, lead; wind, wind; minute, minute; content, content; conduct, conduct; read, read

Homonyms Sort

tear to rip	**tear** a drop from the eye	**bare** not covered	**bear** a large mammal
match to pair	**match** a small stick for fire	**flour** powdery substance	**flower** colorful part of a plant
bark dog sound	**bark** tree covering	**coach** a person who trains	**coach** a type of vehicle
close near	**close** to shut	**write** to form letters or words	**right** a direction opposite left
star celestial object	**star** a famous person	**lead** to guide	**lead** a soft metal
scale a device for weighing	**scale** the size of something	**night** time of day	**knight** person from medieval times
right correct	**right** a direction	**wind** moving air	**wind** to twist
see to look	**sea** large body of salt water	**minute** time	**minute** small
content things inside	**content** happy	**peace** state of calm	**piece** a portion of something
pair two of something	**pear** type of fruit	**bat** animal	**bat** sports equipment
conduct to lead	**conduct** behavior	**spring** season	**spring** to jump
read (present tense)	**read** (past tense)	**light** not heavy	**light** a source of illumination

Homonym Header Cards

multiple-meaning words

same sound, same spelling, two meanings

homophones

same sound, different spelling

homographs

different sound, same spelling

4.J Homophones Bingo

Distribute the Homophones Bingo Board on page 254 to each student. Select 12 sets of age-appropriate homophones from Common Homophones on pages 255–256. Model for students how to *randomly* fill in the words on their board. Once bingo boards are made, read a definition of a word and have students cover the corresponding word on their board, using a dauber or chip. Continue until a student calls "Bingo!" after covering a full line (five words) horizontally, diagonally, or vertically.

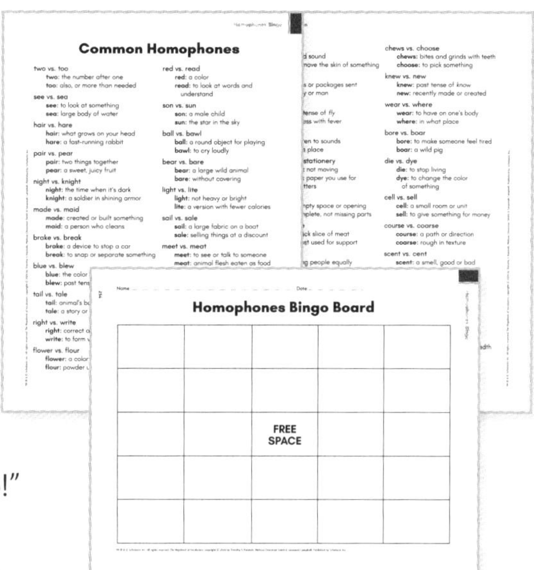

Common Homophones

Homophones Bingo Board

FREE SPACE

Materials	• Homophones Bingo Board, page 254 • Common Homophones, pages 255–256 • bingo daubers or chips
Grade Band	4–8
Length of Activity	15–45 minutes
Differentiation Ideas	**Striving Learners and English Learners:** Review any tricky words beforehand or have them written on a card with the correct spelling. **Striving Learners:** Use a 4-x-4 bingo board and 16 words.
Extension Ideas	• Have the winner get to call the next bingo game after you have copied and highlighted the words being used for the game. • Repeat activity on another day with different words, keeping in any ones that were confusing to the students the last time. • Provide teacher-created sentences with a "blank" instead of the definition.

Strategies for Understanding Relationships Among Words

LANGUAGE DOMAINS

Reading

Writing

Speaking

Listening

Name: ____________________ Date: __________

Homophones Bingo Board

		FREE SPACE		

Common Homophones

two vs. too
- **two:** the number after one
- **too:** also, or more than needed

see vs. sea
- **see:** to look at something
- **sea:** large body of water

hair vs. hare
- **hair:** what grows on your head
- **hare:** a fast-running rabbit

pair vs. pear
- **pair:** two things together
- **pear:** a sweet, juicy fruit

night vs. knight
- **night:** the time when it's dark
- **knight:** a soldier in shining armor

made vs. maid
- **made:** created or built something
- **maid:** a person who cleans

brake vs. break
- **brake:** a device to stop a car
- **break:** to snap or separate something

blue vs. blew
- **blue:** the color of the sky
- **blew:** past tense of *blow*

tail vs. tale
- **tail:** animal's back part; wags
- **tale:** a story or adventure told

right vs. write
- **right:** correct or true
- **write:** to form words on paper

flower vs. flour
- **flower:** a colorful part of a plant
- **flour:** powder used for baking

red vs. read
- **red:** a color
- **read:** to look at words and understand

son vs. sun
- **son:** a male child
- **sun:** the star in the sky

ball vs. bawl
- **ball:** a round object for playing
- **bawl:** to cry loudly

bear vs. bare
- **bear:** a large wild animal
- **bare:** without covering

light vs. lite
- **light:** not heavy or bright
- **lite:** a version with fewer calories

sail vs. sale
- **sail:** a large fabric on a boat
- **sale:** selling things at a discount

meet vs. meat
- **meet:** to see or talk to someone
- **meat:** animal flesh eaten as food

deer vs. dear
- **deer:** a wild animal with antlers
- **dear:** loved or special to someone

bale vs. bail
- **bale:** a big bundle of something
- **bail:** money given to a court to stay out of jail before a trial

stare vs. stair
- **stare:** to look at something hard
- **stair:** a step in a staircase

pail vs. pale
- **pail:** a bucket
- **pale:** lighter than usual in color

peal vs. peel
peal: a loud sound
peel: to remove the skin of something

mail vs. male
mail: letters or packages sent
male: a boy or man

flew vs. flu
flew: past tense of *fly*
flu: a sickness with fever

hear vs. here
hear: to listen to sounds
here: in this place

stationary vs. stationery
stationary: not moving
stationery: paper you use for writing letters

hole vs. whole
hole: an empty space or opening
whole: complete, not missing parts

steak vs. stake
steak: a thick slice of meat
stake: a post used for support

fair vs. fare
fair: treating people equally
fare: the cost of a ticket

knot vs. not
knot: a tied loop in a rope
not: a word used for negation

sole vs. soul
sole: the bottom of a foot
soul: the spiritual part of a person

made vs. maid
made: created or built something
maid: a person who cleans

gait vs. gate
gait: a way of walking
gate: a door or entrance

chews vs. choose
chews: bites and grinds with teeth
choose: to pick something

knew vs. new
knew: past tense of *know*
new: recently made or created

wear vs. where
wear: to have on one's body
where: in what place

bore vs. boar
bore: to make someone feel tired
boar: a wild pig

die vs. dye
die: to stop living
dye: to change the color of something

cell vs. sell
cell: a small room or unit
sell: to give something for money

course vs. coarse
course: a path or direction
coarse: rough in texture

scent vs. cent
scent: a smell, good or bad
cent: a small coin

cite vs. site
cite: to mention or refer to
site: a place or location

do vs. due
do: to perform an action
due: expected to arrive soon

cent vs. sent
cent: a coin worth one hundredth
sent: past tense of *send*

4.K **Homographs**

Choose a pair of sentences from the Homophone Sentences on pages 258–259, project them, and have students read them. In pairs, have students discuss how to pronounce the boldfaced word so it matches the meaning in each sentence. Then have them come up with a definition and part of speech for each form of the word. From there, share the provided definitions and parts of speech with the class. Once students have reviewed the definitions and parts of speech, have student chorally read the sentences with the correct pronunciation of the boldfaced word. Continue with each pair of sentences.

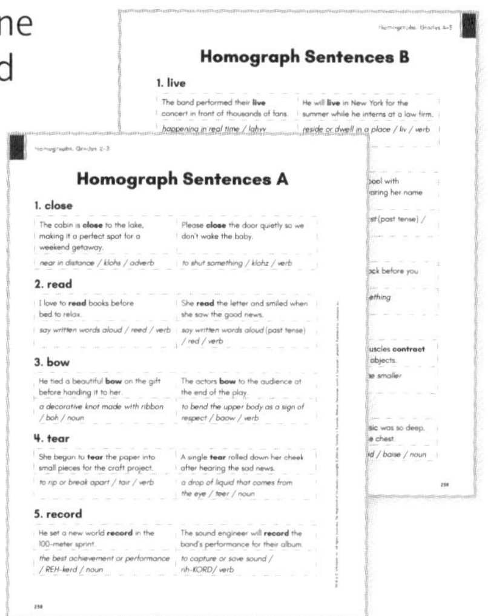

Homograph Sentences B

1. live

The band performed their **live** concert in front of thousands of fans.	He will **live** in New York for the summer while he interns at a law firm.
happening in real time / lahyv	*reside or dwell in a place / liv / verb*

Homograph Sentences A

1. close

The cabin is **close** to the lake, making it a perfect spot for a weekend getaway.	Please **close** the door quietly so we don't wake the baby.
near in distance / klohs / adverb	*to shut something / klohz / verb*

2. read

I love to **read** books before bed to relax.	She **read** the letter and smiled when she saw the good news.
say written words aloud / reed / verb	*say written words aloud (past tense) / red / verb*

3. bow

He tied a beautiful **bow** on the gift before handing it to her.	The actors **bow** to the audience at the end of the play.
a decorative knot made with ribbon / boh / noun	*to bend the upper body as a sign of respect / baow / verb*

4. tear

She began to **tear** the paper into small pieces for the craft project.	A single **tear** rolled down her cheek after hearing the sad news.
to rip or break apart / tair / verb	*a drop of liquid that comes from the eye / teer / noun*

5. record

He set a new world **record** in the 100-meter sprint.	The sound engineer will **record** the band's performance for their album.
the best achievement or performance / REH-kerd / noun	*to capture or save sound / rih-KORD/ verb*

258

Materials	• Homographs Sentences A, Grades 2–3, page 258 • Homographs Sentences B, Grades 4–5, page 259
Grade Band	2–8
Length of Activity	10 minutes
Differentiation Ideas	**Striving Learners and English Learners:** Provide and have students repeat the two pronunciations before sharing the sentences to distinguish the words.
Extension Ideas	Create more examples using AI with these great homographs: *permit, sow, minute, object, content, wound, subject, produce,* and *present.* (Be sure to check any AI results to make sure they are appropriate.)

Strategies for Understanding Relationships Among Words

LANGUAGE DOMAINS

Reading

Writing

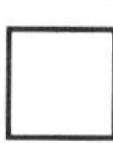

Speaking

Listening

Homograph Sentences A

1. close

The cabin is **close** to the lake, making it a perfect spot for a weekend getaway.	Please **close** the door quietly so we don't wake the baby.
near in distance / klohs / adverb	*to shut something / klohz / verb*

2. read

I love to **read** books before bed to relax.	She **read** the letter and smiled when she saw the good news.
say written words aloud / reed / verb	*said written words aloud* (past tense) */ red / verb*

3. bow

He tied a beautiful **bow** on the gift before handing it to her.	The actors **bow** to the audience at the end of the play.
a decorative knot made with ribbon / boh / noun	*to bend the upper body as a sign of respect / baow / verb*

4. tear

She began to **tear** the paper into small pieces for the craft project.	A single **tear** rolled down her cheek after hearing the sad news.
to rip or break apart / tair / verb	*a drop of liquid that comes from the eye / teer / noun*

5. record

He set a new world **record** in the 100-meter sprint.	The sound engineer will **record** the band's performance for their album.
the best achievement or performance / REH-kerd / noun	*to capture or save sound / rih-KORD / verb*

Homograph Sentences B

1. live

The band performed their **live** concert in front of thousands of fans.	He will **live** in New York for the summer while he interns at a law firm.
happening in real time / lahyv / adjective	*reside or dwell in a place / liv / verb*

2. dove

The white **dove** flew gracefully across the sky, symbolizing peace.	She **dove** into the pool with excitement after hearing her name called for the race.
type of bird / duhv / noun	*jumped into headfirst* (past tense) / *dohv / verb*

3. wind

The **wind** blew fiercely through the trees during the storm.	Please **wind** the clock before you leave for the day.
movement of air / winned / noun	*to twist or turn something / whynd / verb*

4. contract

They signed a **contract** to finalize the business deal.	Your arm and leg muscles **contract** when you lift heavy objects.
a formal agreement / KON-trakt / noun	*to tighten or become smaller / kun-TRAKT / verb*

5. bass

He caught a huge **bass** while fishing at the lake.	The **bass** in the music was so deep, it could be felt in the chest.
a type of fish / bhass / noun	*low-frequency sound / baise / noun*

CHAPTER 4

Exploration of Word Relationships

Strategies for Understanding Relationships Among Words

LANGUAGE DOMAINS

Reading

Writing

Speaking

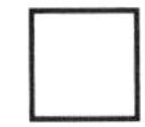

Listening

4.L Multiple-Meaning Sentences

1. **right**

a direction opposite of left We had to go to the gas station and almost missed the right turn

correct or accurate I realized my mom was right and I should have gone to bed earlier.

2. **place**

where something is

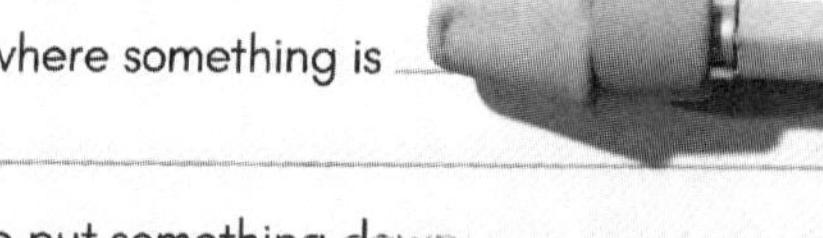

to put something down

Review what a multiple-meaning word is and provide students with an example: *punch* can mean "to hit something" or "a juicy drink." Then distribute a Multiple-Meaning Sentences sheet on pages 261–263. Have students read each word with two meanings and write two sentences that show they understand the difference between the two words. Invite them to share their sentences with a partner.

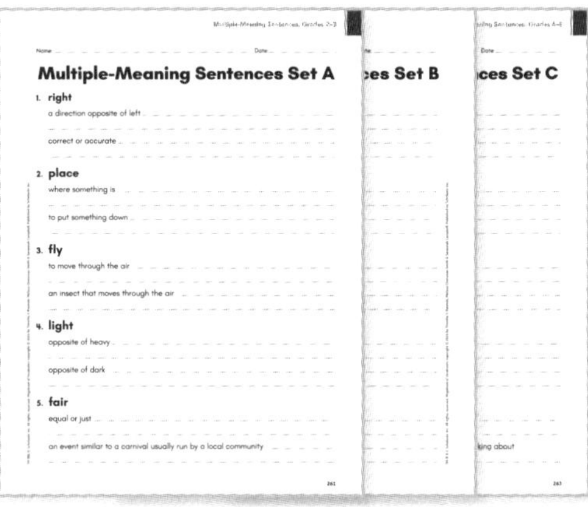

Multiple-Meaning Sentences Set A

1. right
a direction opposite of left
correct or accurate

2. place
where something is
to put something down

3. fly
to move through the air
an insect that moves through the air

4. light
opposite of heavy
opposite of dark

5. fair
equal or just
an event similar to a carnival usually run by a local community

Materials	• Multiple-Meaning Sentences Set A, Grades 2–3, page 261 • Multiple-Meaning Sentences Set B, Grades 4–5, page 262 • Multiple-Meaning Sentences Set C, Grades 6–8, page 263
Grade Band	2–8
Length of Activity	10 minutes
Differentiation Ideas	**Striving Learners and English Learners:** Partner up students with a thriving learner to work together.
Extension Ideas	• Have students also identify each word's part of speech. • Have students do a quick sketch of the word meaning next to each sentence.

Name: ______________________ Date: ______________

Multiple-Meaning Sentences Set A

1. right

a direction opposite of left ______________________

____

correct or accurate ______________________

____

2. place

where something is ______________________

____

to put something down ______________________

____

3. fly

to move through the air ______________________

____

an insect that moves through the air ______________________

____

4. light

opposite of heavy ______________________

____

opposite of dark ______________________

____

5. fair

equal or just ______________________

____

an event similar to a carnival usually run by a local community ______________________

____

Name: ______________________ Date: ____________

Multiple-Meaning Sentences Set B

1. **duck**

a type of waterfowl ______________________

____

to lower your head quickly ______________________

____

2. **rock**

a hard solid material ______________________

____

to move back and forth ______________________

____

3. **match**

a game or competition ______________________

____

a tool used to start a fire ______________________

____

4. **wave**

raised movement of water ______________________

____

to move your hand back and forth to say hello or goodbye ______________________

____

5. **seal**

a marine animal ______________________

____

a way to close something up ______________________

____

Name: ______________________________ Date: ______________

Multiple-Meaning Sentences Set C

1. **jam**

a sweet spread made from fruit ______________________________

____

to squeeze or pack something tightly ______________________________

____

2. **mine**

belonging to me ______________________________

____

a place where minerals or metals are dug up ______________________________

____

3. **spring**

a season of the year ______________________________

____

a coiled-up object ______________________________

____

4. **tire**

a rubber covering on a wheel of a car or bike ______________________________

____

to become worn out due to physical activity ______________________________

____

5. **point**

sharp end of an object ______________________________

____

to use your finger and direct toward something you are talking about ______________________________

____

Strategies for Understanding Relationships Among Words

LANGUAGE DOMAINS

Reading

Writing

Speaking

Listening

4.M **Combining Sentences**

Distribute the Connecting Words and Phrases reference sheet on page 265 and a Combining Sentences sheet on pages 266–267. Explain to students that combining simple sentences can make writing flow better by eliminating repetitive language and showing connections between thoughts. To practice combining sentences, have students read a pair of sentences on the Combining Sentences sheet and combine them using words from the reference sheet. Model the first pair using the reference sheet and adding details or revising language to create the best single sentence possible. For example: *Jack went up a hill. Jill went up a hill* could become *Jack and Jill went up a hill* because the two people are doing the same thing. However, replacing *and* with *but* would not work because it changes the meaning of the sentence. Have students complete Combining Sentences and share their sentences with the class to show the different ways sentences can be combined.

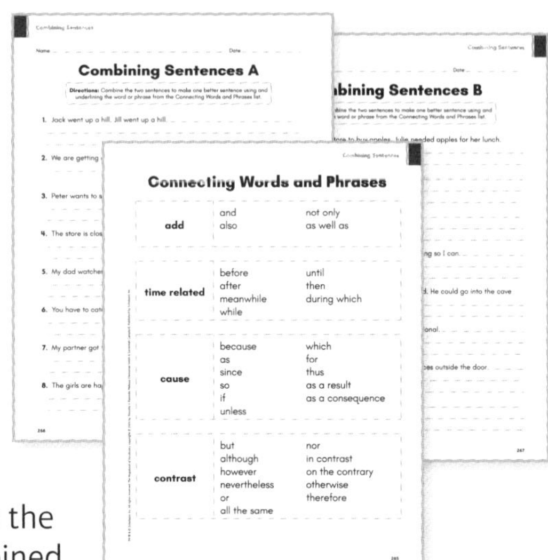

Combining Sentences A

Combining Sentences B

Connecting Words and Phrases

add	and also	not only as well as
time related	before after meanwhile while	until then during which
cause	because as since so if unless	which for thus as a result as a consequence
contrast	but although however nevertheless or all the same	nor in contrast on the contrary otherwise therefore

Materials	• Connecting Words and Phrases, page 265 • Combining Sentences A, page 266 • Combining Sentences B, page 267
Grade Band	2–8
Length of Activity	20 minutes
Differentiation Ideas	**Striving Learners and English Learners:** Introduce a few words at a time for each category, especially for younger learners. Model think-aloud strategies for a couple of examples so students can hear the process for choosing what connecting word or phrase would be appropriate for the sentences.
Extension Ideas	• Have students add extra details to the sentences after they combine them to practice expanding sentences. • Give students three sentences to combine into one. • Create sentences using student names. • Have students keep the Connecting Words and Phrases sheet as a reference guide to use in an upcoming writing assignment, or glue into a writer's notebook.

Connecting Words and Phrases

add	and also	not only as well as
time related	before after meanwhile while	until then during which
cause	because as since so if unless	which for thus as a result as a consequence
contrast	but although however nevertheless or all the same	nor in contrast on the contrary otherwise therefore

Name: ________________ Date: ________

Combining Sentences A

Directions: Combine the two sentences to make one better sentence using and underlining the word or phrase from the Connecting Words and Phrases list.

1. Jack went up a hill. Jill went up a hill. ____________

2. We are getting on the bus. We are going to the zoo. ____________

3. Peter wants to see the bears. Zoe wants to see the penguins. ____________

4. The store is closed today. The park is open. ____________

5. My dad watches the news. He goes to bed. ____________

6. You have to catch the ball. Don't let it hit the ground. ____________

7. My partner got the markers. I got the papers. ____________

8. The girls are happy. They are playing with kittens. ____________

Name: ____________________ Date: ____________

Combining Sentences B

Directions: Combine the two sentences to make one better sentence using and underlining the word or phrase from the Connecting Words and Phrases list.

1. Mom went to the store to buy apples. Julie needed apples for her lunch.

2. Dinner is in five minutes. We are having lasagna.

3. The buffalo wing is too spicy. I need some milk.

4. I can't help you. You need to tell me what's wrong so I can.

5. Marty didn't know if he should wait for his friend. He could go into the cave alone.

6. This restaurant is expensive. The food is exceptional.

7. The dog started to bark. She heard strange voices outside the door.

8. Riley stayed home from school. Riley got sick.

CHAPTER 4
Exploration of Word Relationships

Strategies for Understanding Relationships Among Words

LANGUAGE DOMAINS

Reading

Writing

Speaking

Listening

4.N Word Relationship Word Ladders

Copy and distribute one of the Word Ladders on pages 269–272. Have students read each clue, determine an answer, and fill in the blank. Give additional clues if necessary for students to determine an answer. When they've completed the ladder, have them decide if the first and last words are synonyms or antonyms (for the first two word ladders) and note the homophones (for the last two word ladders).

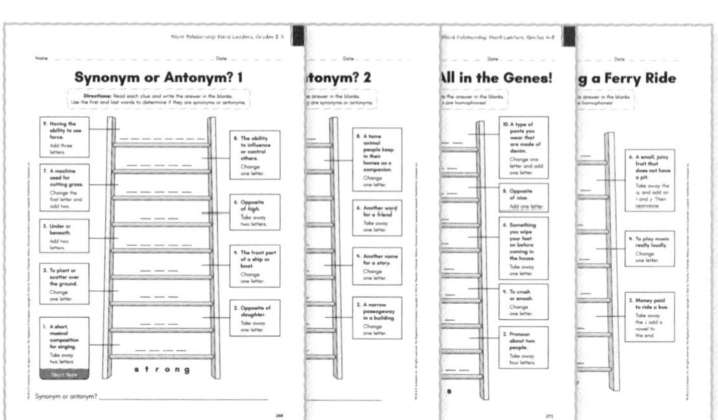
Synonym or Antonym? 1

Materials	• Word Ladder: Synonym or Antonym? 1, Grades 2–5, page 269 • Word Ladder: Synonym or Antonym? 2, Grades 2–5, page 270 • Word Ladder: Homophones: It's All in the Genes!, Grades 4–8, page 271 • Word Ladder: Homophones: Taking a Ferry Ride, Grades 4–8, page 272
Grade Band	2–8
Length of Activity	10 minutes per activity
Differentiation Ideas	• **Striving Learners:** Provide the word for the more challenging parts of the word ladder, or provide the first letter of each word to offer a clue. • **English Learners:** Provide all the words but in a different order so students have a list to choose from and can choose words that match the semantic and letter clues.

Extension Ideas	• Give short lessons along the way about words, tenses, definitions, word relationships, etc., as the opportunity arises.
	• Check out more *Word Ladders* books from Scholastic:
	  • *Daily Word Ladders: Idioms*, Rasinski & Smith
	  • *Daily Word Ladders: Content Areas*, Rasinski & Smith
	  • *Daily Word Ladders: Grades K–1*, Rasinski
	  • *Daily Word Ladders: Grades 2–3*, Rasinski
	  • *Daily Word Ladders: Grades 4–6*, Rasinski
	  • *Partner Poems & Word Ladders for Building Foundational Literacy Skills*, Harrison, Rasinski, & Fresch

Answers	All bottom to top: **Synonym or Antonym? 1:** (synonym) strong, song, son, sow, bow, below, low, mower, power, powerful; **Synonym or Antonym? 2:** (antonym) full, hull, hall, tall, tale, pale, pal, pat, pet, empty; **It's All in the Genes!:** genes, genius, us, mush, mash, mast, mat, man, mean, lean, jeans; **Taking a Ferry Ride:** fairy, fair, fare, flare, blare, bare, berry, ferry

Name: ______________________ Date: ______________

Synonym or Antonym? 1

Directions: Read each clue and write the answer in the blanks. Use the first and last words to determine if they are synonyms or antonyms.

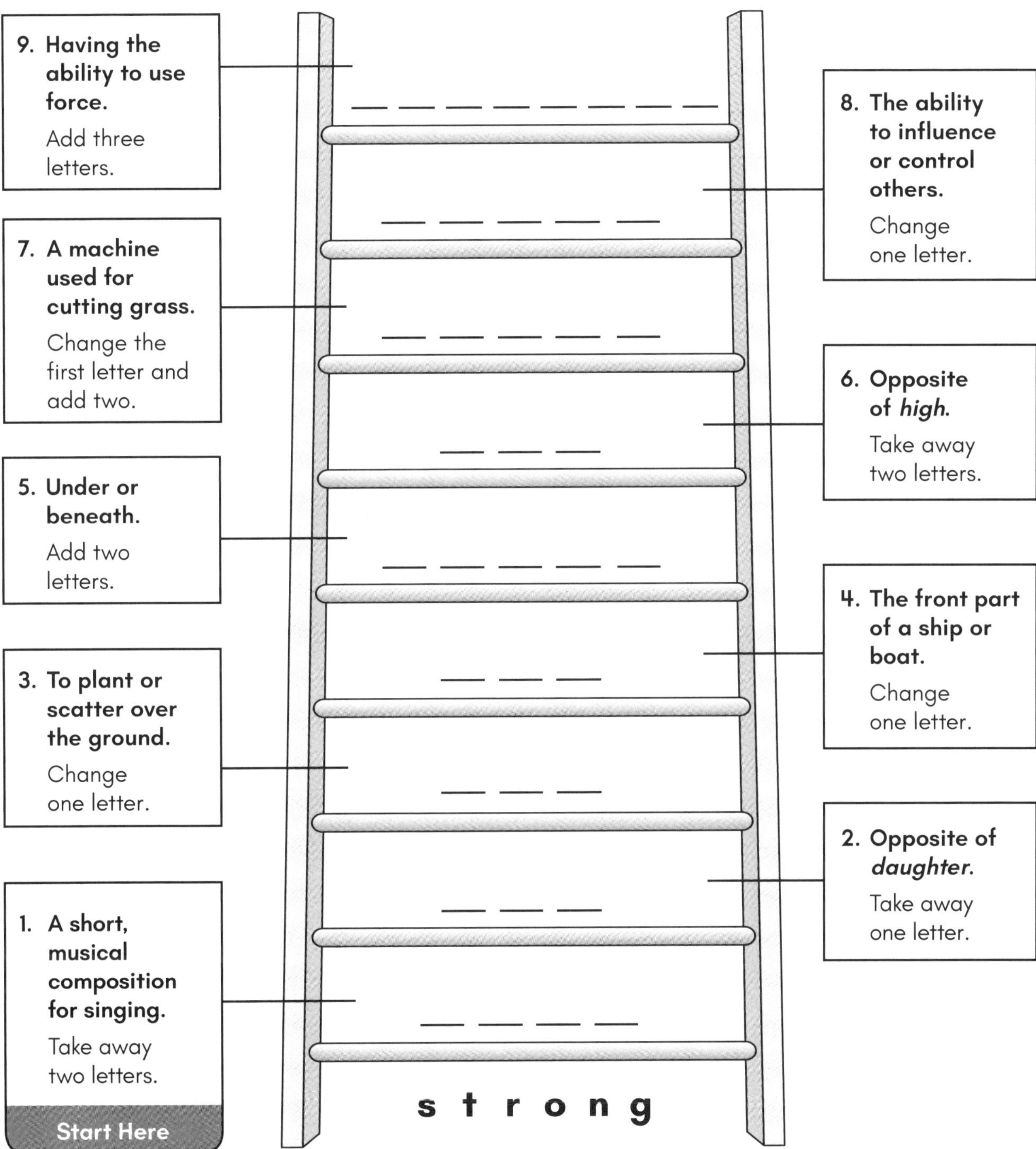

Synonym or antonym? ______________________

Name: ____________________ Date: __________

Synonym or Antonym? 2

Directions: Read each clue and write the answer in the blanks. Use the first and last words to determine if they are synonyms or antonyms.

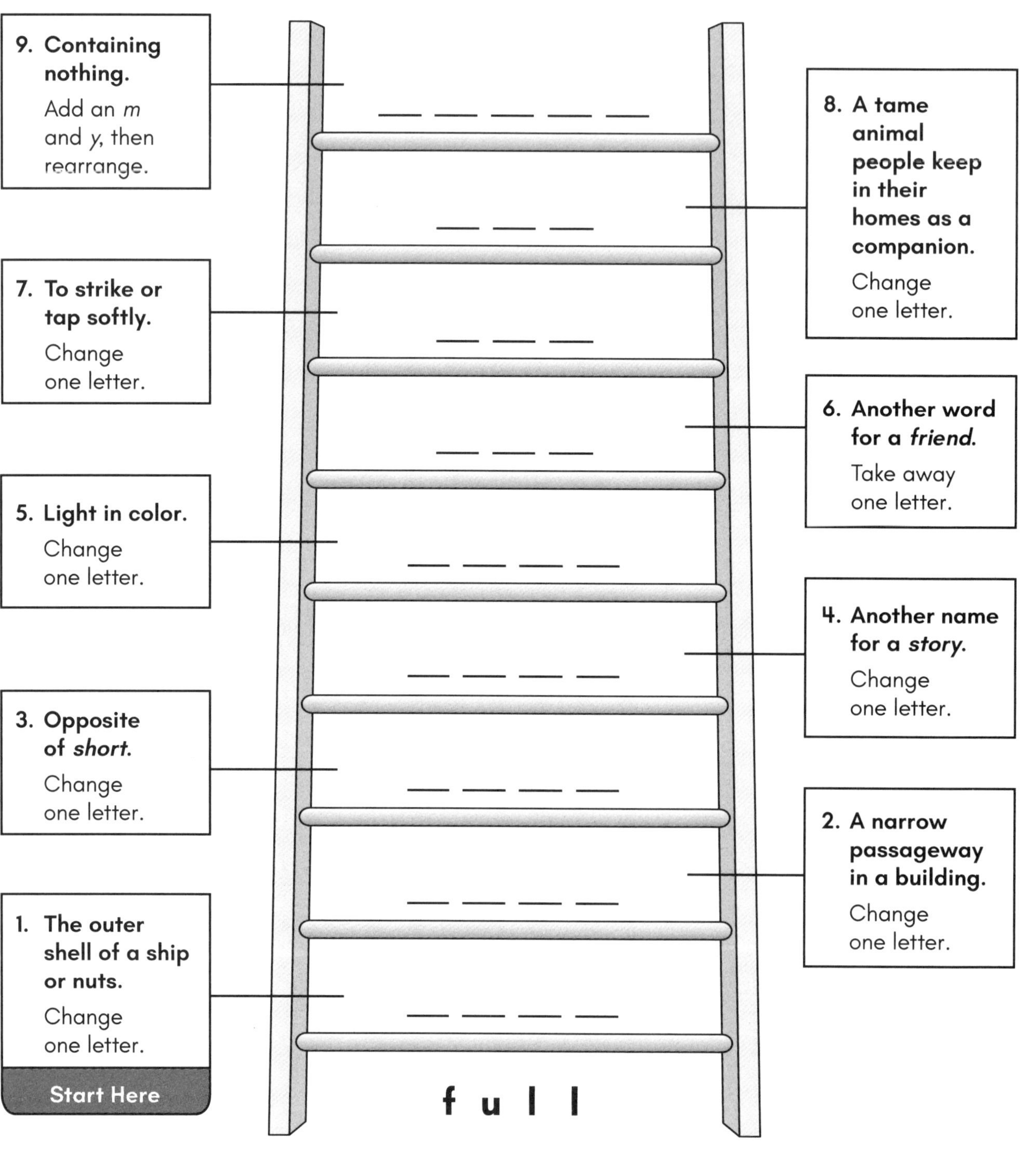

Synonym or antonym? ____________________

Name: ______________________ Date: ____________

Homophones: It's All in the Genes!

Directions: Read each clue and write the answer in the blanks. Notice the first and last words are homophones!

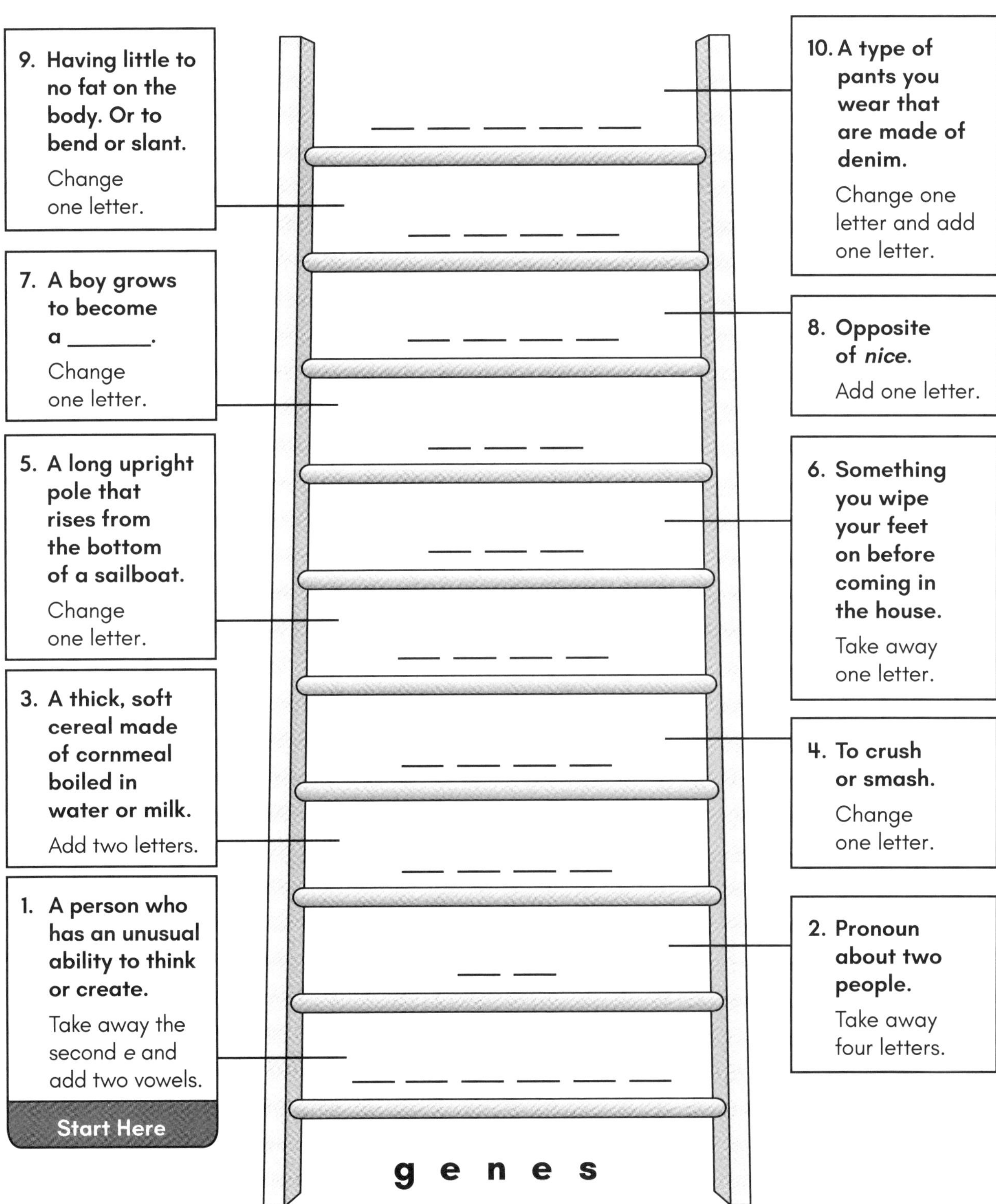

Name: ______________________ Date: ______________

Homophones: Taking a Ferry Ride

Directions: Read each clue and write the answer in the blanks. Notice the first and last words are homophones!

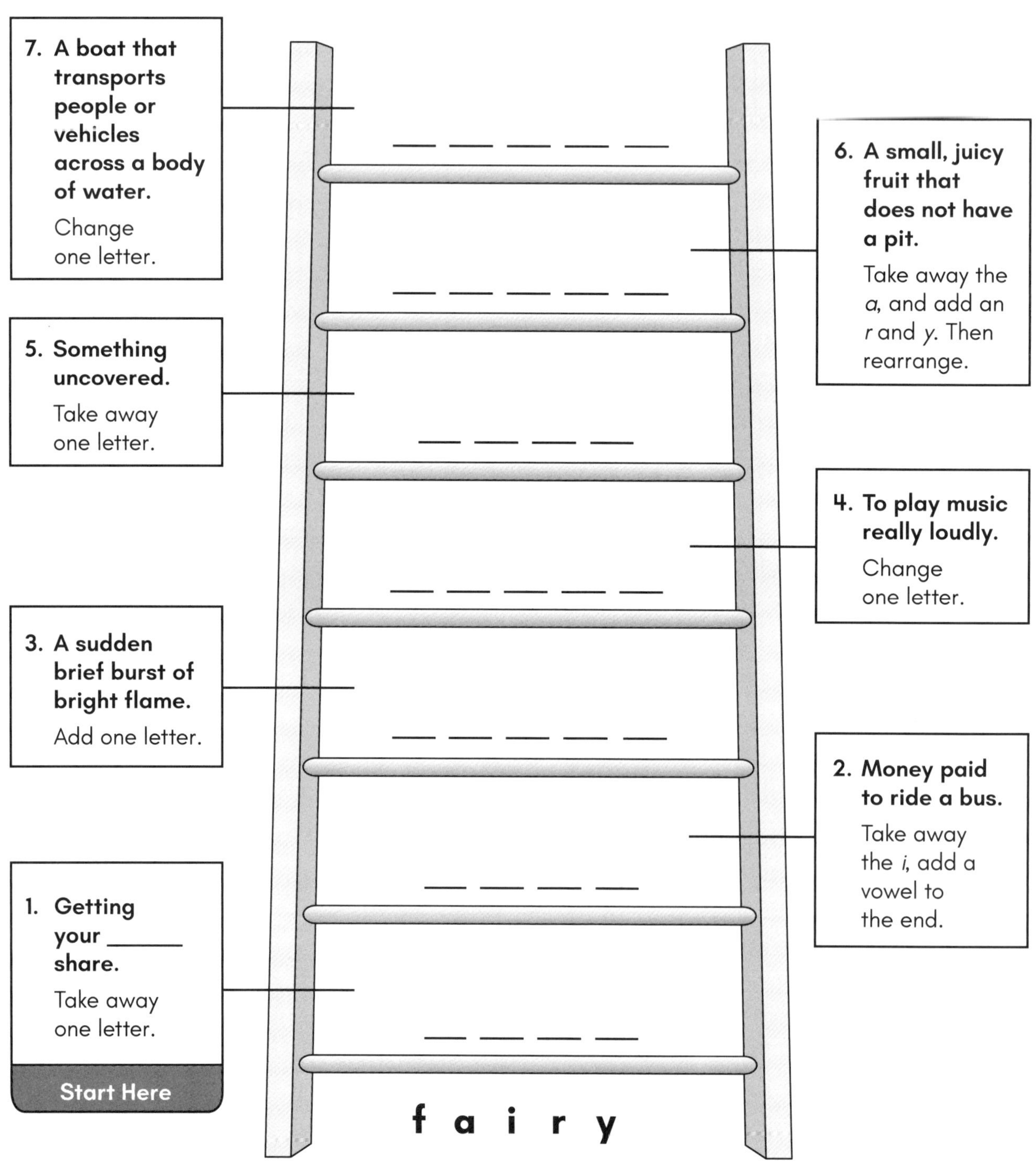

4.0 Commonly Confused Words

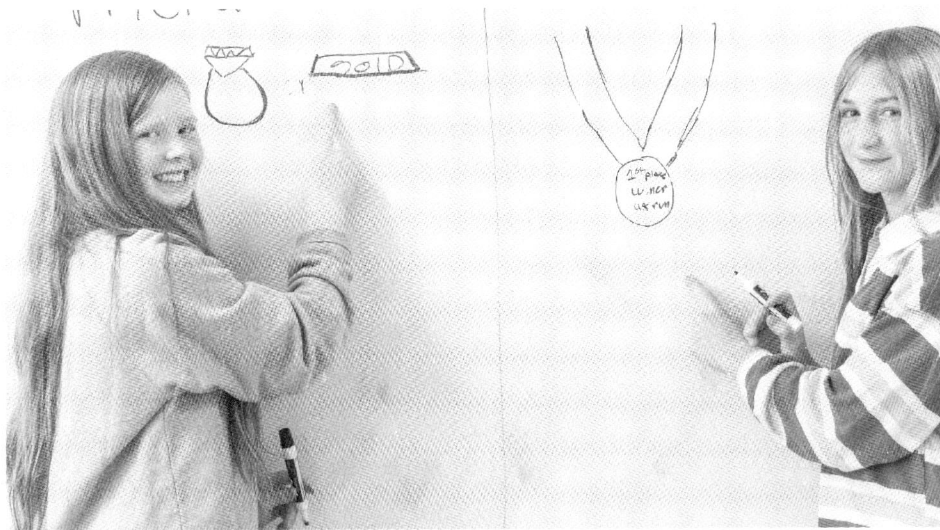

(left) *metal*, (right) *medal*

Distribute one word card from a Commonly Confused Words Set on pages 274–275 to each student. Then have students walk around the room to find a classmate with a card that contains a word that could be easily confused with his or her own word because of spelling or pronunciation. After they find a match, ask both students to research the definitions of their words using a print or online dictionary. On a sheet of paper, have the pair create a mini-poster by writing the two words at the top and creating two separate drawings that capture the meaning of each word. Once the posters are complete, invite students to present them to the class, sharing the definitions of both words and how they might be commonly confused, paying special attention to pronunciation.

Materials	• Commonly Confused Words Set A, Grades 4–5, page 274 • Commonly Confused Words Set B, Grades 6–8, page 275 • paper and colored pencils or markers • print or online dictionary
Grade Band	4–8
Length of Activity	30 minutes
Differentiation Ideas	• **English Learners:** To avoid confusion in the meanings of words, explain the meanings of the words orally rather than looking them up in a dictionary. • **Thriving Learners:** Have students create their drawings digitally.
Extension Ideas	• Compile the drawings into a class book. • Have students write definitions in a word catcher journal. • Direct students to include a clue or something in their picture to help their classmates remember the difference between the two words.
Answers	Answers are paired up next to each other on Commonly Confused Words Sets A and B, pages 274–275

Strategies for Understanding Relationships Among Words

LANGUAGE DOMAINS

Reading

Writing

Speaking

Listening

Commonly Confused Words Set A

breathe	breath	metal	medal
lose	loose	aisle	isle
taught	thought	heal	heel
lightening	lightning	lend	loan
moral	morale	patients	patience
capital	capitol	than	then
dessert	desert	cereal	serial
ant	aunt	advise	advice
accept	except	lay	lie
lead	led	cents	sense

Commonly Confused Words Set B

gallant	gallon	valiant	valance
elimination	illumination	adopt	adapt
chivalry	shivery	incite	insight
indomitable	abominable	decent	descent
site	cite	all ready	already
affect	effect	empathy	sympathy
emigrate	immigrate	mettlesome	meddlesome
complements	compliments	conscience	conscious
confident	confidant	principal	principle
eluded	alluded	regretfully	regrettably

LANGUAGE DOMAINS

Reading

Writing

Speaking

Listening

4.P Homophones: Two Words, One Sentence

Copy a Homophone Cards Set on pages 277–279 and cut apart the cards. Pair students and give them one card and a lined sheet of paper. Have students write down the two homophones on the card and use them both correctly in *one* sentence. When they've finished, have students walk around the room and find a pair of classmates to swap cards with. Then have them go back to their desks and write a sentence with the new card. Continue the process until you call "time." To avoid simple sentences (such as *I have a pair of pears*), show students what a well-written sentence with context and details might look like. Students can share sentences with the class when they've finished writing.

Materials	• Homophone Cards Set A, Grades 2–3, page 277 • Homophone Cards Set B, Grades 4–5, page 278 • Homophone Cards Set C, Grades 6–8, page 279 • lined paper
Grade Band	2–8
Length of Activity	30 minutes
Differentiation Ideas	• **Striving Learners:** Give students simpler homophones. • **English Learners:** Provide extra help by reading students' cards to them before they start creating a sentence.
Extension Ideas	Have students read one of their sentences aloud to the class, leaving out the two homophones and saying "blank" instead. Have the rest of the class guess what the two words are for the blanks and spell each one to be sure the right homophone is used correctly. This promotes critical thinking, as students use the clues in the sentence to figure out the homophones.

Homophone Cards Set A

eight a number between 7 and 9 **ate** past tense of *eat*	**whole** complete, or all of something **hole** empty space or opening	**sea** salt water covering part of Earth **see** to look at something with eyes
which asking to choose one thing **witch** a person with magical powers	**pair** two things that go together **pear** a sweet green fruit	**here** in this place or location **hear** to listen with your ears
right correct, or opposite of left **write** to make words with a pen	**week** seven days in a row **weak** not strong or powerful	**break** to make something stop working **brake** to slow or stop a vehicle
for used to show reason **four** the number after 3	**hi** a friendly way to greet **high** something far up off the ground	**I** refers to yourself, the speaker **eye** the part of the body you see with
new something that has just been made **knew** past tense of *know*	**wood** material from trees used for building **would** shows a choice or possibility	**hour** time: 60 minutes **our** belonging to us
meat the edible parts of animals **meet** to see or talk to someone	**be** to exist or live **bee** a buzzing insect that makes honey	**son** a boy in the family **sun** a star that gives light
tail animal part that wags **tell** to say a story or adventure	**some** a few or part of something **sum** the total when added together	**two** the number after 1 **too** also, or more than needed
dear loved or special to someone **deer** a wild animal with antlers	**no** opposite of *yes* **know** to understand or be aware	**blue** the color of the sky **blew** past tense of *blow*

Homophone Cards Set B

band a group of music players **banned** not allowed, or forbidden	**sail** large fabric on a boat that uses wind **sale** when things are sold at a discount	**tied** fastened with a knot **tide** the rise and fall of the sea
they're contraction for *they are* **their** belonging to them	**wheel** a round object that rolls **we'll** contraction for *we will*	**made** created or built **maid** a person who cleans a house
one a single thing, number before 2 **won** past tense of *win*	**piece** a part of something **peace** calm, or without fighting	**rowed** paddled a boat forward **road** a path for vehicles
stair a step in a staircase **stare** to look for a long time	**flour** powder used for baking **flower** a colorful part of a plant	**through** moving in one side, out the other **threw** past tense of *throw*
knight a soldier in shining armor **night** the time when it's dark	**way** a path or direction **weigh** to measure the weight of something	**pain** a feeling of hurt or discomfort **pane** a flat piece of glass
bear a large wild animal **bare** without covering or clothing	**plane** a flying vehicle **plain** simple, not fancy or decorated	**cent** a coin worth 1/100 **scent** a smell, good or bad
bored feeling uninterested **board** a flat, still surface	**steel** a strong, shiny metal **steal** to take without permission	**flew** past tense of *fly* **flu** a sick feeling with a fever
ball a round object for throwing **bawl** to cry loudly	**wail** a loud, drawn-out cry **whale** a large sea animal	**wait** to stay in one place **weight** how heavy something is

Homophone Cards Set C

pact an agreement between people **packed** something put tightly in place	**beat** to hit or strike repeatedly **beet** a round, red root vegetable	**cereal** breakfast food made of grains **serial** happening over and over
sweet sugary **suite** a set of connected rooms	**peak** the highest point or top **peek** to look at something quickly	**soar** to fly high in the sky **sore** a painful or hurt spot
seam a line where two fabrics join **seem** to appear or look like	**dew** water drops on plants **due** expected to arrive soon	**groan** a sound made from discomfort **grown** bigger or more developed
forth forward or ahead **fourth** the place after third	**pedal** the part of a bike that is pushed **petal** a colorful piece of a flower	**pail** a bucket used for carrying **pale** light in color or shade
heel the back part of the foot **heal** to get better or recover	**sight** the ability to see, or vision **cite** to mention or refer to	**berry** a small, round, juicy fruit **bury** to hide something under the ground
capital a city where government is **capitol** a building where laws are made	**seen** past tense of *see* **scene** a place or part of a story	**steak** a thick slice of meat **stake** a pointed post or support
base the bottom or starting point **bass** the lowest sound in music	**oar** a paddle used for rowing **or** a word used for choice	**sew** to stitch fabric together **sow** to plant seeds in soil
hoarse a rough or scratchy voice **horse** a large animal that is ridden	**principal** the head of a school **principle** a basic rule or truth	**hire** to pay someone for work **higher** at a greater level or height

CHAPTER 4
Exploration of Word Relationships

Strategies for Understanding Relationships Among Words

LANGUAGE DOMAINS

Reading

Writing

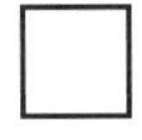

Speaking

Listening

4.Q Find the Relationship

Pair students and provide them with a Find the Relationship Set on pages 281–282. Prompt them to discuss and identify the relationship among the words in each set. Alternatively, structure this strategy as a whole-class game by putting students in groups and giving just ONE word at a time. Have a member of each group say what group members think the relationship is. If they get it on the first try, they get three points; second try, two points; third try, one point.

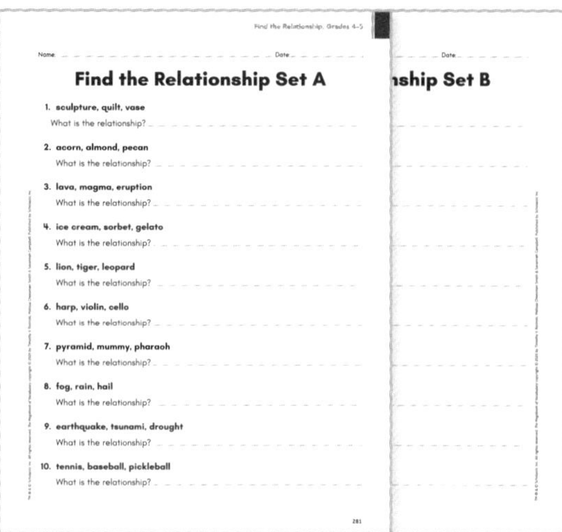

Name ______ Date ______

Find the Relationship Set A

1. sculpture, quilt, vase
What is the relationship? ______
2. acorn, almond, pecan
What is the relationship? ______
3. lava, magma, eruption
What is the relationship? ______
4. ice cream, sorbet, gelato
What is the relationship? ______
5. lion, tiger, leopard
What is the relationship? ______
6. harp, violin, cello
What is the relationship? ______
7. pyramid, mummy, pharaoh
What is the relationship? ______
8. fog, rain, hail
What is the relationship? ______
9. earthquake, tsunami, drought
What is the relationship? ______
10. tennis, baseball, pickleball
What is the relationship? ______

281

Materials	• Find the Relationship Set A, Grades 4–5, page 281 • Find the Relationship Set B, Grades 6–8, page 282
Grade Band	4–8
Length of Activity	20 minutes
Differentiation Ideas	**Striving Learners and English Learners:** Check the list to see if there are any words they may not know beforehand and review as a class or with the students by themselves so they are able to understand each problem.
Extension Ideas	• Have students create their own related groups of words on index cards and share them. • Have students find relationships within groups of words related to the content you are teaching. • Create your own set of word groups using an AI website and prompt: Give me 10 sets of words that each have a category that students must guess to find. (Be sure to check any AI results to make sure they are appropriate.)
Answers	**Set A: 1.** art hobby products **2.** types of nuts **3.** volcanic activity **4.** frozen desserts **5.** wild cats **6.** string instruments **7.** ancient Egypt **8.** types of precipitation **9.** natural disasters **10.** sports with small balls **Set B: 1.** desert life **2.** types of fungi **3.** mythical creatures **4.** space exploration **5.** Latin dance styles **6.** solar phenomena **7.** brain teasers **8.** insects with skinny bodies **9.** sea gods **10.** temperature scales

Name: ____________________ Date: __________

Find the Relationship Set A

1. **sculpture, quilt, vase**

   What is the relationship? ____________________

2. **acorn, almond, pecan**

   What is the relationship? ____________________

3. **lava, magma, eruption**

   What is the relationship? ____________________

4. **ice cream, sorbet, gelato**

   What is the relationship? ____________________

5. **lion, tiger, leopard**

   What is the relationship? ____________________

6. **harp, violin, cello**

   What is the relationship? ____________________

7. **pyramid, mummy, pharaoh**

   What is the relationship? ____________________

8. **fog, rain, hail**

   What is the relationship? ____________________

9. **earthquake, tsunami, drought**

   What is the relationship? ____________________

10. **tennis, baseball, pickleball**

    What is the relationship? ____________________

Name: ________________________ Date: ____________

Find the Relationship Set B

1. **cactus, dune, mirage**

   What is the relationship? ________________________

2. **yeast, mold, mushroom**

   What is the relationship? ________________________

3. **dragon, unicorn, werewolf**

   What is the relationship? ________________________

4. **telescope, astronaut, gravity**

   What is the relationship? ________________________

5. **salsa, tango, cha-cha**

   What is the relationship? ________________________

6. **solar flare, eclipse, meteor shower**

   What is the relationship? ________________________

7. **maze, riddle, puzzle**

   What is the relationship? ________________________

8. **cicada, grasshopper, praying mantis**

   What is the relationship? ________________________

9. **Triton, Neptune, Poseidon**

   What is the relationship? ________________________

10. **Celsius, Fahrenheit, Kelvin**

    What is the relationship? ________________________

Strategies for Interpreting Figurative Language

4.R **Idiom Word Ladders**

Distribute an Idiom Word Ladder on pages 284–285 to students. Have students read each clue, determine an answer, and fill in the blank, giving additional clues if they need support. Then have them use the first and last words to complete the idiom under the ladder.

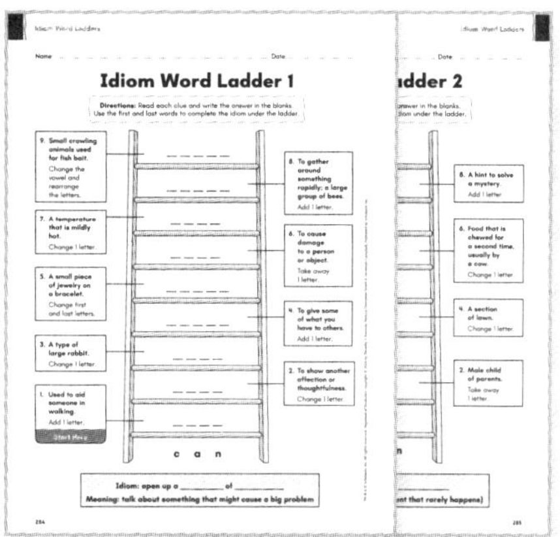

Idiom Word Ladder 1

Idiom: open up a ______ of ______

Meaning: talk about something that might cause a big problem

Materials	• Idiom Word Ladder 1, page 284 • Idiom Word Ladder 2, page 285
Grade Band	4–8
Length of Activity	10 minutes per activity
Differentiation Ideas	• **Striving Learners:** Provide the word for the more challenging parts of the word ladder, or provide the first letter of each word as a clue. • **English Learners:** Give students the words in the ladder, but jumble them, so they have a list to choose from.
Extension Ideas	Check out more Word Ladders from Scholastic: • *Daily Word Ladders: Idioms*, Rasinski & Smith • *Daily Word Ladders: Content Areas*, Rasinski & Smith • *Daily Word Ladders: Grades K–1*, Rasinski • *Daily Word Ladders: Grades 2–3*, Rasinski • *Daily Word Ladders: Grades 4–6*, Rasinski • *Partner Poems & Word Ladders for Building Foundational Literacy Skills*, Harrison, Rasinski & Fresch
Answers	• **Idiom Word Ladder 1:** open a can of worms—can, cane, care, hare, share, charm, harm, warm, swarm, worms • **Idiom Word Ladder 2:** once in a blue moon—moon, soon, son, sob, sod, cod, cud, cue, clue, blue

LANGUAGE DOMAINS

Reading

Writing

Speaking

Listening

Name: ______________________ Date: ______________

Idiom Word Ladder 1

Directions: Read each clue and write the answer in the blanks. Use the first and last words to complete the idiom under the ladder.

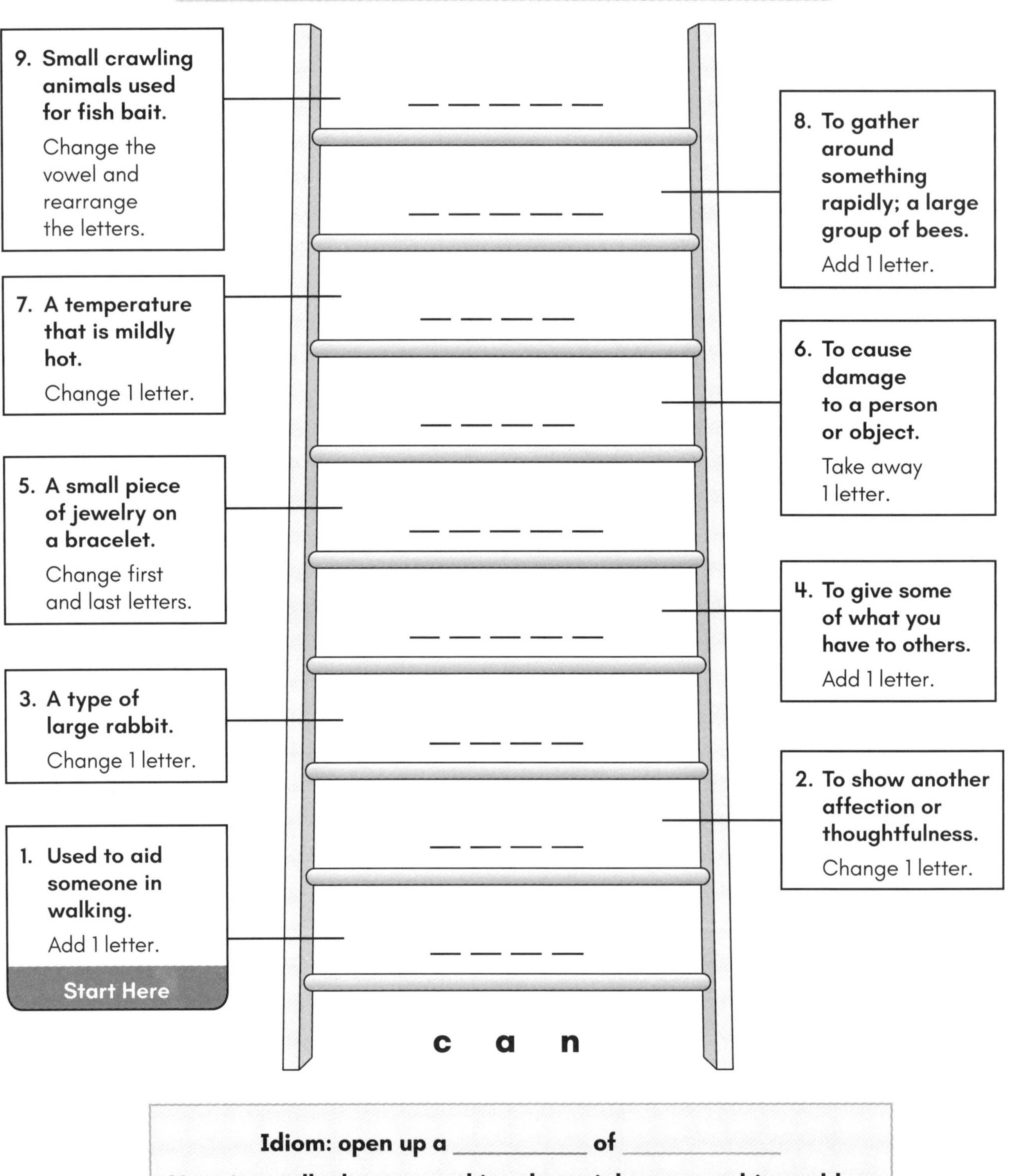

Idiom: open up a __________ of __________

Meaning: talk about something that might cause a big problem

Name: ______________________ Date: ______________

Idiom Word Ladder 2

Directions: Read each clue and write the answer in the blanks. Use the first and last words to complete the idiom under the ladder.

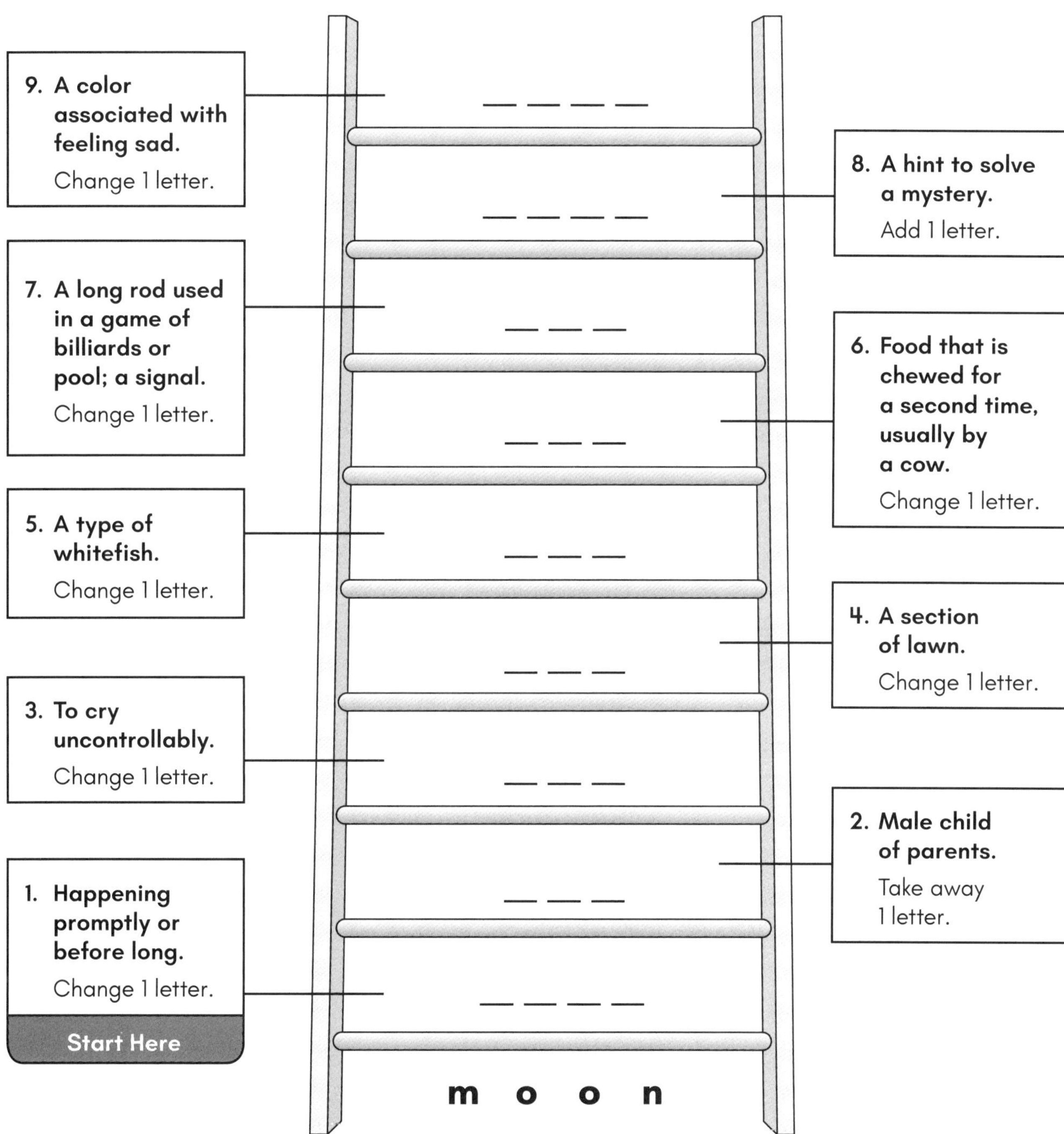

Idiom: once in a ____________ ____________

Meaning: very infrequently (e.g., an event that rarely happens)

Strategies for Interpreting Figurative Language

LANGUAGE DOMAINS

Reading

Writing

Speaking

Listening

4.S Idiom Mini-Posters

Explore the difference between literal and figurative meanings by providing a familiar example such as *raining cats and dogs*. The literal meaning suggests animals falling from the sky, while the figurative meaning suggests raining heavily. Next, choose an idiom and its definition to explore, or select one from the Common Idioms on pages 287–289. Ask each student to fold a blank sheet of paper in half, write the idiom at the top, then label one side *literal* and the other side *figurative*. Then, have students use colored pencils to illustrate both interpretations. From there, ask students to share their drawings and explanations with the class or in small groups.

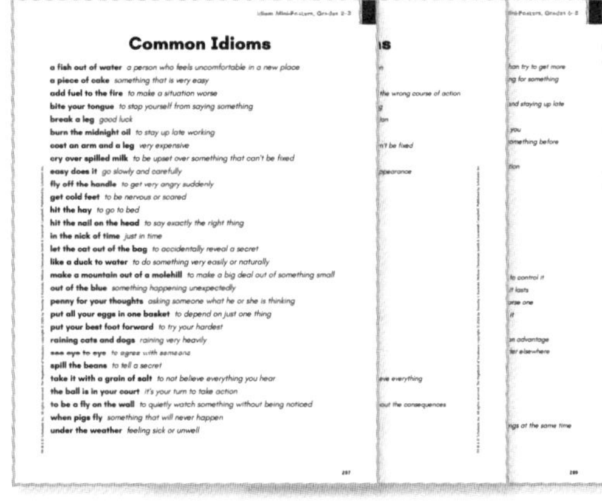

Common Idioms

a fish out of water *a person who feels uncomfortable in a new place*
a piece of cake *something that is very easy*
add fuel to the fire *to make a situation worse*
bite your tongue *to stop yourself from saying something*
break a leg *good luck*
burn the midnight oil *to stay up late working*
cost an arm and a leg *very expensive*
cry over spilled milk *to be upset over something that can't be fixed*
easy does it *go slowly and carefully*
fly off the handle *to get very angry suddenly*
get cold feet *to be nervous or scared*
hit the hay *to go to bed*
hit the nail on the head *to say exactly the right thing*
in the nick of time *just in time*
let the cat out of the bag *to accidentally reveal a secret*
like a duck to water *to do something very easily or naturally*
make a mountain out of a molehill *to make a big deal out of something small*
out of the blue *something happening unexpectedly*
penny for your thoughts *asking someone what he or she is thinking*
put all your eggs in one basket *to depend on just one thing*
put your best foot forward *to try your hardest*
raining cats and dogs *raining very heavily*
see eye to eye *to agree with someone*
spill the beans *to tell a secret*
take it with a grain of salt *to not believe everything you hear*
the ball is in your court *it's your turn to take action*
to be a fly on the wall *to quietly watch something without being noticed*
when pigs fly *something that will never happen*
under the weather *feeling sick or unwell*

Materials	• sheets of white paper • colored pencils or markers • Common Idioms, Grades 2–3, page 287 • Common Idioms, Grades 4–5, page 288 • Common Idioms, Grades 6–8, page 289
Grade Band	2–8
Length of Activity	30 minutes
Differentiation Ideas	**Striving Learners and English Learners:** Be sure students understand the meaning of the idiom before they begin drawing. Brainstorm with students ideas of what to draw to ensure they understand not only the idiom, but the difference between literal and figurative.
Extension Ideas	• Find 5–8 idioms related to a content area and let students choose one. For example, when the class is studying the solar system, idioms could be: *over the moon* or *shoot for the stars*. • Investigate one idiom each week. Display students' drawings on a rotating basis, placing each week's drawing at the front of the classroom in a sheet protector. Have students keep a binder of their drawings throughout the year as a keepsake to take home at the end of the year.

Common Idioms

a fish out of water *a person who feels uncomfortable in a new place*

a piece of cake *something that is very easy*

add fuel to the fire *to make a situation worse*

bite your tongue *to stop yourself from saying something*

break a leg *good luck*

burn the midnight oil *to stay up late working*

cost an arm and a leg *very expensive*

cry over spilled milk *to be upset over something that can't be fixed*

easy does it *go slowly and carefully*

fly off the handle *to get very angry suddenly*

get cold feet *to be nervous or scared*

hit the hay *to go to bed*

hit the nail on the head *to say exactly the right thing*

in the nick of time *just in time*

let the cat out of the bag *to accidentally reveal a secret*

like a duck to water *to do something very easily or naturally*

make a mountain out of a molehill *to make a big deal out of something small*

out of the blue *something happening unexpectedly*

penny for your thoughts *asking someone what he or she is thinking*

put all your eggs in one basket *to depend on just one thing*

put your best foot forward *to try your hardest*

raining cats and dogs *raining very heavily*

see eye to eye *to agree with someone*

spill the beans *to tell a secret*

take it with a grain of salt *to not believe everything you hear*

the ball is in your court *it's your turn to take action*

to be a fly on the wall *to quietly watch something without being noticed*

when pigs fly *something that will never happen*

under the weather *feeling sick or unwell*

Common Idioms

at the drop of a hat *to do something immediately, without hesitation*

back to square one *to start over after a failure*

barking up the wrong tree *to make a wrong assumption or pursue the wrong course of action*

bite the bullet *to do something unpleasant that you've been avoiding*

break the ice *to make people feel more comfortable in a new situation*

by the book *to do something exactly as the rules or instructions say*

cry over spilled milk *to worry or get upset about something that can't be fixed*

cut to the chase *to get to the point without wasting time*

don't judge a book by its cover *don't make judgments based on appearance*

fish out of water *a person who feels out of place in a situation*

get cold feet *to feel nervous or scared about doing something*

go the extra mile *to do more than what is expected*

have a heart of gold *to be kind and caring*

hit the jackpot *to get something unexpectedly good or valuable*

in a nutshell *explained in a very short and simple way*

jump through hoops *to do something difficult or complicated*

keep your chin up *to stay positive and not give up*

let off steam *to release pent-up emotions or energy*

look before you leap *to think carefully before doing something*

miss the boat *to miss an opportunity*

on cloud nine *feeling extremely happy or excited*

on the ball *to be quick to understand and respond*

out of the blue *something happening unexpectedly*

put a sock in it *to tell someone to be quiet*

take with a grain of salt *to not take something too seriously or believe everything*

the ball is in your court *it's your turn to take action*

throw caution to the wind *to take a risk or act without worrying about the consequences*

turn over a new leaf *to start fresh or change one's behavior*

under your nose *right in front of you, but you didn't notice*

with flying colors *to succeed or pass something easily*

Common Idioms

a bird in the hand is worth two in the bush *keep what you have rather than try to get more*

a watched pot never boils *time seems to move slower when you are waiting for something*

bite off more than you can chew *to take on more than you can handle*

burn the candle at both ends *to work too hard by doing too many things and staying up late*

cry wolf *to raise a false alarm*

don't bite the hand that feeds you *don't be ungrateful to those who help you*

don't count your chickens before they hatch *don't assume you will get something before it happens*

every cloud has a silver lining *there is something good in every bad situation*

hit the road *to leave or begin a journey*

if the shoe fits, wear it *if something applies to you, accept it*

in hot water *in trouble*

jump on the bandwagon *to join others in doing something popular*

jump the gun *to start something too early*

keep an eye on *to watch something carefully*

keep your fingers crossed *to hope for good luck*

let sleeping dogs lie *don't stir up trouble that has already been settled*

let the chips fall where they may *to let something happen without trying to control it*

make hay while the sun shines *take advantage of a good situation while it lasts*

out of the frying pan and into the fire *going from a bad situation to a worse one*

practice makes perfect *the more you do something, the better you get at it*

put your money where your mouth is *to take action on what you say*

the early bird catches the worm *the person who arrives or acts first has an advantage*

the grass is always greener on the other side *things are not always better elsewhere*

through thick and thin *to support someone in good and bad times*

throw in the towel *to give up or quit*

under someone's thumb *to be controlled by someone*

walking on air *feeling extremely happy*

wear your heart on your sleeve *to openly show your emotions*

you can't have your cake and eat it too *you can't have two opposing things at the same time*

your guess is as good as mine *I don't know either*

Strategies for Interpreting Figurative Language

LANGUAGE DOMAINS

Reading
☐

Writing
☐

Speaking
☑

Listening
☑

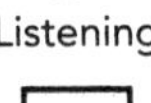

4.T Mystery Idioms Game

Choose a set of idioms from the Mystery Idioms list on page 291, or create a set yourself made up of words that relate to a unit of study. Organize students into small groups and provide each group a dry-erase board and marker. Then reveal the topic of the mystery idioms (space, geography, etc.). To begin the game, read the boldfaced keyword and definition for each idiom. Prompt groups to discuss and guess an idiom that matches the clues. Have each group write the idiom they think is being described on the dry-erase board, and have all groups reveal their answers simultaneously. From there, give the answer, or "the mystery idiom." Tally correct responses on the board and continue the process until all idioms have been revealed and a winner is determined.

Materials	• Mystery Idioms, page 291 • dry-erase boards and markers
Grade Band	4–8
Length of Activity	Varies
Differentiation Ideas	**Striving Learners and English Learners:** Provide the list of idioms instead of just the word.
Extension Ideas	• Have students come up with other idioms that fit into this theme. • Encourage students to come up with sentences or situations where this idiom can be used in context. • Give students a new keyword each week and ask them to figure out the mystery idiom, perhaps as part of a weekly class riddle. • The mystery idioms from the game can also be used with the Idioms Mini-Posters strategy on page 286.

Mystery Idioms

Environment and Nature

- blow off **steam**: to release pent-up stress, often through physical activity
- make **waves**: to cause a disturbance or controversy
- a drop in the **ocean**: a very small amount compared to what is needed
- going **green**: to adopt environmentally friendly practices
- sink or **swim**: to either succeed or fail, depending on one's efforts
- the tip of the **iceberg**: only a small part of a much larger issue or situation
- under the **weather**: feeling ill or unwell
- a **storm** is brewing: trouble or conflict is about to happen

Space Exploration

- shoot for the **stars**: to aim for something very high or difficult to achieve
- the **sky's** the limit: there's no limit to what can be achieved
- over the **moon**: extremely happy or delighted
- a **star** is born: someone who is becoming very successful or famous
- lost in **space**: feeling disoriented or confused
- catch a falling **star**: to achieve something rare or unattainable
- out of this **world**: extraordinary or amazing
- to be in **orbit**: to be very focused or engaged in something

Land and Water

- a flat-**earther**: a person who refuses to acknowledge common facts or ideas
- a **mountain** to climb: a difficult task or obstacle to overcome
- **climbing** the ladder: moving up in a career or social status
- a **drop** in the bucket: a small or insignificant amount
- walking on **air**: feeling extremely happy or euphoric
- in hot **water**: in trouble or difficulty
- on top of the **world**: feeling very happy and successful
- in the same **boat**: facing the same challenges or difficulties together

Human Anatomy

- back on your **feet**: to recover from a setback or illness
- get under someone's **skin**: to irritate or annoy someone
- a pain in the **neck**: something or someone that is irritating
- head over **heels**: completely in love or infatuated
- keep your **head**: to stay calm in a stressful situation
- with all your **heart**: doing something with great passion or enthusiasm
- a **heart** of gold: a kind and compassionate disposition
- lend a **hand**: to offer help
- bite your **tongue**: to hold back from saying something, often hurtful

Physics

- a butterfly **effect**: a small change leading to large consequences
- at the speed of **light**: very quickly, almost instantly
- full **throttle**: to go at maximum speed or intensity
- **bend** over backward: to make a great effort to do something
- **pull** the plug: to stop something abruptly
- under **pressure**: to feel stress or tension in a situation
- change **gears**: to switch or adjust to a different activity or way of thinking
- a **balancing** act: to juggle multiple responsibilities without letting any fail

Habitats and Ecosystems

- a **fish** out of water: a person who feels uncomfortable or out of place in a particular situation
- **home** is where the heart is: when a place where you feel most comfortable is your home
- a **nest** egg: money saved for the future, often for emergencies or retirement
- bury your head in the **sand**: to ignore an obvious problem or situation
- birds of a feather **flock** together: people with similar characteristics stick together
- the **lion's** share: the largest portion or most significant part of something
- in the lion's **den**: in a very dangerous or challenging situation
- a **home** away from home: a place that feels as comfortable as your own home

Psychology

- **mind** over matter: the ability to overcome physical limitations using mental strength
- on the same **wavelength**: to think or understand things in the same way
- in the back of your **mind**: being aware of but not thinking about consciously
- a gut **feeling**: a strong instinct or intuition about something
- out of sight, out of **mind**: forgetting about something when it is no longer present
- a roller coaster of **emotions**: experiencing strong, changing emotions
- in the **moment**: fully engaged in or focused on what is happening right now
- lightbulb **moment**: a sudden realization or understanding of something

Genes and Heredity

- like **father**, like son: when children tend to resemble or behave like their parents
- a **chip** off the old block: a person who is very similar to one of his or her parents
- run in the **family**: a trait or condition that is common among members of a family
- **blood** is thicker than water: family bonds are stronger than other relationships
- **born** with a silver spoon in your mouth: to be born into a privileged family
- cut from the **same** cloth: people who are very similar in appearance or behavior
- a spitting **image**: someone who looks exactly like another related person
- the apple doesn't fall far from the **tree**: when children act like or resemble their parents

CHAPTER 4

Exploration of Word Relationships

Strategies for Interpreting Figurative Language

LANGUAGE DOMAINS

Reading

Writing

Speaking

Listening

4.U Identifying Similes and Metaphors

Review the definitions of *simile* (comparison of two unlike things, using *like* or *as*) and *metaphor* (comparison of two unlike things, stating one is another). Distribute a Similes and Metaphors Set on pages 293–294. Have students identify each sentence as a simile or a metaphor, and ask them to put a box around the two things being compared.

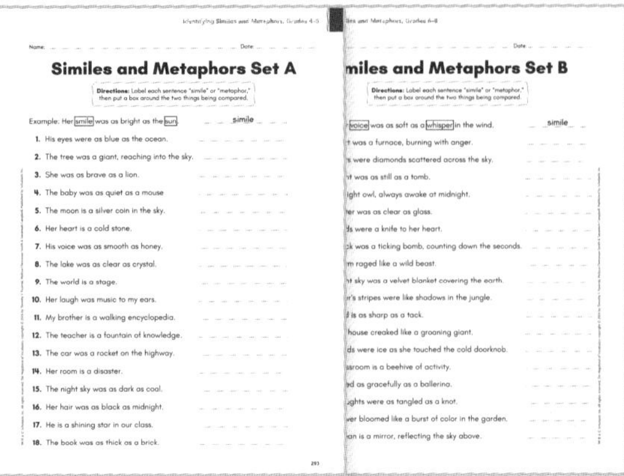

Identifying Similes and Metaphors, Grades 4-5

Name: Date:

Similes and Metaphors Set A

Directions: Label each sentence "simile" or "metaphor," then put a box around the two things being compared.

Example: Her smile was as bright as the sun. simile

1. His eyes were as blue as the ocean.
2. The tree was a giant, reaching into the sky.
3. She was as brave as a lion.
4. The baby was as quiet as a mouse
5. The moon is a silver coin in the sky.
6. Her heart is a cold stone.
7. His voice was as smooth as honey.
8. The lake was as clear as crystal.
9. The world is a stage.
10. Her laugh was music to my ears.
11. My brother is a walking encyclopedia.
12. The teacher is a fountain of knowledge.
13. The car was a rocket on the highway.
14. Her room is a disaster.
15. The night sky was as dark as coal.
16. Her hair was as black as midnight.
17. He is a shining star in our class.
18. The book was as thick as a brick.

293

...iles and Metaphors, Grades 6-8

Date:

...miles and Metaphors Set B

Directions: Label each sentence "simile" or "metaphor," then put a box around the two things being compared.

...voice was as soft as a whisper in the wind. simile

...t was a furnace, burning with anger.

...s were diamonds scattered across the sky.

...t was as still as a tomb.

...ight owl, always awake at midnight.

...er was as clear as glass.

...ds were a knife to her heart.

...k was a ticking bomb, counting down the seconds.

...m raged like a wild beast.

...t sky was a velvet blanket covering the earth.

...r's stripes were like shadows in the jungle.

...d is as sharp as a tack.

...house creaked like a groaning giant.

...ds were ice as she touched the cold doorknob.

...sroom is a beehive of activity.

...d as gracefully as a ballerina.

...ghts were as tangled as a knot.

...ver bloomed like a burst of color in the garden.

...an is a mirror, reflecting the sky above.

Materials	• Similes and Metaphors Set A, Grades 4–5, page 293 • Similes and Metaphors Set B, Grades 6–8, page 294
Grade Band	4–8
Length of Activity	15 minutes
Differentiation Ideas	**Striving Learners and English Learners:** Brainstorm and write a couple of similes and metaphors with them first so they understand how to tell the difference between the two.
Extension Ideas	Direct students to choose one to expand with more details, then create a drawing of the simile or metaphor. These can then be displayed on a bulletin board with their drawings and sentences.
Answers	Answer states simile or metaphor, then boxed words: **Set A: 1.** simile, eyes/ocean **2.** metaphor, tree/giant **3.** simile, she/lion **4.** simile, baby/mouse **5.** metaphor, moon/coin **6.** metaphor, heart/stone **7.** simile, voice/honey **8.** simile, lake/crystal **9.** metaphor, world/stage **10.** metaphor, laugh/music **11.** metaphor, brother/encyclopedia **12.** metaphor, teacher/fountain **13.** metaphor, car/rocket **14.** metaphor, room/disaster **15.** simile, sky/coal **16.** simile, hair/midnight **17.** metaphor, he/star **18.** simile, book/brick **Set B: 1.** metaphor, heart/furnace **2.** metaphor, stars/diamonds **3.** simile, night/tomb **4.** metaphor, he/owl **5.** simile, water/glass **6.** metaphor, words/knife **7.** metaphor, clock/bomb **8.** simile, storm/beast **9.** metaphor, sky/blanket **10.** simile, stripes/shadows **11.** simile, mind/tack **12.** simile, house/giant **13.** metaphor, hands/ice **14.** metaphor, classroom/beehive **15.** simile, he/ballerina **16.** simile, thoughts/knot **17.** simile, flower/burst **18.** metaphor, ocean/mirror

Name: ______________________ Date: ____________

Similes and Metaphors Set A

Directions: Label each sentence "simile" or "metaphor," then put a box around the two things being compared.

Example: Her [smile] was as bright as the [sun]. simile

1. His eyes were as blue as the ocean. ____________
2. The tree was a giant, reaching into the sky. ____________
3. She was as brave as a lion. ____________
4. The baby was as quiet as a mouse. ____________
5. The moon is a silver coin in the sky. ____________
6. Her heart is a cold stone. ____________
7. His voice was as smooth as honey. ____________
8. The lake was as clear as crystal. ____________
9. The world is a stage. ____________
10. Her laugh was music to my ears. ____________
11. My brother is a walking encyclopedia. ____________
12. The teacher is a fountain of knowledge. ____________
13. The car was a rocket on the highway. ____________
14. Her room is a disaster. ____________
15. The night sky was as dark as coal. ____________
16. Her hair was as black as midnight. ____________
17. He is a shining star in our class. ____________
18. The book was as thick as a brick. ____________

Name: ______________________ Date: __________

Similes and Metaphors Set B

Directions: Label each sentence "simile" or "metaphor," then put a box around the two things being compared.

Example: Her [voice] was as soft as a [whisper] in the wind. simile

1. His heart was a furnace, burning with anger. ______
2. The stars were diamonds scattered across the sky. ______
3. The night was as still as a tomb. ______
4. He's a night owl, always awake at midnight. ______
5. The water was as clear as glass. ______
6. His words were a knife to her heart. ______
7. The clock was a ticking bomb, counting down the seconds. ______
8. The storm raged like a wild beast. ______
9. The night sky was a velvet blanket covering the earth. ______
10. The tiger's stripes were like shadows in the jungle. ______
11. His mind is as sharp as a tack. ______
12. The old house creaked like a groaning giant. ______
13. Her hands were ice as she touched the cold doorknob. ______
14. The classroom is a beehive of activity. ______
15. He moved as gracefully as a ballerina. ______
16. Her thoughts were as tangled as a knot. ______
17. The flower bloomed like a burst of color in the garden. ______
18. The ocean is a mirror, reflecting the sky above. ______

4.V Writing Similes and Metaphors

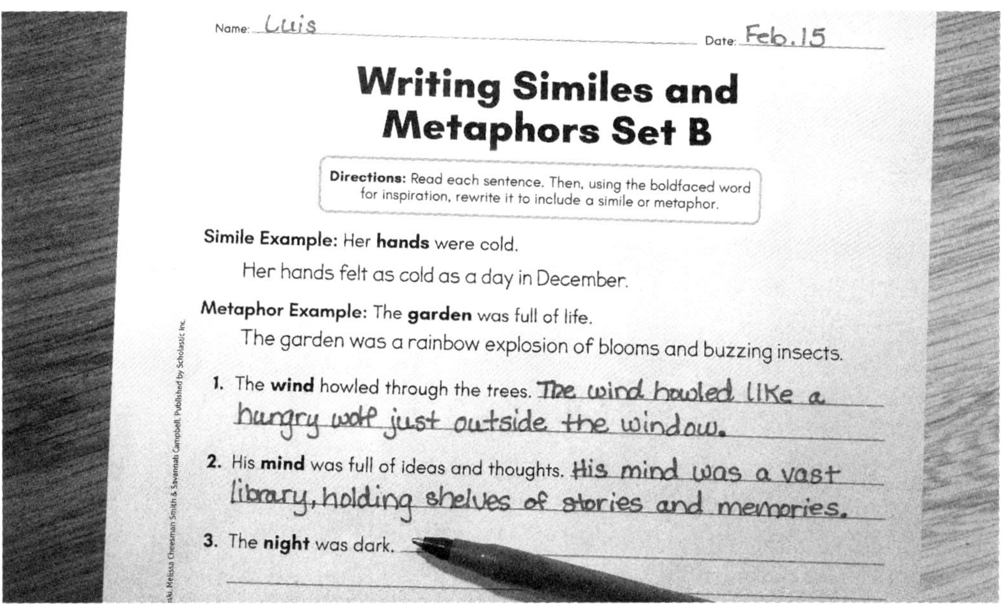
Name: Luis Date: Feb. 15

Writing Similes and Metaphors Set B

Directions: Read each sentence. Then, using the boldfaced word for inspiration, rewrite it to include a simile or metaphor.

Simile Example: Her **hands** were cold.

Her hands felt as cold as a day in December.

Metaphor Example: The **garden** was full of life.

The garden was a rainbow explosion of blooms and buzzing insects.

1. The **wind** howled through the trees. The wind howled like a hungry wolf just outside the window.
2. His **mind** was full of ideas and thoughts. His mind was a vast library, holding shelves of stories and memories.
3. The **night** was dark.

Remind students of the difference between similes and metaphors. (A simile is a comparison using *like* or *as*; a metaphor is a comparison saying one thing is another.) Distribute the Writing Similes and Metaphors Sets on pages 296–297, and review the examples with the students. Then have students read the sentences and rewrite them as a simile or metaphor.

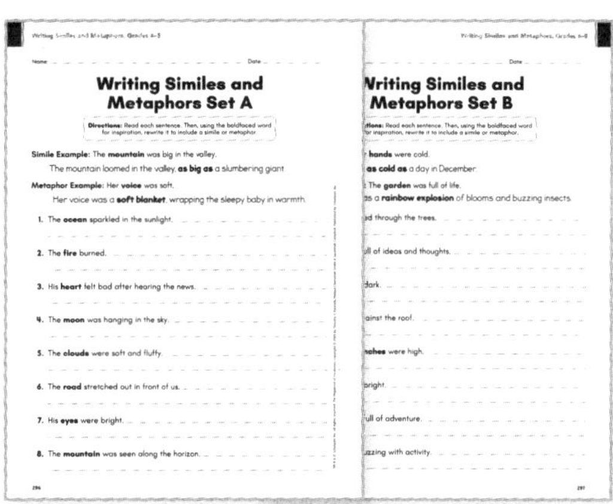
Writing Similes and Metaphors Set A

Simile Example: The **mountain** was big in the valley.

The mountain loomed in the valley, **as big as** a slumbering giant.

Metaphor Example: Her **voice** was soft.

Her voice was a **soft blanket**, wrapping the sleepy baby in warmth.

1. The **ocean** sparkled in the sunlight.
2. The **fire** burned.
3. His **heart** felt bad after hearing the news.
4. The **moon** was hanging in the sky.
5. The **clouds** were soft and fluffy.
6. The **road** stretched out in front of us.
7. His **eyes** were bright.
8. The **mountain** was seen along the horizon.

Writing Similes and Metaphors Set B

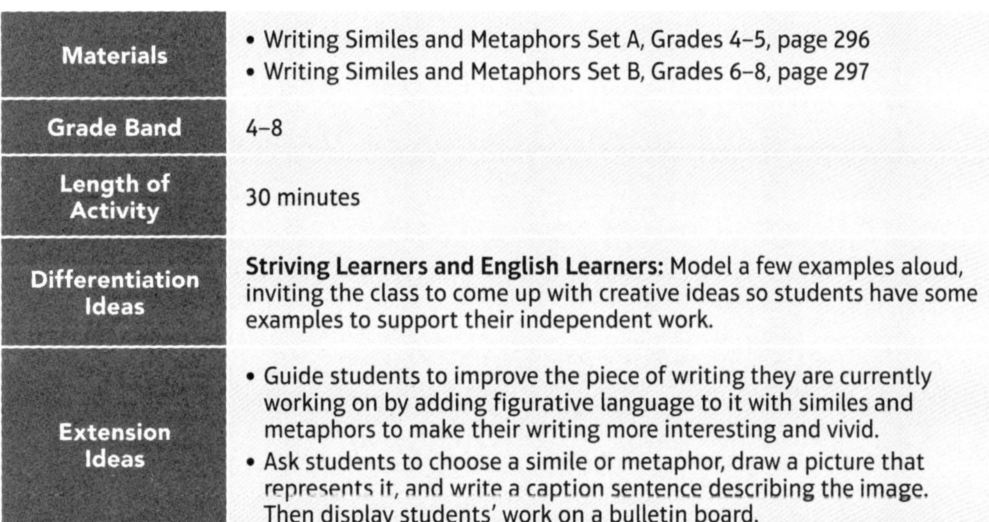

Materials	• Writing Similes and Metaphors Set A, Grades 4–5, page 296 • Writing Similes and Metaphors Set B, Grades 6–8, page 297
Grade Band	4–8
Length of Activity	30 minutes
Differentiation Ideas	**Striving Learners and English Learners:** Model a few examples aloud, inviting the class to come up with creative ideas so students have some examples to support their independent work.
Extension Ideas	• Guide students to improve the piece of writing they are currently working on by adding figurative language to it with similes and metaphors to make their writing more interesting and vivid. • Ask students to choose a simile or metaphor, draw a picture that represents it, and write a caption sentence describing the image. Then display students' work on a bulletin board.

LANGUAGE DOMAINS

Reading

Writing

Speaking

Listening

Name: ______________________ Date: __________

Writing Similes and Metaphors Set A

Directions: Read each sentence. Then, using the boldfaced word for inspiration, rewrite it to include a simile or metaphor.

Simile Example: The **mountain** was big in the valley.

The mountain loomed in the valley, **as big as** a slumbering giant.

Metaphor Example: Her **voice** was soft.

Her voice was a **soft blanket**, wrapping the sleepy baby in warmth.

1. The **ocean** sparkled in the sunlight. ______________________

2. The **fire** burned. ______________________

3. His **heart** felt bad after hearing the news. ______________________

4. The **moon** was hanging in the sky. ______________________

5. The **clouds** were soft and fluffy. ______________________

6. The **road** stretched out in front of us. ______________________

7. His **eyes** were bright. ______________________

8. The **mountain** was seen along the horizon. ______________________

Name: ______________________ Date: ______________

Writing Similes and Metaphors Set B

Directions: Read each sentence. Then, using the boldfaced word for inspiration, rewrite it to include a simile or metaphor.

Simile Example: Her **hands** were cold.

Her hands felt **as cold as** a day in December.

Metaphor Example: The **garden** was full of life.

The garden was a **rainbow explosion** of blooms and buzzing insects.

1. The **wind** howled through the trees. ______________________

2. His **mind** was full of ideas and thoughts. ______________________

3. The **night** was dark. ______________________

4. The **rain** fell against the roof. ______________________

5. The **trees' branches** were high. ______________________

6. Her **smile** was bright. ______________________

7. The **book** was full of adventure. ______________________

8. The **city** was buzzing with activity. ______________________

CHAPTER 4
Exploration of Word Relationships

Strategies for Interpreting Figurative Language

LANGUAGE DOMAINS

Reading

Writing

Speaking

Listening

4.W **Types of Irony**

Distribute Types of Irony on page 299. Define irony and its three types. See definitions of the types under the "Answers" section below. Give examples of the three types.

- **Verbal irony:** someone gets a flat tire and says, "This is just what I needed today."
- **Dramatic irony:** someone thinking nobody remembered their birthday then walking into their surprise birthday party.
- **Situational irony:** a baker being allergic to flour.

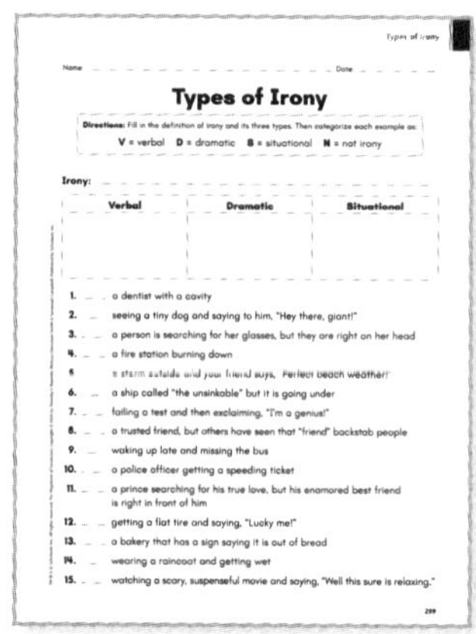

Types of Irony

Name ________ Date ________

Types of Irony

Directions: Fill in the definition of irony and its three types. Then categorize each example as:
V = verbal **D** = dramatic **S** = situational **N** = not irony

Irony: ________

Verbal	Dramatic	Situational

1. ___ a dentist with a cavity
2. ___ seeing a tiny dog and saying to him, "Hey there, giant!"
3. ___ a person is searching for her glasses, but they are right on her head
4. ___ a fire station burning down
5. ___ a storm outside and your friend says, "Perfect beach weather!"
6. ___ a ship called "the unsinkable" but it is going under
7. ___ failing a test and then exclaiming, "I'm a genius!"
8. ___ a trusted friend, but others have seen that "friend" backstab people
9. ___ waking up late and missing the bus
10. ___ a police officer getting a speeding ticket
11. ___ a prince searching for his true love, but his enamored best friend is right in front of him
12. ___ getting a flat tire and saying, "Lucky me!"
13. ___ a bakery that has a sign saying it is out of bread
14. ___ wearing a raincoat and getting wet
15. ___ watching a scary, suspenseful movie and saying, "Well this sure is relaxing."

299

Have students write the definition of each type in the boxes at the top of the sheet, and then work in pairs to discuss each example and decide its type of irony. Discuss answers as a class, providing clarification as needed.

Materials	Types of Irony, page 299
Grade Band	6–8
Length of Activity	15 minutes
Differentiation Ideas	**Striving Learners and English Learners:** Give multiple examples of each type of irony and explain to students the key indicators of each type: **Verbal**: something sarcastic someone is saying; **Dramatic**: the reader knows something the character does not; **Situational**: the opposite of what you predicted happens, based on who a person is or where they are.
Extension Ideas	Have students come up with their own examples of each type of irony, and then share; the class can guess which type of irony it is.
Answers	**Irony:** events or words that are the opposite of what is expected; **Verbal:** When someone says something but means something else, often in a sarcastic way. **Dramatic:** When the audience, reader, or observer knows something the character does not. **Situational:** The opposite of what you predict happens, based on who a person is or where they are. **1.** S, **2.** V, **3.** D, **4.** S, **5.** V, **6.** D, **7.** V, **8.** D, **9.** N, **10.** S, **11.** S, **12.** V, **13.** S, **14.** N, **15.** V

Name: ______________________ Date: ______________

Types of Irony

Directions: Fill in the definition of irony and its three types. Then categorize each example as:

V = verbal **D** = dramatic **S** = situational **N** = not irony

Irony: ______________________

Verbal	Dramatic	Situational

1. ____ a dentist with a cavity
2. ____ seeing a tiny dog and saying to him, "Hey there, giant!"
3. ____ a person is searching for her glasses, but they are right on her head
4. ____ a fire station burning down
5. ____ a storm outside and your friend says, "Perfect beach weather!"
6. ____ a ship called "the unsinkable" but it is going under
7. ____ failing a test and then exclaiming, "I'm a genius!"
8. ____ a trusted friend, but others have seen that "friend" backstab people
9. ____ waking up late and missing the bus
10. ____ a police officer getting a speeding ticket
11. ____ a prince searching for his true love, but his enamored best friend is right in front of him
12. ____ getting a flat tire and saying, "Lucky me!"
13. ____ a bakery that has a sign saying it is out of bread
14. ____ wearing a raincoat and getting wet
15. ____ watching a scary, suspenseful movie and saying, "Well this sure is relaxing."

CHAPTER 4
Exploration of Word Relationships

Strategies for Capturing Nuances and Connotations

LANGUAGE DOMAINS

Reading

Writing
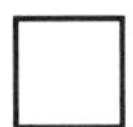

Speaking

Listening

4.X Nuance Match-Up

In this introduction to word nuances, students work with pairs of related words (e.g., *cold* and *freezing*) to explore subtle differences in meaning. Guide students in understanding that "word buddies" are words with similar meanings, but one may be stronger or more intense than the other. Copy and cut apart the Word Buddy Cards on page 301. Then have students match each pair and explain how the words are alike and how they are different. Model a pair aloud. Say both words, act them out, and ask the provided questions or your own questions. Place the cards in a pocket chart and identify the more intense word. From there, invite students to choose a word pair and draw simple illustrations to show the difference in meaning.

Materials	Word Buddy Cards, page 301
Grade Band	K–1
Length of Activity	30 minutes
Differentiation Ideas	• **Striving Readers:** Use image-supported cards to illustrate the meaning of the words in small groups before introducing them as a whole group. • **English Learners:** Focus on concrete vocabulary that can be easily demonstrated (*cold, big, happy*) for one of the words. • **Thriving Readers:** Add a third word to some sets and ask students to rank them by intensity (*mad, angry, furious*).
Extension Ideas	• Play charades. Have students act out the matched words. The class has to decide who acted out the most intense word. *Who was soaked versus just wet?* • Use image-supported cards to create a matching or memory game. Students flip the cards over, searching for word buddies. When one is found, the students get to keep the cards.

Word Buddy Cards

cold	**freezing**	**cold/freezing** • Which word would better describe ice? • Which word would describe how it feels when you can still play outside?
wet	**soaked**	**wet/soaked** • Which word would you use if your shirt got a little splash on it from a puddle? • Which word would describe your clothes if you fell in a pool?
tired	**exhausted**	**tired/exhausted** • Which one would you use if you could barely keep your eyes open? • Which word means you just need a little nap?
happy	**excited**	**happy/excited** • You might giggle if you are happy, but what might you do if you are excited? • Which word would you use if you got exactly what you wanted for your birthday?
fast	**speedy**	**fast/speedy** • A bike can be fast, but what can be speedy? • Which word might describe how fast a superhero can fly?
mad	**furious**	**mad/furious** • When you are mad you might frown, but what might you do if you are furious? • Which word would you use if someone had taken your scooter?
little	**tiny**	**little/tiny** • Which word would you use to describe an ant? • Which word would you use to describe how you looked as a baby?
big	**huge**	**big/huge** • Which word would best describe a dinosaur? • What would be something that could happen to you that would be a huge surprise?
clean	**spotless**	**clean/spotless** • Which word would describe your bedroom if you put all your toys away? • Which word would describe something that looks almost brand new?

Strategies for Capturing Nuances and Connotations

LANGUAGE DOMAINS

Reading

Writing

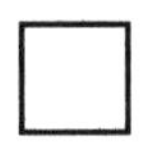

Speaking

Listening

4.Y **Odd One Out**

Put students in small groups and give each group a dry-erase board and marker. Tell students they will be looking for word nuances: *slight differences in meanings of similar words*. Project or call out one set of words at a time from an Odd One Out Word Set on pages 303–304 and challenge students to choose the word that is the odd one out, or doesn't belong. Then have them choose a category name for the rest of the words. From there, have them write the category name and words on their dry-erase boards, and share them with the class for discussion. (Strategy inspired by teacher Sean Morrisey and featured in Melissa Loftus and Lori Sappington's *The Literacy 50*.)

Odd One Out Word Set B

3.	4.
silly	gracious
eerie	tactful
terrifying	playful
spooky	respectful
7.	**8.**
illustrate	puzzling
imaginative	curious
inventive	interesting
inspired	unclear
11.	**12.**
fog	startled
breeze	fearful
hurricane	shocked
windstorm	astonished

Odd One Out Word Set A

1.	2.	3.	4.
crawl	colorful	dim	disappointed
stand	fragile	radiant	upset
trot	sturdy	dazzling	excited
dash	powerful	rainy	heartbroken
5.	**6.**	**7.**	**8.**
soft	full	easy	lately
hard	hungry	tricky	slowly
silent	tired	challenging	quickly
noisy	starving	lazy	instantly
9.	**10.**	**11.**	**12.**
damp	curious	quiet	flood
soaked	shy	smooth	tornado
drenched	courageous	loud	cloud
dusty	fearless	booming	hurricane

Materials	• Odd One Out Word Set A, Grades 2–3, page 303 • Odd One Out Word Set B, Grades 4–5, page 304 • dry-erase boards and markers for each small group
Grade Band	2–5
Length of Activity	30 minutes
Differentiation Ideas	**Striving Readers and English Learners:** Focus on two of the remaining words in each set and have students describe why they are different to help understand the nuance. For example, "What's the difference between *smart* and *brilliant*?"
Extension Ideas	• Have students create their own Odd One Out Word sets in groups to share and do with the class. • Challenge students to choose one of the word sets and add more words to the category, then order the words from an established continuum from one end to the other: *weakest to strongest, smallest to largest*, etc.
Answers	Listed category, then odd one out: **Set A: 1.** movement, stand **2.** strength, colorful. **3.** brightness, rainy **4.** sadness, excited **5.** loudness, hard **6.** hunger, tired **7.** effort/work, lazy **8.** speed of action, lately **9.** wetness, dusty **10.** bravery, curious **11.** loudness, smooth **12.** natural disasters, cloud **Set B: 1.** confidence, clumsy **2.** learning, frozen **3.** scariness, silly **4.** politeness, playful **5.** influence, question **6.** trouble/danger, solution **7.** creativity, illustrate **8.** mystery, interesting **9.** travel, pause **10.** humor, joke **11.** strength of wind, fog **12.** surprise, fearful (Accept all reasonable answers.)

Odd One Out Word Set A

1.	2.	3.	4.
crawl stand trot dash	colorful fragile sturdy powerful	dim radiant dazzling rainy	disappointed upset excited heartbroken
5. soft hard silent noisy	**6.** full hungry tired starving	**7.** easy tricky challenging lazy	**8.** lately slowly quickly instantly
9. damp soaked drenched dusty	**10.** curious shy courageous fearless	**11.** quiet smooth loud booming	**12.** flood tornado cloud hurricane

Odd One Out Word Set B

1.	2.	3.	4.
unsure	confused	silly	gracious
clumsy	proficient	eerie	tactful
confident	mastered	terrifying	playful
boastful	frozen	spooky	respectful

5.	6.	7.	8.
suggest	problem	illustrate	puzzling
question	crisis	imaginative	curious
convince	disaster	inventive	interesting
manipulate	solution	inspired	unclear

9.	10.	11.	12.
stroll	witty	fog	startled
journey	hilarious	breeze	fearful
expedition	joke	hurricane	shocked
pause	comical	windstorm	astonished

4.Z Shades of Meaning Continuum

Choose one set of words from the Continuum Words List on page 306 and write each word on a piece of cardstock. Select two students to hold the "end words" (in bold) on the list, leaving ample space between them. Then, one at a time, choose a student to hold a listed word, and have the rest of the class decide where each student should stand along the continuum of meaning—from low to high or weak to strong. As more words are added, encourage the class to adjust the positions of their classmates as necessary. Once all words are placed, have the class guess the category. This strategy may be challenging at first because the category is a mystery, so encourage discussion and make adjustments as needed.

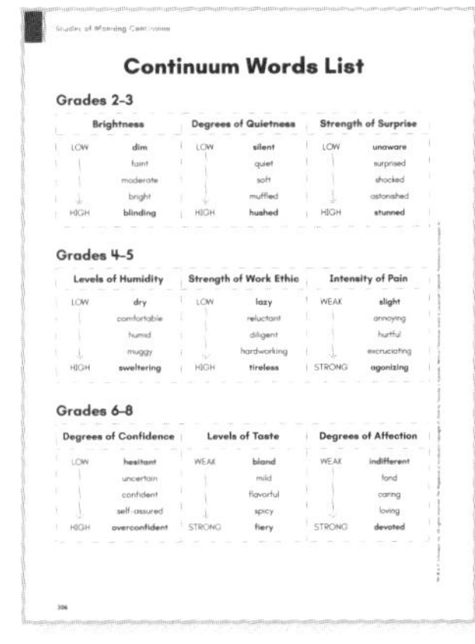

Continuum Words List

Grades 2–3

Brightness		Degrees of Quietness		Strength of Surprise	
LOW	**dim**	LOW	**silent**	LOW	**unaware**
	faint		quiet		surprised
	moderate		soft		shocked
	bright		muffled		astonished
HIGH	**blinding**	HIGH	**hushed**	HIGH	**stunned**

Grades 4–5

Levels of Humidity		Strength of Work Ethic		Intensity of Pain	
LOW	**dry**	LOW	**lazy**	WEAK	**slight**
	comfortable		reluctant		annoying
	humid		diligent		hurtful
	muggy		hardworking		excruciating
HIGH	**sweltering**	HIGH	**tireless**	STRONG	**agonizing**

Grades 6–8

Degrees of Confidence		Levels of Taste		Degrees of Affection	
LOW	**hesitant**	WEAK	**bland**	WEAK	**indifferent**
	uncertain		mild		fond
	confident		flavorful		caring
	self-assured		spicy		loving
HIGH	**overconfident**	STRONG	**fiery**	STRONG	**devoted**

306

Materials	• Continuum Words List, page 306 • cardstock
Grade Band	2–8
Length of Activity	15 minutes per set
Differentiation Ideas	**Striving Learners and English Learners:** Choose these students to hold the signs for the first round to get them involved and help them understand the activity without the pressure of knowing the answers.
Extension Ideas	Use your own set of words from a text or unit of study, or generate word list ideas using AI. (Be sure to check any AI results to make sure they are appropriate.)

Strategies for Capturing Nuances and Connotations

LANGUAGE DOMAINS

Reading

Writing

Speaking

Listening

Continuum Words List

Grades 2–3

Brightness		Degrees of Quietness		Strength of Surprise	
LOW	**dim**	LOW	**silent**	LOW	**unaware**
	faint		quiet		surprised
	moderate		soft		shocked
	bright		muffled		astonished
HIGH	**blinding**	HIGH	**hushed**	HIGH	**stunned**

Grades 4–5

Levels of Humidity		Strength of Work Ethic		Intensity of Pain	
LOW	**dry**	LOW	**lazy**	WEAK	**slight**
	comfortable		reluctant		annoying
	humid		diligent		hurtful
	muggy		hardworking		excruciating
HIGH	**sweltering**	HIGH	**tireless**	STRONG	**agonizing**

Grades 6–8

Degrees of Confidence		Levels of Taste		Degrees of Affection	
LOW	**hesitant**	WEAK	**bland**	WEAK	**indifferent**
	uncertain		mild		fond
	confident		flavorful		caring
	self-assured		spicy		loving
HIGH	**overconfident**	STRONG	**fiery**	STRONG	**devoted**

4.AA Nuance Ladders

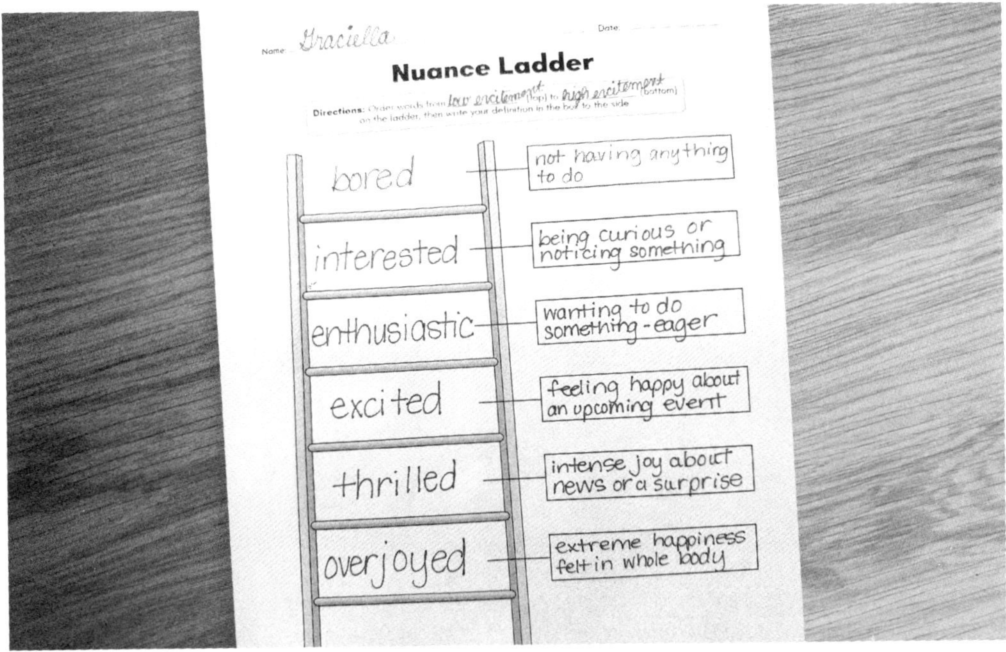

Give small groups of students a copy of the Nuance Ladder on page 309 and six words to sequence from one end of a continuum to another. If any of the words are unfamiliar to students, have them look them up in a dictionary or discuss them as a group. Ask students to agree on the order of the words and write them on the ladder. From there, have them write a definition of each word in the box next to it.

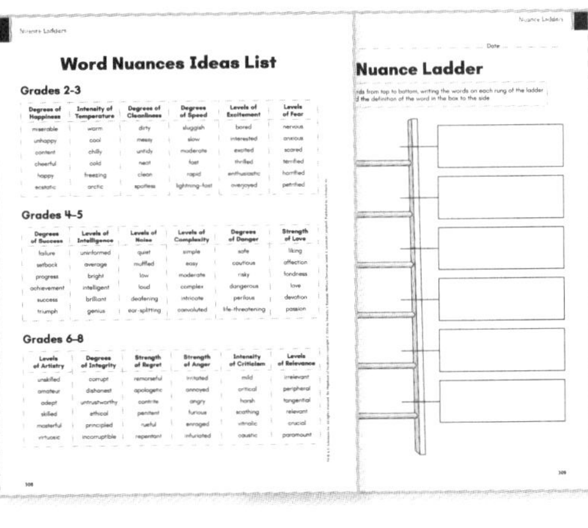

Materials	• Word Nuances Ideas List, page 308 • Nuance Ladder, page 309
Grade Band	2–8
Length of Activity	30 minutes
Differentiation Ideas	**Striving Learners and English Learners:** Define unknown words with student-friendly definitions.
Extension Ideas	• Use words from a text or unit of study to create more continuums of words. • Use an AI website to help create more word lists. (Be sure to check any AI results to make sure they are appropriate.)
Answers	Answers provided on Word Nuances Ideas List, page 308

LANGUAGE DOMAINS

Reading

Writing

Speaking

Listening

Word Nuances Ideas List

Grades 2-3

Degrees of Happiness	Intensity of Temperature	Degrees of Cleanliness	Degrees of Speed	Levels of Excitement	Levels of Fear
miserable	warm	dirty	sluggish	bored	nervous
unhappy	cool	messy	slow	interested	anxious
content	chilly	untidy	moderate	excited	scared
cheerful	cold	neat	fast	thrilled	terrified
happy	freezing	clean	rapid	enthusiastic	horrified
ecstatic	arctic	spotless	lightning-fast	overjoyed	petrified

Grades 4-5

Degrees of Success	Levels of Intelligence	Levels of Noise	Levels of Complexity	Degrees of Danger	Strength of Love
failure	uninformed	quiet	simple	safe	liking
setback	average	muffled	easy	cautious	affection
progress	bright	low	moderate	risky	fondness
achievement	intelligent	loud	complex	dangerous	love
success	brilliant	deafening	intricate	perilous	devotion
triumph	genius	ear-splitting	convoluted	life-threatening	passion

Grades 6-8

Levels of Artistry	Degrees of Integrity	Strength of Regret	Strength of Anger	Intensity of Criticism	Levels of Relevance
unskilled	corrupt	remorseful	irritated	mild	irrelevant
amateur	dishonest	apologetic	annoyed	critical	peripheral
adept	untrustworthy	contrite	angry	harsh	tangential
skilled	ethical	penitent	furious	scathing	relevant
masterful	principled	rueful	enraged	vitriolic	crucial
virtuosic	incorruptible	repentant	infuriated	caustic	paramount

Name: ______________________________ Date: ______________

Nuance Ladder

Directions: Order words from top to bottom, writing the words on each rung of the ladder and the definition of the word in the box to the side.

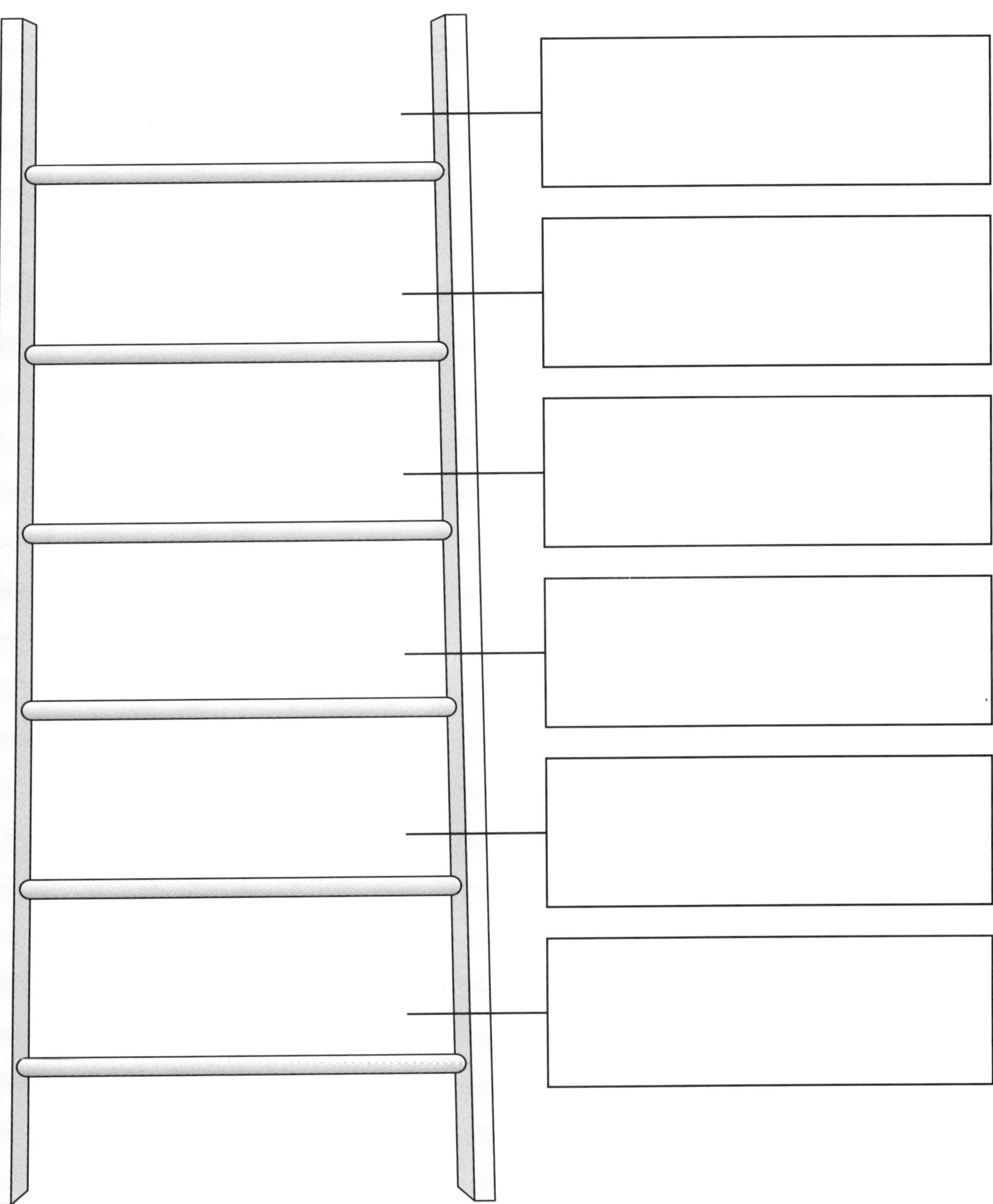

LANGUAGE DOMAINS

Reading

Writing

Speaking

Listening

4.BB **Tone and Connotation**

Distribute the Tones List on page 311. Review the definitions of tone (the attitude or emotional vibe the reader feels when reading a text) and connotation (the positive or negative feeling associated with a word). In pairs, have students read each tone on the list and mark a **+** for positive or **-** for negative to describe its connotation.

Follow with a class discussion to clear up any misconceptions about words that are unfamilar to students. Then distribute a Tone and Connotation Set on pages 312–313 and have students read the scenarios aloud, identify the tone using the Tones List, identify the connotation (**+** or **-**), and fill in their answers. Then ask them to highlight the words from the passage that helped them determine the tone.

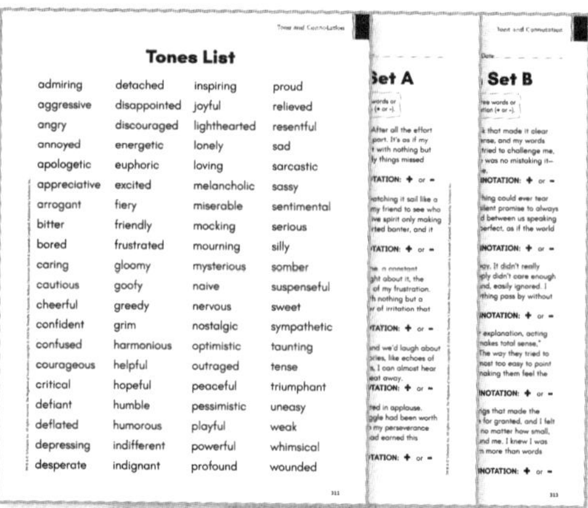

Tones List

admiring	detached	inspiring	proud
aggressive	disappointed	joyful	relieved
angry	discouraged	lighthearted	resentful
annoyed	energetic	lonely	sad
apologetic	euphoric	loving	sarcastic
appreciative	excited	melancholic	sassy
arrogant	fiery	miserable	sentimental
bitter	friendly	mocking	serious
bored	frustrated	mourning	silly
caring	gloomy	mysterious	somber
cautious	goofy	naive	suspenseful
cheerful	greedy	nervous	sweet
confident	grim	nostalgic	sympathetic
confused	harmonious	optimistic	taunting
courageous	helpful	outraged	tense
critical	hopeful	peaceful	triumphant
defiant	humble	pessimistic	uneasy
deflated	humorous	playful	weak
depressing	indifferent	powerful	whimsical
desperate	indignant	profound	wounded

Set A

Set B

Materials	• Tones List, page 311 • Tone and Connotation Set A, page 312 • Tone and Connotation Set B, page 313
Grade Band	4–8
Length of Activity	30 minutes for first activity 15 minutes for each worksheet
Differentiation Ideas	**Striving Learners and English Learners:** Read the passage aloud to scaffold the decoding and focus on the meaning.
Extension Ideas	• Direct students to write their own paragraph, choosing one of the tones from the list. They should have 3+ words/phrases that match the tone they chose. Then have them trade paragraphs with a partner who will try to figure out the intended tone and identify the words that helped set the tone. • Ask students to find the best emoji to fit the tones on the Tones List to cement learning with a visual representation. • Have students do an open sort (sorting by a category they choose) with words on the Tones List.
Answers	**Possible Answers: Set A: 1.** disappointed; possible highlighted words: disheartened, letdown, regret **2.** playful; possible highlighted words: grinning, tossed, laughed, lighthearted **3.** resentful; possible highlighted words: bitter, unfair, angrier, frustration, injustice, irritation **4.** nostalgic; possible highlighted words: memories, old, almost hear **5.** triumphant; possible highlighted words: stood tall, rush of pride, struggle, victory, perseverance, moment of glory **Set B: 1.** sassy; possible highlighted words: smirk, tossed my hair, shot a look, sharp, attitude, raised an eyebrow **2.** loving; possible highlighted words: wrapped my arms, holding them close, gentle, warmth, heart swelled, affection **3.** indifferent; possible highlighted words: shrugged, not particularly bothered, didn't really matter, simply didn't care, ignored, without any real interest, pass by **4.** mocking; possible highlighted words: roll my eyes, hide my smirk, ridiculous, sarcasm **5.** appreciative; possible highlighted words: smile, truly grateful, kindness, didn't take for granted, sense of thankfulness, reminded me of the goodness, lucky, thoughtful acts, cherished them

Tones List

admiring
aggressive
angry
annoyed
apologetic
appreciative
arrogant
bitter
bored
caring
cautious
cheerful
confident
confused
courageous
critical
defiant
deflated
depressing
desperate

detached
disappointed
discouraged
energetic
euphoric
excited
fiery
friendly
frustrated
gloomy
goofy
greedy
grim
harmonious
helpful
hopeful
humble
humorous
indifferent
indignant

inspiring
joyful
lighthearted
lonely
loving
melancholic
miserable
mocking
mourning
mysterious
naive
nervous
nostalgic
optimistic
outraged
peaceful
pessimistic
playful
powerful
profound

proud
relieved
resentful
sad
sarcastic
sassy
sentimental
serious
silly
somber
suspenseful
sweet
sympathetic
taunting
tense
triumphant
uneasy
weak
whimsical
wounded

Name: ______________________________ Date: ______________

Tone and Connotation Set A

Directions: Read each passage, identify its tone, highlight three words or phrases that helped you identify its tone, and circle a connotation (+ or -).

1. I can't help but feel disheartened by how everything turned out. After all the effort and hope I put into this, it feels like a letdown to see things fall apart. It's as if my expectations were nothing more than an illusion, and now I'm left with nothing but regret. The feeling continues to linger, reminding me of how badly things missed the mark.

   TONE: ______________________ **CONNOTATION: +** or **-**

2. I couldn't stop grinning as I tossed the frisbee high into the air, watching it sail like a bird with a mind of its own. With a wink, I darted after it, racing my friend to see who could catch it first. We both stumbled and laughed, our competitive spirit only making the game more ridiculous. Every moment was filled with lighthearted banter, and it felt like the whole world was in on the joke.

   TONE: ______________________ **CONNOTATION: +** or **-**

3. I couldn't shake the bitter feeling that had been building inside me, a constant reminder of how unfair everything had become. The more I thought about it, the angrier I grew, as if every little thing was designed to remind me of my frustration. They always seem to take more than they give, and I was left with nothing but a sense of injustice. It felt impossible to move past the quiet simmer of irritation that lingered after every encounter.

   TONE: ______________________ **CONNOTATION: +** or **-**

4. The smell of freshly baked cookies would drift from the kitchen, and we'd laugh about stories from years ago. Every corner of that old house held memories, like echoes of voices that once filled the rooms. Even now, when I close my eyes, I can almost hear the soft hum of those simpler times, as if they were just a heartbeat away.

   TONE: ______________________ **CONNOTATION: +** or **-**

5. I stood tall, a rush of pride flooding through me as the crowd erupted in applause. After months of hard work and determination, it felt like every struggle had been worth it. The victory was sweet, each step leading up to it a testament to my perseverance and strength. With a smile that couldn't be wiped away, I knew I had earned this moment of glory.

   TONE: ______________________ **CONNOTATION: +** or **-**

Name: __________ Date: __________

Tone and Connotation Set B

Directions: Read each passage, identify its tone, highlight three words or phrases that helped you identify its tone, and circle a connotation (+ or -).

1. With a smirk, I tossed my hair over my shoulder and shot a look that made it clear I wasn't about to back down. I wasn't here for anyone's nonsense, and my words came out sharp, each one dripping with attitude. When they tried to challenge me, I just raised an eyebrow, daring them to say something. There was no mistaking it—if they wanted a fight, I was more than ready to give them one.
   TONE: __________ **CONNOTATION: +** or **-**

2. I wrapped my arms around them, holding them close as if nothing could ever tear us apart. Every touch was gentle, full of warmth and care, a silent promise to always be there. My heart swelled with affection, each glance shared between us speaking more than words ever could. In that moment, everything felt perfect, as if the world outside didn't matter at all.
   TONE: __________ **CONNOTATION: +** or **-**

3. I shrugged, not particularly bothered by the situation either way. It didn't really matter to me whether things went one way or the other; I simply didn't care enough to get involved. Their opinions were just noise in the background, easily ignored. I moved through the day without any real interest, letting everything pass by without a second thought.
   TONE: __________ **CONNOTATION: +** or **-**

4. I couldn't help but roll my eyes as they stumbled through their explanation, acting like it was the most profound thing ever said. "Oh, sure, that makes total sense," I said, dragging out each word as if I was utterly convinced. The way they tried to act so serious only made it harder to hide my smirk. It was almost too easy to point out how ridiculous their words sounded, and I couldn't resist making them feel the full weight of my sarcasm.
   TONE: __________ **CONNOTATION: +** or **-**

5. I couldn't help but smile, feeling truly grateful for the little things that made the day special. The kindness shown to me was a gift I didn't take for granted, and I felt a deep sense of thankfulness in every moment. Each gesture, no matter how small, filled me with warmth and reminded me of the goodness around me. I knew I was lucky to experience such thoughtful acts, and I cherished them more than words could express.
   TONE: __________ **CONNOTATION: +** or **-**

CHAPTER 4

Exploration of Word Relationships

Strategies for Capturing Nuances and Connotations

LANGUAGE DOMAINS

Reading

Writing

Speaking

Listening

4.CC Connotation in Context

Review the meaning of connotation (the *positive* or *negative* feeling associated with a word) and give students a few examples. **positive:** *brave, unique, creative;* **negative:** *nosy, childish, disappointed.* Then distribute a Connotation in Context activity on pages 315–316 and have students read each sentence. Then have them determine what the boldfaced word means and its connotation (positive or negative), and fill in the information in the blanks provided.

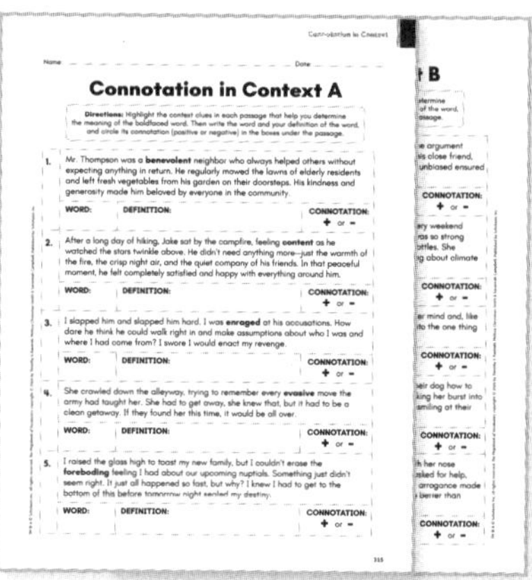

Connotation in Context

Name ______ Date ______

Connotation in Context A

Directions: Highlight the context clues in each passage that help you determine the meaning of the boldfaced word. Then write the word and your definition of the word, and circle its connotation (positive or negative) in the boxes under the passage.

1. Mr. Thompson was a **benevolent** neighbor who always helped others without expecting anything in return. He regularly mowed the lawns of elderly residents and left fresh vegetables from his garden on their doorsteps. His kindness and generosity made him beloved by everyone in the community.

WORD:	DEFINITION:	CONNOTATION: + or −

2. After a long day of hiking, Jake sat by the campfire, feeling **content** as he watched the stars twinkle above. He didn't need anything more—just the warmth of the fire, the crisp night air, and the quiet company of his friends. In that peaceful moment, he felt completely satisfied and happy with everything around him.

WORD:	DEFINITION:	CONNOTATION: + or −

3. I slapped him and slapped him hard. I was **enraged** at his accusations. How dare he think he could walk right in and make assumptions about who I was and where I had come from? I swore I would enact my revenge.

WORD:	DEFINITION:	CONNOTATION: + or −

4. She crawled down the alleyway, trying to remember every **evasive** move the army had taught her. She had to get away, she knew that, but it had to be a clean getaway. If they found her this time, it would be all over.

WORD:	DEFINITION:	CONNOTATION: + or −

5. I raised the glass high to toast my new family, but I couldn't erase the **foreboding** feeling I had about our upcoming nuptials. Something just didn't seem right. It just all happened so fast, but why? I knew I had to get to the bottom of this before tomorrow night sealed my destiny.

WORD:	DEFINITION:	CONNOTATION: + or −

315

Materials	• Connotation in Context A, page 315 • Connotation in Context B, page 316
Grade Band	6–8
Length of Activity	15 minutes
Differentiation Ideas	**Striving Learners and English Learners:** Read aloud the example sentences with expression to help students pick up on the tone and connotation.
Extension Ideas	• Allow students to choose a word that describes the mood of the passages, having them think more deeply about the connotation of that work. • Assign students a vocabulary word they are currently studying and have them write their own.
Answers	**A: 1.** benevolent; being kind and wanting to help others; positive **2.** content; feeling happy and satisfied with what you have; positive **3.** enraged; very angry or furious; negative **4.** evasive; avoiding something difficult or not giving a clear answer; negative **5.** foreboding; a feeling that something bad or unpleasant is going to happen; negative **B: 1.** impartial; being fair and not taking sides; positive **2.** zealous; being very excited and enthusiastic about something; positive **3.** placid; peaceful, calm and not easily upset; positive **4.** amused; feeling happy or entertained because something is funny or enjoyable; positive **5.** haughty; acting like you are better than others and being rude about it; negative

Name: ______________________ Date: __________

Connotation in Context A

Directions: Highlight the context clues in each passage that help you determine the meaning of the boldfaced word. Then write the word and your definition of the word, and circle its connotation (positive or negative) in the boxes under the passage.

1.	Mr. Thompson was a **benevolent** neighbor who always helped others without expecting anything in return. He regularly mowed the lawns of elderly residents and left fresh vegetables from his garden on their doorsteps. His kindness and generosity made him beloved by everyone in the community.		
	WORD:	**DEFINITION:**	**CONNOTATION:** + or −
2.	After a long day of hiking, Jake sat by the campfire, feeling **content** as he watched the stars twinkle above. He didn't need anything more—just the warmth of the fire, the crisp night air, and the quiet company of his friends. In that peaceful moment, he felt completely satisfied and happy with everything around him.		
	WORD:	**DEFINITION:**	**CONNOTATION:** + or −
3.	I slapped him and slapped him hard. I was **enraged** at his accusations. How dare he think he could walk right in and make assumptions about who I was and where I had come from? I swore I would enact my revenge.		
	WORD:	**DEFINITION:**	**CONNOTATION:** + or −
4.	She crawled down the alleyway, trying to remember every **evasive** move the army had taught her. She had to get away, she knew that, but it had to be a clean getaway. If they found her this time, it would be all over.		
	WORD:	**DEFINITION:**	**CONNOTATION:** + or −
5.	I raised the glass high to toast my new family, but I couldn't erase the **foreboding** feeling I had about our upcoming nuptials. Something just didn't seem right. It just all happened so fast, but why? I knew I had to get to the bottom of this before tomorrow night sealed my destiny.		
	WORD:	**DEFINITION:**	**CONNOTATION:** + or −

Connotation in Context B

Directions: Highlight the context clues in each passage that help you determine the meaning of the boldfaced word. Then write the word and your definition of the word, and circle its connotation (positive or negative) in the boxes under the passage.

1. The judge remained **impartial**, carefully listening to both sides of the argument before making a fair decision. Even though one of the lawyers was his close friend, he did not let that influence his ruling. His ability to stay neutral and unbiased ensured that justice was served.

WORD:	DEFINITION:	CONNOTATION: + or −

2. Emma was **zealous** about protecting the environment, spending every weekend cleaning up parks and organizing recycling drives. Her enthusiasm was so strong that she convinced her entire school to start using reusable water bottles. She never missed an opportunity to educate others, passionately speaking about climate change whenever she could.

WORD:	DEFINITION:	CONNOTATION: + or −

3. Everything was clear now; no ripples, no waves. She had made up her mind and, like the **placid** lake before her, her indecision had smoothed itself out into the one thing that must be done.

WORD:	DEFINITION:	CONNOTATION: + or −

4. Lena was **amused** when she saw her little brother trying to teach their dog how to dance. The dog clumsily lifted its paws, following the boy's lead, making her burst into laughter. She found the whole scene entertaining and couldn't stop smiling at their silly attempts.

WORD:	DEFINITION:	CONNOTATION: + or −

5. Olivia's **haughty** attitude was clear as she walked into the room with her nose slightly in the air, ignoring everyone around her. When a classmate asked for help, she scoffed and said, "I don't waste my time on easy questions." Her arrogance made it hard for others to befriend her, as she always acted as if she were better than everyone else.

WORD:	DEFINITION:	CONNOTATION: + or −

Children's Books With Great Vocabulary Words

***Alexander and the Terrible, Horrible, No Good, Very Bad Day* by Judith Viorst**
horrible / miserable / horrendous / cavity / numbness / draining / hurdle / exhausted / demoted / suffocating / absurd / exasperated

***A Bad Case of Stripes* by David Shannon**
fretting / examine / extraordinary / twitching / contagious / jabbed / prodded / remedies

***Barnyard Banter* by Denise Fleming**
henhouse / paddock / wallow / banter / cacophony / niche / careens / flits / textile

***Be You!* by Peter H. Reynolds**
journey / curious / comfort zone / kindred / persistent / quirky / plunge / compassionate / voyage

***The Boy with Big, Big Feelings* by Britney Winn Lee**
feathery / bursting / reeling / rumble / clench / over-equipped / quiver / dramatic / marveled

***Chicks and Salsa* by Aaron Reynolds**
pilfered / enticing / aromas / savory / sumptuous / cuisine / fiesta / delectable / garnish / tantalizing / simmer / succulent

***Cloudy with a Chance of Meatballs* by Judi Barrett**
uneventfully / prediction / varied / frankfurters / drizzle / gradual / sanitation / fog / portions / accompanied / abandon / stale / necessities / coastal / temporary

***The Couch Potato* by Jory John**
slouch / comfy / cozy / activates / gadget / fetches / spectacular / bliss / react / kingdom / high-resolution / realistic / massive / horizon / balance

***Diary of a Spider* by Doreen Cronin**
insects / rumble / faraway / molted / breeze

***Enemy Pie* by Derek Munson**
enemy / faded / squinted / relieved / mumbled / common

***Eyes that Kiss in the Corners* by Joanna Ho**
sweeping / crinkle / serene / baubles / toddle / revolution

***Giraffes Can't Dance* by Giles Andreae**
crooked / munching / buckled / prance / waltz / tango / clumsy / sneered / clearing / shuffling / sway

***The Girl Who Thought in Pictures* by Julia Finley Mosca**
frilly / tantrum / feats / prototype / advocate

***Give Bees a Chance* by Bethany Barton**
gather / processed / convinced / defend / designed / impact / unparalleled / interest

***Granddaddy's Turn: A Journey to the Ballot Box* by Michael S. Bandy and Eric Stein**
figured / complain / patience / beaming / proudly / clutched / temper

***The Hello, Goodbye Window* by Norton Juster**
barrel / frighten / olden / harmonica / reflections / specialty / expect / extinct

***I Need My Monster* by Amanda Noll**
ragged / scrambling / panting / creaking / inspection / shaggy / peered / slithering / menacing / ominous

***Just Ask!* by Sonia Sotomayor**
trimmed / fragile / chatty / stutter / express / distracted / unique

***Last Stop on Market Street* by Matt de la Peña**
freckled / pool / creaked / sagged / lurched / swirling / glanced

***Library Mouse* by Daniel Kirk**
brimmed / posing / tucked / streamed / scurried / immensely / flattered

***The Little Ships* by Louise Borden**
trapped / nudge / echoing / lugged / frayed / convoy / gazed / stray / thundered

***Mother Bruce* by Ryan T. Higgins**
grump / drizzled / prepared / stern / pesky / stubborn / migration

***Mars!: Earthlings Welcome* by Stacy McAnulty**
inhabitants / marvelous / magnificent / ginormous / stunning / rugged / operated / scampered

***The Smart Cookie* by Jory John**
community / supportive / confident / occasionally / requested / original / splintered / sculpture / chaotic / revealed / pressure / finale

***Stone Soup* by Jon J Muth**
gather / processed / convinced / defend / designed / impact / unparalleled / interest

***Sylvester and the Magic Pebble* by William Steig**
gratified / ceased / frightened / bounding / frantic / inquiring / concluded / exclamation

***The Talking Eggs* by Robert D. San Souci**
sassafras / springhouse / corncrib / woodpile / fetched / kindling / gawked / contrary

***Thunder Cake* by Patricia Polacco**
sultry / tumbling / surveyed / exclaimed / croaked / jagged / bellowed / luscious / rumbled

***A Ticket Around the World* by Natalia Diaz & Melissa Owens**
customs / landmark / climate / culture / tradition / diversity

***Too Many Tamales* by Gary Soto**
glittered / tamales / knead / glob / confess / desperate / plateful / drift / dusk / reappeared / nudge

***The Web Files* by Margie Palatini**
racket / investigate / hysterical / alibi / stakeout / clamored / debrief

***What Do You Do With a Tail Like This?* by Steve Jenkins**
platypus / underground / pesky / chameleon / ledge / termites

***When the Beat Was Born* by Laban Carrick Hill**
jiving / sorrowful / toasting / belonged / mumbling / trickled / turntables / mellow / strobe

***The Word Collector* by Peter H. Reynolds**
drift / motif / hover / aromatic / torrential / jumbled / cascading / gaggle / scurrying

***The Yellow Star: The Legend of King Christian X of Denmark* by Carmen Agra Deedy**
legend / loyal / curious / astonished / fierce / discovering / threatened / resistance / summoned / defiance

***You Make the World* by Muon Thi Văn**
turbulent / fantastical / amplify / entwined / palpable / ripple / immerse / tumult / illuminate / exile / tether / resonance / evoke / infinite

References

Altalhab, S. (2018). Short- and long-term effects of repetition strategies on vocabulary retention. *Advances in Language and Literary Studies, 9*(2), 1–10.

Baumann, J. F., & Kame'enui, E. J. (1991). Research on vocabulary instruction: Ode to Voltaire. In J. Flood et al. (Eds.), *Handbook of research on teaching the English language arts* (pp. 604–632). Macmillan.

Beck, I. L., & Graves, M. F. (2009). *Teaching vocabulary: Lessons from research and practice*. Guilford Press.

Beck, I. L., & Graves, M. F. (2010). *Vocabulary instruction: A research-based guide for classroom teachers* (2nd ed.). Guilford Press.

Beck, I. L., & McKeown, M. G. (2007a). *Teaching vocabulary: Focus on words and their meanings*. Guilford Press.

Beck, I. L., & McKeown, M. G. (2007b). Vocabulary development: A morphologically informed approach. *Language and Literacy 1*(1), 1–12.

Beck, I. L., McKeown, M. G., & Kucan, L. (2013). *Bringing words to life: Robust vocabulary instruction* (2nd ed.). Guilford Press.

Blachowicz, C., & Cobb, C. (2021). *Vocabulary naturally: Raising word wizards!* Independently published.

Blachowicz, C. L. Z., & Fisher, P. J. L. (2010). *Teaching vocabulary in all classrooms* (4th ed.). Pearson.

Bowers, P. N., Kirby, J. R., & Deacon, S. H. (2010). The effects of morphological instruction on literacy skills: A systematic review of the literature. *Review of Educational Research, 80*(2), 144–179.

Brackett, M. A. (2019). *Permission to feel: Unlocking the power of emotions to help our kids, ourselves, and our society thrive*. Celadon Books.

Burkins, J., & Yates, K. (2021). *Shifting the balance: 6 ways to bring the science of reading into the balanced literacy classroom*. Stenhouse Publishers.

Carlisle, J. F. (2010a). Effects of instruction in morphological awareness on literacy achievement: An integrative review. *Reading Research Quarterly, 45*(4), 464–487.

Carlisle, J. F. (2010b). Effects of instruction in morphological awareness on literacy achievement: An integrative review. *Reading Research Quarterly, 45*(4), 464–487.

Cunningham, A. E., & Stanovich, K. E. (1997). Early reading acquisition and its relation to reading experience and ability 10 years later. *Developmental Psychology, 33*(6), 934–945.

David, S. (2016). *Emotional agility: Get unstuck, embrace change, and thrive in work and life*. Avery.

Duke, N. K., & Pearson, P. D. (2002). Effective practices for developing reading comprehension. *Journal of Education, 189*(1/2), 107–122.

Fisher, D., & Frey, N. (2014). *Checking for understanding: Formative assessment techniques for your classroom*. ASCD.

Fraser, C. A. (1999). The role of consulting a dictionary in reading and vocabulary learning. *Canadian Journal of Applied Linguistics, 2*(1–2), 73–89.

Galea, C., Jones, A., Ko, K., Salins, A., Robidoux, S., Noble, C., & McArthur, G. (2025). Home-based shared book reading and developmental outcomes in young children: A systematic review with meta-analyses. *Frontiers in Language Sciences*, Article 1540562.

Gallagher, M. A., Barber, A. T., Beck, J. S., & Buehl, M. M. (2019). Academic vocabulary: Explicit and incidental instruction for students of diverse language backgrounds. *Reading & Writing Quarterly, 35*(2), 84–102.

Golinkoff, R. M., Hoff, E., Rowe, M. L., Tamis-LeMonda, C. S., & Hirsh-Pasek, K. (2019). Language matters: Denying the existence of the 30-million-word gap has serious consequences. *Child Development, 90*(3), 985–992.

Graves, M. F. (2016). *The vocabulary book: Learning and instruction* (2nd ed.). Teachers College Press.

Greenwood, S. C., & Flanigan, K. (2007). Overlapping vocabulary and comprehension: Context clues complement semantic gradients. *The Reading Teacher, 61*(3), 249–254.

Hart, B., & Risley, T. R. (1995). *Meaningful differences in the everyday experience of young American children*. Paul H. Brookes Publishing.

Hoff, E. (2003). The specificity of environmental influence: Socioeconomic status affects early vocabulary development via maternal speech. *Child Development, 74*(5), 1368–1378.

Imhof, A., Liu, S., Schlueter, L., Phu, T., Watamura, S., & Fisher, P. (2022). Improving children's expressive language and auditory comprehension through responsive caregiving: Evidence from a randomized controlled trial of a strength-based video-coaching intervention. *Prevention Science, 24*(1), 254–267.

Kame'enui, E. J., & Baumann, J. F. (2012). Context for vocabulary instruction. In E. J. Kame'enui & J. F. Baumann (Eds.), *Vocabulary instruction: Research to practice* (2nd ed., pp. 3–14). Guilford Press.

Kieffer, M. J., & Lesaux, N. K. (2012). The role of vocabulary knowledge in comprehension: Implications for reading instruction for English language learners. *Reading & Writing Quarterly, 28*(1), 23–51.

Kirby, J. R., & Bowers, P. N. (2018). The effects of morphological instruction on vocabulary learning, reading, and spelling. In R. Berthiaume, D. Daigle, & A. Desrochers (Eds.), *Morphological processing and literacy development* (Chapter 10). Routledge.

Lane, H. B., & Allen, S. A. (2010). The vocabulary-rich classroom: Modeling sophisticated word use to promote word consciousness and vocabulary growth. *The Reading Teacher, 63*(5), 362–370.

Li, Z., Li, J. Z., Zhang, X., & Reynolds, B. L. (2024). Mastery of listening and reading vocabulary levels in relation to CEFR: Insights into student admissions and English as a medium of instruction. *Languages, 9*(7), 239.

Mak, E., Mauer, E., Luo, R., Zhou, Q., & Uchikoshi, Y. (2024). Cognitive demand in parent–child shared book reading and home language development among dual language learners in low-income immigrant families. *International Journal of Bilingual Education and Bilingualism, 29*(3), 792–812.

Manyak, P., Manyak, A., & Kappus, E. (2021). Lessons from a decade of research on multifaceted vocabulary instruction. *The Reading Teacher, 75*(1), 27–39.

Marzano, R. J. (2004). *Building background knowledge for academic achievement: Research on what works in schools*. ASCD.

McKeown, M. G. (2019). Effective vocabulary instruction fosters knowing words, using words, and understanding how words work. *Language, Speech, and Hearing Services in Schools, 50*(4), 466–476.

Moats, L. C. (2004). *Speech to print: Language essentials for teachers*. Brookes Publishing.

Nagy, W. E., & Scott, J. A. (2000). Vocabulary processes. In M. L. Kamil et al. (Eds.), *Handbook of reading research* (Vol. 3, pp. 269–284). Lawrence Erlbaum Associates.

Nagy, W. E., & Townsend, D. (2012). Words as tools: Learning academic vocabulary as language acquisition. *Reading Research Quarterly, 47*(1), 91–108.

Nation, I. S. P. (2013). *Learning vocabulary in another language* (2nd ed.). Cambridge University Press.

National Early Literacy Panel. (2008). *Developing early literacy: Report of the National Early Literacy Panel*. National Institute for Literacy.

National Reading Panel. (2000). *Teaching children to read: An evidence-based assessment of the scientific research literature on reading and its implications for reading instruction*. National Institute of Child Health and Human Development.

Ness, M., & Miles, K. P. (2025). *Making words stick: A four-step instructional routine to power up orthographic mapping*. Scholastic.

Neugebauer, S., Gamez, P., Coyne, M., Colon, I., McCoach, D., & Ware, S. (2017). Promoting word consciousness to close the vocabulary gap in young word learners. *The Elementary School Journal, 118*(1), 28–54.

Owens, R. E. (2020). *Language development: An introduction* (10th ed.). Pearson.

Paul, R., & Norbury, C. F. (2012). *Language disorders from infancy through adolescence: Listening, speaking, reading, writing, and communicating* (4th ed.). Elsevier.

Peters, E. (2014). The effects of repetition and time of posttest administration on EFL learners' form recall of single words and collocations. *Language Teaching Research, 18*(1), 1–21.

Quinn, J. M., Wagner, R. K., Petscher, Y., & Lopez, D. (2015). Developmental relations between vocabulary knowledge and reading comprehension: A latent change score modeling study. *Child Development, 86*(1), 159–175.

Rasinski, T. V., Padak, N., Newton, J., & Newton, E. (2011). The Latin–Greek connection: Building vocabulary through morphological study. *The Reading Teacher, 65*(2), 133–141.

Rasinski, T. V., Padak, N., Newton, R., & Newton, E. (2020). *Building vocabulary with Greek and Latin roots* (2nd ed.). Shell Educational Publishing.

Rowe, M. L. (2012). A longitudinal investigation of the role of quantity and quality of language in vocabulary development. *Child Development, 83*(5), 1561–1576.

Schmitt, N. (2014). Size and depth of vocabulary knowledge: What the research shows. *Language Learning, 64*(4), 913–951.

Schuth, E., Köhne, J., & Weinert, S. (2017). The influence of academic vocabulary knowledge on school performance. *Learning and Instruction, 49*, 157–165.

Scott, J. A., Nagy, W. E., & Flinspach, S. L. (2008). *Text complexity: The influence of vocabulary knowledge on reading comprehension*. Guilford Press.

Scott, J. A., Skobel, B. J., & Wells, J. (2008). *The word-conscious classroom: Building the vocabulary readers and writers need*. Teachers College Press.

Scott, L. H. (2025). *The words that shape us*. Scholastic.

Shanahan, T. (2014, August 4). Academic vocabulary – Part II. *Shanahan on Literacy Blog*. https://www.shanahanonliteracy.com/blog/academic-vocabulary-part-ii

Snow, C. E. (2010). Academic language and the challenge of reading for learning about science. *Science, 328*(5977), 450–452.

Spencer, M., Quinn, J., & Wagner, R. (2017). Vocabulary, morphology, and reading comprehension. In K. Cain, D. Compton, & R. Parrila (Eds.), *Theories of reading development* (pp. 239–256). John Benjamins Publishing Company.

Stahl, S. (1983). Differential word knowledge and reading comprehension. *Journal of Reading Behavior, 15*(4), 33–50.

Stahl, S. A., & Nagy, W. E. (2006). *Teaching word meanings*. Lawrence Erlbaum Associates.

Tuyen, L., & Huyen, V. (2019). Effects of using contextual clues on English vocabulary retention and reading comprehension. *International Journal of English Literature and Social Science, 4*(5), 1342–1347.

Wexler, N. (2019). *The knowledge gap: The hidden cause of America's broken education system—and how to fix it*. Avery.

Zukowski, A. (2020). *Language development and literacy: Foundations for learning*. Routledge.

Index

Other Titles in the Megabook Series

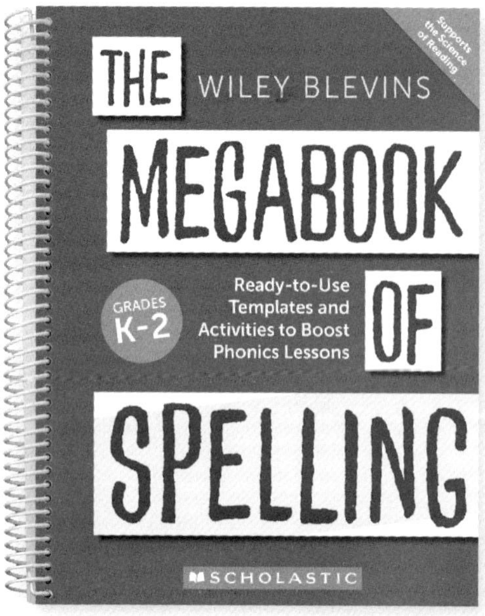

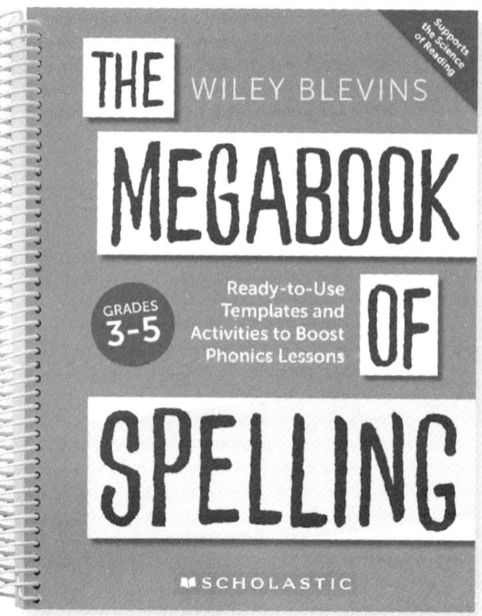

"Megabooks" are research-informed, classroom ready, and loaded with actionable strategies from leading scholars and educators. They're easy to use, inspiring to read, and guaranteed to energize your teaching and engage your students! No professional library is complete without them.